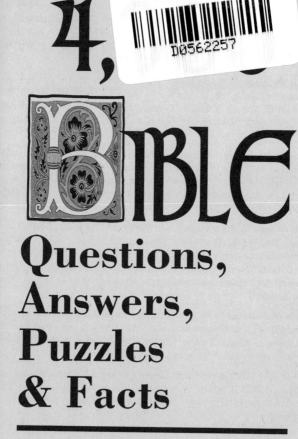

4,

BIBLE

Questions, Answers, Puzzles & Facts

CONTRIBUTING WRITERS:
June Eaton
Cecil Murphey
Carol Smith
Jeffery Scott Wallace
Linda M. Washington

PUBLICATIONS INTERNATIONAL, LTD.

June Eaton is a teacher and freelance writer with an M.A. from Northwestern University. Her published work includes Sunday school curriculum, devotional columns, stories, and articles in more than 60 Christian publications, including *Charisma*, *Christian Life*, *Christian Living*, and *Evangel*. She has also contributed to ten books, including *Bible-in-Life Series* and *Guidebook to Successful Christian Writing*.

Cecil Murphey, M.A. and M. Div. from Columbia Theological Seminary, is an ordained minister and the author of 72 books. He served as editor and compiler for *Dictionary of Biblical Literacy*, *Encyclopedia of Christian Marriage*, and *Encyclopedia for Today's Christian Woman*, and was a contributing writer on *The Bible A to Z*.

Carol Smith is a freelance writer with an M.A. in Religious Education. She has served as an Educational Minister, a Sunday school curriculum writer, and a Children's Minister. Her published works include *The Baker Bible Handbook for Kids*, *Bible Brain Busters*, *The Baker Bible Dictionary for Kids*, *Bibleland.Com*, and *The Treasure Bible*.

Jeffery Scott Wallace is pastor of the Dyers Creek First Church of God in Dover, Tennessee. He holds an M.A. in religion from the University of Tennessee and has served as product developer and editor at Cook Communications Ministries. He has also completed numerous freelance writing and editing projects, including *Understanding the Bible Leader's Guide* and *Discovering the Four Seasons*.

Linda M. Washington is a freelance writer and editor. She served for six years as editor at Cook Communications Ministries and two years as a writer/editor at Ligature Creative Studios. Her published work includes *Bible Discoveries*, *Comprehensive Bible Study*, and *Bible Quiz Masters*.

Scripture quotations are from the New Revised Standard Version of the Bible, copyright © 1989, by the Division of Christian Education of the National Council of the Churches of Christ in the USA. Used by permission. All rights reserved.

ISBN: 0-7853-3481-5

Contents

Welcome

There are many reasons why the Bible is the best-selling book of all time. For believers it has been a source of wisdom and inspiration for thousands of years. It contains a fascinating wealth of details about the people, places, and events of Bible times. Today, the Bible is relied upon by archeologists and scientists to study the past, understand the present, and look to the future of our expanding universe. It is a dynamic book that can be read again and again, each time bringing new insight and understanding.

4000 Bible Questions, Answers, Puzzles & Facts is an interesting tool to test your knowledge of the Bible—and help you learn more in the process. Through multiple choice, true/false, fill-in-the-blanks, quiz questions, and all sorts of puzzles and games, you will be able to focus your attention on facts and phenomena that you've perhaps already read or heard about. Each chapter builds on the previous one, allowing you to reinforce what you've learned and giving you confidence regarding what you already know.

Before you get started, you should know that every chapter has some easy questions and some tough questions, with a whole lot that are somewhere in between. You'll have a great time whether you're going through this book alone, with a friend, or in a group.

At the end of each chapter is a chart that will help you gauge your knowledge and enable you to see how your comprehension is increasing from chapter to chapter. At the end of the book there is one last chart by which you can figure out your overall score. Good luck and have fun.

CHAPTER ONE
Life of Jesus

1. Who was Jesus' earthly father? *JOSEPH*

2. True or False: At the Last Supper, Jesus told his disciples that the bread he wanted them to eat was his body. *TRUE*

3. Fill in the blanks: Jesus said, "Go into all the *world* and proclaim the _____ news to the whole creation" (Mark 16:15).

4. True or False: Jesus was born in Nazareth.

5. Who called Jesus' attention to the fact that there was no more wine at the wedding of Cana? (a) the bridegroom; (b) the banquet master; (c) his mother; (d) a servant.

6. True or False: Jesus called James and Nathanael the "Sons of Thunder."

---

7. UNSCRAMBLE AND SOLVE: WEDDING AT CANA (JOHN 2:1–11)

Then rearrange the boxed letters to form the answer to the question. The answer is a play on words.

What did the host say to his unhappy guests at the wedding at Cana?

He told them _ _ _ _ _ "_ _ _ _."

1. ROHU _ ☐ _ _

2. DEWDING ☐ _ _ _ _ _ _

3. TEARW _ _ _ ☐ _

4. ONEST _ _ ☐ _ _

5. ILLF _ ☐ _ _

6. THERMO _ _ ☐ _ _ _ _

7. STIRE _ _ ☐ _ _

8. KRUND _ _ _ ☐ _

9. GINS _ _ ☐ _

Answers for this page: **1.** *Joseph* **2.** *True* **3.** *world, good* **4.** *False (Bethlehem)* **5.** *(c) his mother* **6.** *False (John, not Nathanael)* **7.** *. . . not to "wine."* 1. *hour;* 2. *wedding;* 3. *water;* 4. *stone;* 5. *fill;* 6. *mother;* 7. *rites;* 8. *drunk;* 9. *sing*

8. Just before Jesus was born, the Roman emperor decreed that the world needed to be registered for what?

9. Which apostle said, "Can anything good come out of Nazareth?" (John 1:46) when he learned of Jesus' hometown? (a) Nathanael; (b) Peter; (c) Thomas; (d) Andrew.

10. Fill in the blanks: Jesus said, "For God so loved the _____ that he gave his only _____" (John 3:16).

11. What two sisters hosted Jesus in their home?

12. True or False: Jesus gave the Beatitudes during his Sermon on the Mount.

13. What criminal was released while Jesus was crucified?

14. Jesus was "amazed" at the faith of this Gentile: (a) Cornelius; (b) a Roman centurion; (c) Luke; (d) Quirinius.

15. Fill in the blanks: "No one has greater _____ than this, to lay down one's _____ for one's friends" (John 15:13).

16. True or False: God did not allow the devil to tempt Jesus after his baptism.

17. Fill in the blank: Jesus said, "Blessed are those who mourn, for they will be _____" (Matt 5:4).

18. This elderly prophetess, the daughter of Phanuel, spoke about Jesus in the temple: (a) Anna; (b) Miriam; (c) Deborah; (d) Huldah.

---

19. CRYPTOGRAM: AT THE TEMPLE

Decode the letters in the words of this Bible verse. Each letter corresponds to a different letter in the alphabet.

TBZXF ZJFXX KTVU ZJXV BEGIK JCY CI ZJX ZXYQDX,
UCZZCIW TYEIW ZJX ZXTAJXFU, DCUZXICIW ZE ZJXY TIK
TUSCIW ZJXY NGXUZCEIU. TIK TDD RJE JXTFK JCY
RXFX TYTLXK TZ JCU GIKXFUZTIKCIW TIK JCU TIURXFU.

Answers for this page: **8.** taxation **9.** *(a)* Nathanael **10.** world, Son **11.** Mary, Martha **12.** True **13.** Barabbas **14.** *(b)* a Roman centurion **15.** love, life **16.** False **17.** comforted **18.** *(a)* Anna **19.** "After three days they found him in the temple, sitting among the teachers, listening to them and asking them questions. And all who heard him were amazed at his understanding and his answers" (Luke 2:46–47).

20. MATCHING

Match the miracle with the place.

1. Calming of the storm   A. Synagogue

2. Water into wine   B. Pool of Bethesda

3. Healing of a blind man   C. Sea of Galilee

4. Man ill for 38 years   D. Bethsaida

5. Healing of a withered hand   E. Cana

21. When Jesus visited the home of friends in Bethany, whom did Jesus gently rebuke for being critical of a family member?

22. True or False: When Jesus healed ten lepers, nine returned to thank him.

23. Which of these men was *not* an apostle of Jesus? (a) Lazarus; (b) Peter; (c) James; (d) Nathanael.

24. Fill in the blanks: "Go therefore and make _____ of all _____, baptizing them in the name of the Father and of the Son and of the Holy Spirit" (Matt 28:19).

25. Who came to Jesus by night to ask about being born again?

26. True or False: During Jesus' transfiguration, Abraham and Moses appeared with Jesus up a high mountain.

27. Fill in the blanks: "_____ to others as you would have them _____ to you" (Luke 6:31).

28. What substance did Mary use to anoint Jesus' feet in her home? (a) frankincense; (b) nard; (c) water; (d) milk.

29. True or False: Satan told Jesus to throw himself off the Mount of Olives to prove he was God's Son.

30. By whose power did the Pharisees claim Jesus cast out demons?

Answers for this page: **20.** *1C; 2E; 3D; 4B; 5A* **21.** *Martha* **22.** *False (one)* **23.** *(a) Lazarus* **24.** *disciples, nations* **25.** *Nicodemus* **26.** *False (Elijah, not Abraham)* **27.** *Do; do* **28.** *(b) nard* **29.** *False (temple)* **30.** *Beelzebub's*

31. QUOTATION PUZZLE: A BRIEF BIOGRAPHY

To find the verse, put the letters that appear in the bottom half of the puzzle into the column of boxes above them. The letters may not be listed in the exact order in which they appear in the quote. Mark off used letters at the bottom. A letter may be used only once. The black boxes represent the space between words.

32. Jesus cursed this kind of tree for its lack of fruit: (a) apple; (b) pomegranate; (c) fig; (d) lemon.

33. True or False: Judas betrayed Jesus for 20 pieces of silver.

34. Jesus used what tiny item as a symbol of the kingdom of heaven?

35. What did the broken bread at the Last Supper symbolize? (a) Jesus' time on earth; (b) Jesus' body; (c) sins of humanity; (d) triumph of evil.

36. True or False: Jesus was a descendant of King David.

37. Fill in the blanks: "If anyone strikes you on the right _____, _____ the other also" (Matt 5:39).

38. What former tax collector became one of Jesus' apostles?

39. True or False: During his triumphal entry, Jesus rode on a horse.

40. Fill in the blanks: Jesus said, "I am the good _____. The good _____ lays down his life for the _____" (John 10:11).

41. Who was Jesus' forerunner, the one sent to prepare the way for him?

Answers for this page: **31.** *"Here is the Lamb of God who takes away the sin of the world!" (John 1:29).* **32.** *(c) fig* **33.** *False (30)* **34.** *mustard seed* **35.** *(b) Jesus' body* **36.** *True* **37.** *cheek, turn* **38.** *Matthew (Levi)* **39.** *False (donkey)* **40.** *shepherd, shepherd, sheep* **41.** *John the Baptist*

42. Which Old Testament prophet prophesied the birthplace of Jesus? (a) Isaiah; (b) Jeremiah; (c) Nahum; (d) Micah.

43. Fill in the blanks: "The Word became _____ and lived among us, and we have seen his glory, the glory as of a father's only son, full of _____ and _____" (John 1:14).

44. Where was Jesus arrested? (a) Jerusalem; (b) upper room; (c) Garden of Gethsemane; (d) Kidron Valley.

45. True or False: Jesus was told to come down off the cross and save himself.

46. Fill in the blanks: "Come to me, all you that are _____ and are carrying heavy burdens, and I will give you _____" (Matt 11:28).

47. For how many days did Jesus appear to his disciples after his resurrection? (a) 10; (b) 20; (c) 30; (d) 40.

48. What person was beheaded, which caused Jesus to grieve?

49. Which apostle vowed to lay down his life for Jesus? (a) Peter; (b) James; (c) John; (d) Philip.

50. True or False: When Jesus was in the wilderness, the devil told Jesus to turn stones into bread.

---

51. MATCHING

Match the parable with the truth Jesus taught.

1. Friend at midnight
2. The soils (sower)
3. Ten bridesmaids
4. Lost son
5. The rich fool

A. God's love
B. Persistence in prayer
C. Kingdom of God
D. Beware of greed
E. Christ's second coming

Answers for this page: **42.** *(d) Micah* **43.** *flesh, grace, truth* **44.** *(c) Garden of Gethsemane* **45.** *True* **46.** *weary, rest* **47.** *(d) 40* **48.** *John the Baptist* **49.** *(a) Peter* **50.** *True* **51.** *1B; 2C; 3E; 4A; 5D*

52. CRYPTOGRAM: CROWDS OF NEEDY PEOPLE

MYDLN HYRUFW HLKD NR ACK, JYCPMCPM UCNA
NADK NAD ILKD, NAD KLCKDF, NAD JICPF, NAD KZND,
LPF KLPQ RNADYW. NADQ TZN NADK LN ACW BDDN,
LPF AD HZYDF NADK.

53. Fill in the blanks: After chasing out the money changers, Jesus told the Jews, "Destroy this _____, and in ___ days I will raise it up" (John 2:19).

54. True or False: The apostles misunderstood what Jesus meant when he said Lazarus was "asleep" and he would "awaken" him.

55. How many apostles did Jesus call?

56. John the Baptist said he was not even worthy to do this for Jesus: (a) baptize him; (b) wash his feet; (c) untie his sandals; (d) talk to him.

57. What is the only miracle of Jesus told in all four Gospels that occured prior to his death?

58. Fill in the blanks: Jesus said, "I am the _____ and the _____. Those who believe in me, even though they die, will _____" (John 11:25).

59. True or False: Pilate was governor of Syria during the time of Jesus' birth.

60. Fill in the blanks: "This will be a sign for you: you will find a _____ wrapped in bands of cloth and lying in a _____" (Luke 2:12).

61. Which apostle verbally expressed doubt concerning Jesus' resurrection? (a) Judas Iscariot; (b) Nathanael; (c) Thomas; (d) James.

62. Fill in the blank: Jesus cautioned: "No one puts new _____ into old wineskins" (Mark 2:22).

Answers for this page: *52.* *"Great crowds came to him, bringing with them the lame, the maimed, the blind, the mute, and many others. They put them at his feet, and he cured them" (Matt 15:30).* **53.** *temple, three* **54.** *True* **55.** *12* **56.** *(c) untie his sandals* **57.** *feeding of the 5,000* **58.** *resurrection, life, live* **59.** *False (appointed over Judah much later)* **60.** *child, manger* **61.** *(c) Thomas* **62.** *wine*

63. Who denied Jesus three times?

64. What leader searched for the infant "king of the Jews" to put him to death?

65. True or False: Jesus told only the Apostle John about his upcoming suffering and death.

---

66. HIDDEN WORDS: THE BOY JESUS

These words appear in Luke 2:41–52. Find them hidden in the sentences below:

temple   teacher   parent   search   mother

festival   Passover   father   heart   wisdom

1. It takes many light years for a ray of sun to reach earth.

2. Grandma ordered tea, cherry pie, and ice cream for dessert.

3. The bus driver complained that his ear, cheek, and chin were sunburned on his left side.

4. I was asked to take part in an ecumenical songfest. I valued the experience.

5. When you look through the prize catalog, I'm sure you'll find an item pleasing to your taste.

6. I agree; kiwis do make a colorful garnish for salads.

7. Karen bought a new cage for her pet marmot. Her old one fell apart.

8. If you wish to lose a few pounds of fat, here are some exercises you can try.

9. The hunter left his compass over there under the tree.

10. We'll pick up a rental car at the airport.

Answers for this page: **63.** *Peter* **64.** *Herod* **65.** *False (told all his apostles)*
66. *1. heart; 2. teacher; 3. search; 4. festival; 5. temple; 6. wisdom; 7. mother;*
8. father; 9. Passover; 10. parent

67. Fill in the blanks: Jesus said, "There will be more _____ in heaven over one sinner who _____ than over ninety-nine righteous persons who need no repentance" (Luke 15:7).

68. Who declared, "Let us go, that we may die with him" when Jesus made plans to go to Lazarus? (a) Peter; (b) Thomas; (c) Philip; (d) John.

69. True or False: During Jesus' transfiguration, the apostles' clothes became dazzling white.

70. Fill in the blank: Jesus said, "I am the _____ of life. Whoever comes to me will never be hungry" (John 6:35).

71. True or False: Peter said he could not believe in Jesus' resurrection until he touched Jesus' wounds.

72. The name *Christ* means this: (a) God with us; (b) bread of life; (c) anointed one; (d) Mighty God.

73. Fill in the blanks: Jesus warned, "Do not store up for yourselves treasures on _____, where _____ and rust consume and where _____ break in and steal" (Matt 6:19).

74. Who were the wise individuals who traveled from the East to see the infant "king of the Jews"?

75. True or False: Even the evil spirits acknowledged that Jesus was the Son of God.

76. He became a reformed tax collector after Jesus came to his house: (a) Joseph; (b) Simon; (c) Zacchaeus; (d) Nicodemus.

77. What was placed on Jesus' head prior to his crucifixion?

78. True or False: When Herod heard about Jesus' popularity, he wondered if John the Baptist had returned from the dead.

79. Jesus drove the money changers out of what building?

Answers for this page: **67.** *joy, repents* **68.** *(b) Thomas* **69.** *False* **70.** *bread* **71.** *False (Thomas)* **72.** *(c) anointed one* **73.** *earth, moth, thieves* **74.** *the magi* **75.** *True* **76.** *(c) Zacchaeus* **77.** *crown of thorns* **78.** *True* **79.** *the temple*

80. MATCHING

Match what Jesus said to someone he healed or to that person's family member.

1. "Come out!"
2. "Go in peace."
3. "Get up!"
4. "Your sins are forgiven."
5. "Go home."
6. "Do not weep."
7. "If you are able!"

A. Paralyzed man
B. Lazarus
C. Gadarenes demoniac
D. Father of boy with demon
E. Widow of Nain
F. Bleeding woman
G. Jairus's daughter

81. While Jesus did this, the accusers of the woman caught in adultery drifted away: (a) observed them closely; (b) wrote on the ground; (c) forgave the woman; (d) prayed.

82. Prior to Jesus' birth, Mary and Joseph traveled to what town in obedience to the Roman emperor's decree?

83. Fill in the blank: Jesus said, "Where your _____ is, there your heart will be also" (Luke 12:34).

84. What did Jesus allow a legion of demons to enter when he cast them out of a man?

85. What Old Testament prophet predicted that a virgin would give birth to Jesus? (a) Isaiah; (b) Jeremiah; (c) Ezekiel; (d) Micah.

86. Fill in the blanks: Jesus gave this assurance: "You will know the _____, and the _____ will make you _____" (John 8:32).

87. Jesus advised against looking this way when one fasts: (a) happy; (b) dismal; (c) content; (d) angry.

88. True or False: The Pharisees once criticized Jesus because his disciples did not wash their hands before eating.

Answers for this page: **80.** 1B; 2F; 3G; 4A; 5C; 6E; 7D **81.** *(b) wrote on the ground* **82.** *Bethlehem* **83.** *treasure* **84.** *herd of swine* **85.** *(a) Isaiah* **86.** *truth, truth, free* **87.** *(b) dismal* **88.** *True*

89. Fill in the blanks: Jesus said, "Just as _____ lifted up the serpent in the wilderness, so must the Son of _____ be lifted up" (John 3:14).

90. Who appeared both to Zechariah the priest and to Mary with birth announcements?

91. Fill in the blank: Jesus said, "Blessed are the _____, for they will be called children of God" (Matt 5:9).

92. After Jesus healed the man with the withered hand, the Pharisees conspired with this group to destroy Jesus: (a) chief priests; (b) Sadducees; (c) Herodians; (d) scribes.

93. True or False: The Apostle John baptized Jesus.

94. What affliction did Peter's mother-in-law have that Jesus cured? (a) deafness; (b) issue of blood; (c) fever; (d) blindness.

95. Fill in the blank: Jesus told Pilate, "My _____ is not from this world" (John 18:36).

96. Jesus was crucified at what place?

97. True or False: Peter walked on water until he feared the elements and failed to trust Jesus.

98. Fill in the blank: Jesus said, "I watched _____ fall from heaven like a flash of lightning" (Luke 10:18).

99. In Jesus' parable of the lost sheep, how many were not lost? (a) 1; (b) 50; (c) 99; (d) 100

---

100. Cryptogram: Believe in Him

"MYLR LR LUGXXG MYX CLOO TW EH WPMYXK, MYPM POO CYT RXX MYX RTU PUG JXOLXQX LU YLE EPH YPQX XMXKUPO OLWX; PUG L CLOO KPLRX MYXE AB TU MYX OPRM GPH."

---

101. MATCHING

How did some of the influential leaders respond to Jesus? Match the leader or leaders with the response.

1. Pilate
2. Herod
3. Pharisees
4. Magi
5. Nicodemus

A. Sought to worship him
B. Accused him of blasphemy
C. Wanted him dead as a child
D. Considered him a good teacher
E. Found him "not guilty"

102. Who was the *official* high priest before whom Jesus was tried?

103. True or False: The Pharisees were outraged that Jesus ate with tax collectors and sinners.

104. Who did Jesus say he would send after he returned to heaven?

105. Of the following events, which came first? (a) Last Supper; (b) clearing of the temple; (c) prayer in Gethsemane; (d) triumphal entry.

106. True or False: Jesus rebuked the apostles for lack of faith after he calmed the storm.

107. Fill in the blanks: Jesus said, "Do not let your _____ be troubled. Believe in God, believe also in _____" (John 14:1).

108. Jesus' parents discovered that he was missing when he was 12 during which festival? (a) New Moon; (b) Day of Atonement; (c) Passover; (d) Purim.

109. What elderly prophet did God say would not die until he saw the Messiah?

110. True or False: Simon the Zealot, one of Jesus' apostles, was also called Cephas (the Rock).

111. What guided the wise men to the infant Jesus?

Answers for this page: **101.** *1E; 2C; 3B; 4A; 5D* **102.** *Caiaphas* **103.** *True* **104.** *Holy Spirit* **105.** *(d) triumphal entry* **106.** *True* **107.** *hearts, me* **108.** *(c) Passover* **109.** *Simeon* **110.** *False* **111.** *a star*

112. QUOTATION PUZZLE: THE MEETING PLACE

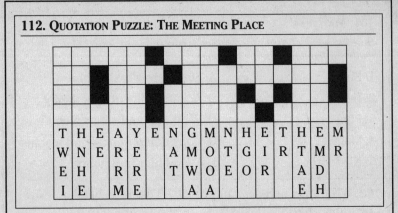

113. Jesus raised to life the dead daughter of this synagogue leader: (a) Jairus; (b) Zechariah; (c) Jason; (d) Nicodemus.

114. True or False: Andrew led his brother, Peter, to Jesus.

115. Fill in the blank: Jesus declared, "Very truly, I tell you, before _____ was, I am" (John 8.58).

116. Of what race was the woman with whom Jesus conversed at Jacob's well?

117. True or False: While in prison, John the Baptist questioned whether Jesus was the Messiah.

118. While in Nain, Jesus raised from the dead the son of which person? (a) a widow; (b) a Pharisee; (c) an apostle; (d) a noble.

119. What occupation did Jesus' earthly father teach him?

120. True or False: Jesus predicted his death but not his resurrection.

121. Jesus said he did not come to bring peace but to bring this: (a) love; (b) joy; (c) a sword; (d) hope.

122. Who carried Jesus' cross after Jesus could no longer carry it?

Answers for this page: **112.** *"Where two or three are gathered in my name, I am there among them" (Matt 18:20).* **113.** *(a) Jairus* **114.** *True* **115.** *Abraham* **116.** *Samaritan* **117.** *True* **118.** *(a) a widow* **119.** *carpentry* **120.** *False (predicted his resurrection as well)* **121.** *(c) a sword* **122.** *Simon of Cyrene*

123. What was Jesus doing while a fierce storm terrified the apostles on the Sea of Galilee? (a) teaching; (b) sleeping; (c) eating; (d) none of the above.

124. What did Jesus say that Jairus's daughter was doing that caused the mourners to laugh at Jesus?

125. Fill in the blanks: Jesus said, "Blessed are the _____ in heart, for they will see _____" (Matt 5:8).

126. True or False: The Pharisees were angry at Jesus because he healed a man with a withered hand on the sabbath.

127. In the parable of the talents, who was faithful? The man with: (a) 1 talent; (b) 2 talents; (c) 4 talents; (d) b and c.

128. Fill in the blanks: Jesus advised, "Let your light shine before others, so that they may see your _____ works and give _____ to your Father in heaven" (Matt 5:16).

129. What tore in two when Jesus died?

130. True or False: The rich young ruler who came to Jesus gave up everything to follow him.

131. When Elizabeth heard Mary's greeting, who leaped for joy in the womb of Elizabeth?

132. Jesus' triumphal entry into Jerusalem was the fulfillment of a prophecy recorded in what Old Testament book? (a) Isaiah; (b) Jeremiah; (c) Zechariah; (d) Ezekiel.

---

133. CRYPTOGRAM: WAY TO GOD

ZAYBY YXEW FR TEU, "E XU FTA VXG, XCW FTA FDBFT, XCW FTA SEHA. CR RCA IRUAY FR FTA HXFTAD AQIAJF FTDRBPT UA."

Answers for this page: **123.** *(b) sleeping* **124.** *sleeping* **125.** *pure, God* **126.** *True* **127.** *(b) 2 talents* **128.** *good, glory* **129.** *the curtain of the temple* **130.** *False* **131.** *John the Baptist* **132.** *(c) Zechariah* **133.** *Jesus said to him, "I am the way, and the truth, and the life. No one comes to the Father except through me" (John 14:6).*

134. MATCHING

Match Jesus' statement to the person, group, or occasion.

1. "Do you love me?"

2. "Woe to you!"

3. "Be silent!"

4. "Where is your faith?"

5. "Away with you!"

A. The apostles in a storm

B. Peter

C. Pharisees

D. Satan

E. Unclean spirit

135. True or False: The crowd responded favorably when Jesus announced that those who eat of his flesh will have life.

136. Who was the blind man who persistently called out to Jesus for healing even though the crowd rebuked him? (a) Barabbas; (b) Bartimaeus; (c) Bartholomew; (d) Baruch.

137. Who bribed the guards to say that Jesus' body was stolen after his crucifixion?

138. True or False: Jesus was without any sin.

139. How many days and nights did Jesus fast in the wilderness, where the devil tempted him?

140. Fill in the blanks: At Jesus' baptism, God said, "This is my Son, the _____, with whom I am well _____" (Matt 3:17).

141. The Pharisees tried to trap Jesus by asking him whether this should be given to Caesar: (a) homage; (b) taxes; (c) sacrifices; (d) none of these.

142. True or False: Jesus was unable to carry his cross all the way to the place where he would be crucified.

143. Fill in the blank: Jesus told his disciples, "The Advocate, the Holy _____, whom the Father will send in my name, will teach you everything" (John 14:26).

Answers for this page: **134.** *1B; 2C; 3E; 4A; 5D* **135.** *False* **136.** *(b) Bartimaeus* **137.** *the chief priests* **138.** *True* **139.** *40* **140.** *Beloved, pleased* **141.** *(b) taxes* **142.** *True* **143.** *Spirit*

144. What apostle besides Peter and John witnessed Jesus' transfiguration?

145. What did the woman use to bathe Jesus' feet in the house of Simon, the Pharisee? (a) aloes; (b) tears; (c) water; (d) none of these.

146. True or False: Some religious leaders accused Jesus of being possessed with a demon.

147. Who climbed a sycamore tree in order to see Jesus? (a) Salome; (b) Martha; (c) Mary; (d) Zacchaeus.

148. After Jesus asked, "Who do you say that I am?" who declared that Jesus is "the Christ"?

149. True or False: People in Nazareth did not take Jesus seriously, because they knew his family.

150. What of Jesus' did the woman who had been hemorrhaging touch in order to be healed? (a) robe; (b) hand; (c) foot; (d) staff.

151. In one of his strongest rebukes, Jesus compared the Pharisees to what whitewashed objects?

152. True or False: Jesus wanted to share the Passover meal with his closest disciples the night before his crucifixion.

153. Fill in the blanks: Jesus said, "Do not give what is holy to _____; and do not throw your _____ before swine" (Matt 7:6).

154. True or False: The guards were so stunned at the appearance of an angel at Jesus' tomb that two of them dropped dead on the spot.

---

155. Cryptogram: Healed by His Wounds

PU HZI HVFAEUE MVD VFD RDZAIXDUIIJVAI, LDFIPUE MVD
VFD JAJKFJRJUI; FWVA PJO HZI RPU WFAJIPOUAR RPZR
OZEU FI HPVNU, ZAE TQ PJI TDFJIUI HU ZDU PUZNUE.

Answers for this page: **144.** *James* **145.** *(b) tears* **146.** *True* **147.** *(d) Zacchaeus* **148.** *Peter* **149.** *True* **150.** *(a) robe* **151.** *tombs* **152.** *True* **153.** *dogs, pearls* **154.** *False* **155.** *"He was wounded for our transgressions, crushed for our iniquities; upon him was the punishment that made us whole, and by his bruises we are healed" (Isa 53:5).*

156. Who was the friend of Jesus and the brother of Martha and Mary?

157. True or False: Jesus taught that the first and greatest commandment is to love one's neighbor as one's self.

158. A Canaanite (Syrophoenician) woman sought Jesus' help for this member of her family: (a) daughter; (b) husband; (c) son; (d) mother.

159. What sign did Jesus' betrayer use to indicate who was to be arrested on the Mount of Olives?

160. What did Jesus eat to prove to the apostles that he had been resurrected and was not a ghost? (a) dried figs; (b) roasted lamb; (c) broiled fish; (d) none of the above.

161. Fill in the blank: Jesus said, "Love your _____ and pray for those who persecute you" (Matt 5:44).

162. What did Jesus find his disciples doing in the Garden of Gethsemane after his agonizing prayer? (a) hiding; (b) arguing; (c) singing; (d) sleeping.

---

163. WORD SEARCH: MIRACLES OF JESUS   *Answers on page 36.*

In the puzzle on the next page, find the 23 words or phrases related to Jesus' miracles. Find only the words in bold capitals. You can find words diagonally, vertically, horizontally, backward, and forward. When you find a word in the puzzle, cross it off the list.

Blind **BARTIMAEUS**
BOY WITH DEMON
CALMING the **STORM**
CANAANITE GIRL
COIN in fish's mouth
Daughter of **JAIRUS**
Feeding of **FIVE THOUSAND**
FIG TREE withered
HEAL
Healing **CRIPPLED** woman
Healing servant of **CENTURION**
Healing **TEN LEPERS**

Large catch of **FISH**
MAN AT POOL of Bethesda
Man **BORN BLIND**
Man with **DROPSY**
OFFICIAL's SON
PARALYZED MAN
Raising of **LAZARUS**
Walking on **WATER**
Water into **WINE**
Widow of **NAIN's SON** (raising of)
Woman with **BLEEDING**

WORD SEARCH: MIRACLES OF JESUS

```
                                    T  O
                                 F  U  L  L
                              J  A  I  R  U  S  R
              F  U  N  D  E  L  P  P  I  R  C  I
              P  I  D  N  I  L  B  N  R  O  B  G
              O  A  V  N  S  R  E  P  E  L  N  E  T  H
        C  N  F  R  E  O  F  U  N  N  O  A  T  G  H
     B  F  A  O  F  A  T  I  A  O  I  O  I  I  N  S
  B  E  A  I  L  M  I  L  H  R  E  W  P  N  N  I  U
  E  W  E  R  S  M  E  C  Y  O  U  P  T  S  A  D  R
     H  A  R  T  H  I  D  I  Z  U  T  A  O  A  E  A
        E  T  T  I  Y  N  H  A  E  S  N  N  N  E  Z
           A  E  G  M  S  G  T  L  D  A  E  A  L  A
           O  L  R  I  A  P  S  I  S  M  N  C  B  L
                    F  E  O  T  W  O  A  D
                       U  R  O  Y  N  N
                       S  D  R  O  E
                       T  O  M  B  B
                       X  A
                       B
```

164. True or False: After Jesus was brought before Herod and Pilate, these two officials ceased being enemies and became friends.

165. In Capernaum, what did Jesus tell the paralytic to do? (a) stand up; (b) carry his mat; (c) go home; (d) all of the above.

Answers for pages 20 and 21: **156.** *Lazarus* **157.** *False (love God)* **158.** *(a) daughter* **159.** *a kiss* **160.** *(c) broiled fish* **161.** *enemies* **162.** *(d) sleeping* **164.** *True* **165.** *(d) all of the above*

166. MATCHING

Match Aramaic phrases spoken by Jesus with their meanings.

1. *Talitha cum*   A. "Father [Daddy]."

2. *Eli*   B. "Why have you forsaken me?"

3. *Abba*   C. "Be opened!"

4. *Ephphatha*   D. "My God."

5. *Lema sabachthani*   E. "Little girl, get up."

167. True or False: Jesus was called the "Son of Man."

168. What items belonging to Jesus did the soldiers divide among themselves at his crucifixion?

169. When the rich young ruler came to Jesus, what did Jesus advise him to do? (a) sell all his possessions; (b) follow him; (c) give to the poor; (d) all of the above.

170. True or False: One of Jesus' apostles was a Cananaean.

171. Who cut off the ear of the high priest's servant when the crowd arrived to arrest Jesus?

172. True or False: Jesus told the woman at Jacob's well that he was the Messiah.

173. What was the name of the Jewish ruling council, which was headed by the chief priest and which put Jesus on trial?

174. Fill in the blanks: Jesus warned, "I say to you that everyone who looks at a woman with _____ has already committed _____ with her in his heart" (Matt 5:28).

175. Which of the following individuals was *not* raised from the dead by Jesus? (a) Lazarus; (b) the son of the widow in Nain; (c) Jairus's daughter; (d) Dorcas.

176. What wedding term did Jesus use to refer to himself?

177. True or False: Two bandits were crucified with Jesus.

Answers for this page: **166.** *1E; 2D; 3A; 4C; 5B* **167.** *True* **168.** *his clothes* **169.** *(d) all of the above* **170.** *True (Simon)* **171.** *Peter* **172.** *True* **173.** *Sanhedrin* **174.** *lust, adultery* **175.** *(d) Dorcas* **176.** *bridegroom* **177.** *True*

178. Whom did Jesus commend for giving all in the temple treasury?

179. The Pharisees were appalled because Jesus claimed equality with whom?

---

180. UNSCRAMBLE AND MATCH: JESUS' LIFE

Unscramble the names of locations on the right, then match each event of Jesus' life with the place it occurred.

1. The Spirit of God descended on Jesus like a dove. Luke 3:21–22

_____ A. THANZEAR

2. Jesus turned water into wine. John 2:1–11

_____ B. JANDOR

3. Jesus read from a scroll in the synagogue. Luke 4:16–20

_____ C. ILEGALE

4. Jesus rode into the city on a colt. Mark 11:1–11

_____ D. THEMESANGE

5. Jesus walked on water. Mark 6:45–51

_____ E. ANAC

6. Jesus healed a centurion's servant. Matthew 8:5–13

_____ F. MEARSLUJE

7. Jesus' feet were anointed by Mary. John 12:1–8

_____ G. UNCAMPERA

8. Jesus was betrayed and arrested. Mark 14:32–50

_____ H. UMASEM

9. Jesus walked along a road with two disciples Luke 24:13–15.

_____ I. ANYTHEB

10. Jesus commissioned 11 disciples. Matthew 28:16–20

_____ J. BADSETHIA

Answers for this page: 178. *the poor widow* **179.** *God* **180.** *1. Jordan/B; 2. Cana/E; 3. Nazareth/A; 4. Jerusalem/F; 5. Bethsaida/J; 6. Capernaum/G; 7. Bethany/I; 8. Gethsemane/D; 9. Emmaus/H; 10. Galilee/C.*

181. Cryptogram: One Sacrifice

LFOZ MO WZ WO MXXIWDZJU SIG HIGZMRO ZI UWJ
IDAJ, MDU MSZJG ZKMZ ZKJ LFUYHJDZ, OI AKGWOZ,
KMBWDY EJJD ISSJGJU IDAJ ZI EJMG ZKJ OWDO IS
HMDT, VWRR MXXJMG M OJAIDU ZWHJ, DIZ ZI UJMR
VWZK OWD.

182. Fill in the blank: Jesus said, "Did I not choose you, the twelve? Yet one of you is a _____" (John 6:70).

183. What did the apostles think Jesus was when they saw him walk on water?

184. About how long did Jesus' ministry on earth last? (a) one year; (b) two years; (c) three years; (d) five years.

185. Which apostle kept the common purse of Jesus' band and stole from it?

186. True or False: When Jesus called Andrew to be his apostle, Andrew requested permission to bury his father before joining Jesus' band.

187. What was Peter's occupation before he became Jesus' disciple?

188. In Jesus' parable about the woman who owns ten silver coins, how many of them did she lose? (a) one; (b) three; (c) five; (d) all of them.

189. Fill in the blank: Jesus told the apostles, "Whoever wants to be first must be _____ of all and servant of all" (Mark 9:35).

190. Where did Thomas have to place his hand in order to believe Jesus was truly alive? (a) Jesus' side; (b) Jesus' head; (c) Jesus' feet; (d) none of the above.

191. True or False: When Jesus was told that his mother and brothers waited to see him, Jesus replied he had no family.

Answers for this page: **181.** *"Just as it is appointed for mortals to die once, and after that the judgment, so Christ, having been offered once to bear the sins of many, will appear a second time, not to deal with sin" (Heb 9:27–28).* **182.** *devil* **183.** *a ghost* **184.** *(c) three years* **185.** *Judas Iscariot* **186.** *False* **187.** *fisherman* **188.** *(a) one* **189.** *last* **190.** *(a) Jesus' side* **191.** *False*

192. What Old Testament prophet predicted that a young woman would be with child and name him "Immanuel"? (a) Isaiah; (b) Jeremiah; (c) Ezekiel; (d) Micah.

193. True or False: While on the cross, Jesus' legs were broken to ensure that he would die quickly.

194. When asked about divorce, who was the individual Jesus said permitted it because of the hardness of the people's hearts?

195. Fill in the blanks: "In the beginning was the _____ , and the _____ was with God and the _____ was God" (John 1:1).

196. True or False: Jesus refused to explain the parable of the sower because of the apostles' lack of faith.

197. What basic necessity did foxes and birds have that Jesus mentioned a lack of? (a) food; (b) place to live; (c) clothing; (d) none of the above.

198. Besides Joseph of Arimathea, who laid Jesus' body in the tomb?

199. True or False: After John baptized Jesus, John became one of Jesus' 12 apostles.

200. Jesus called himself this type of bread: (a) of heaven; (b) of life; (c) of souls; (d) of God.

---

201. MATCHING

Match the site of praise for Jesus with the person who praised him.

1. Praise at the cross
2. Praise in the upper room
3. Praise from the womb
4. Praise at Jacob's well
5. Praise at a tomb

A. John the Baptist
B. Martha
C. Samaritans
D. Roman centurion
E. Thomas

Answers for this page: **192.** *(a) Isaiah* **193.** *False (not broken)* **194.** *Moses* **195.** *Word, Word, Word* **196.** *False* **197.** *(b) place to live* **198.** *Nicodemus* **199.** *False* **200.** *(b) of life* **201.** *1D; 2E; 3A; 4C; 5B*

202. QUOTATION PUZZLE: A WAY TO OBEY

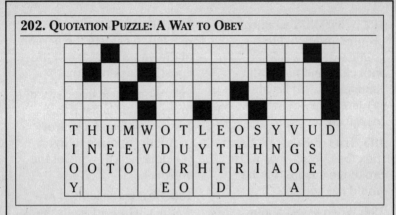

T	H	U	M	W	O	T	L	E	O	S	Y	V	U	D
I	N	E	E	V	D	U	Y	T	H	H	N	G	S	
O	O	T	O		O	R	H	T	R	I	A	O	E	
Y					E	O		D				A		

203. In Jesus' parable of the rich man and Lazarus, to whose "side" was Lazarus taken after death? (a) Moses'; (b) Abraham's; (c) David's; (d) Jacob's.

204. True or False: Every member of the Sanhedrin opposed Jesus.

205. Fill in the blanks: "I am sending you out like sheep into the midst of wolves; so be wise as _____ and innocent as _____" (Matt 10:16).

206. True or False: Saul of Tarsus became friends with Jesus shortly before Jesus was crucified.

207. The apostles feared for Jesus' life when Jesus decided to go to Judea in response to whose illness?

208. Fill in the blanks: "Strive first for the _____ of God and his _____, and all these things will be given to you as well" (Matt 6:33).

209. True or False: Jesus said no one would marry or be given in marriage in heaven.

210. Which apostle asked Jesus how many times one should forgive someone? (a) Peter; (b) James; (c) John; (d) Philip.

211. In what person did Jesus say "there is no deceit"?

Answers for this page: **202.** *"In everything do to others as you would have them do to you" (Matt 7:12).* **203.** *(b) Abraham's* **204.** *False (Nicodemus and Joseph of Arimathea didn't)* **205.** *serpents, doves* **206.** *False* **207.** *Lazarus's* **208.** *kingdom, righteousness* **209.** *True* **210.** *(a) Peter* **211.** *Nathanael*

212. About how much time had passed between the return of the Jewish exiles to Jerusalem and the birth of Christ? (a) 100 years; (b) 200 years; (c) 300 years; (d) 400 years.

213. True or False: The wine Jesus miraculously made in Cana was almost as good as the first wine served at the wedding feast.

214. Young Jesus and his family stayed in Egypt until the death of what person?

215. The woman at Jacob's well called Jesus a prophet when he told her she did not currently have what? (a) children; (b) a husband; (c) a home; (d) a good reputation.

216. True or False: Jesus compared himself to a mother hen.

217. What took Jesus out of the sight of his followers when he ascended into heaven?

218. Fill in the blanks: Jesus promised, "Take my _____ upon you, and learn from me; for I am gentle and humble in heart, and you will find rest for your _____" (Matt 11:29).

219. Jesus referred to John the Baptist as which prophet? (a) Isaiah; (b) Elijah; (c) Jeremiah; (d) Micah.

220. When Jesus sent out the 12 apostles, he told them to shake what from their feet if people in a town did not welcome them?

221. True or False: Jesus asked God to remove the cup of his suffering from him.

222. Where was Jesus baptized? (a) Sea of Galilee; (b) Jordan River; (c) Dead Sea; (d) Lake of Gennesaret.

223. During what Jewish feast was Jesus crucified?

224. Whom did Jesus call the "father of lies"? (a) the chief priest; (b) Herod; (c) the devil; (d) none of the above.

Answers for this page: **212.** *(d) 400 years* **213.** *False (better)* **214.** *Herod* **215.** *(b) a husband* **216.** *True* **217.** *a cloud* **218.** *yoke, souls* **219.** *(b) Elijah* **220.** *dust* **221.** *True* **222.** *(b) Jordan River* **223.** *Passover* **224.** *(c) the devil*

225. True or False: When the apostles told a man to stop casting out demons in Jesus' name, Jesus rebuked the man and told him to repent.

226. The inscription on Jesus' cross was written in what language? (a) Hebrew; (b) Latin; (c) Greek; (d) all of the above.

227. Fill in the blank: After announcing Jesus' upcoming birth, the angel Gabriel told Mary, "For nothing will be _____ with God" (Luke 1:37).

228. Many members of this Jewish group were Jesus' adversaries throughout his ministry: (a) Essenes; (b) Sadducees; (c) zealots; (d) none of the above.

229. True or False: Jesus predicted the destruction of the temple in Jerusalem.

230. Who was the Roman emperor at the time of Jesus' birth?

231. True or False: Jesus warned that blasphemy against the Holy Spirit could not be forgiven.

232. To whom did Jesus entrust the care of his mother while dying on the cross?

233. The two disciples who met Jesus on the road to Emmaus recognized him when he did this: (a) explained Scripture; (b) broke bread; (c) ate fish; (d) talked to them.

234. True or False: Because of a dream, Pilate's wife encouraged Pilate to condemn Jesus.

235. Where in Jerusalem did Jesus' parents find the 12-year-old Jesus after he had been missing for three days?

---

236. CRYPTOGRAM: OUR ADVOCATE

HB KGQB GD GIQNOGUB HVUK UKB EGUKBC, ZBTYT
OKCVTU UKB CVAKUBNYT; GDI KB VT UKB GUNDVDA
TGOCVEVEVOB ENC NYC TVDT, GDI DNU ENC NYCT
NDRX PYU GRTN ENC UKB TVDT NE UKB HKNRB
HNCRI.

---

237. MATCHING

Jesus had six trials before being crucified. Match with those who officiated at each trial.

1. First religious trial	A. Caiaphas
2. Second religious trial	B. Herod
3. Third religious trial	C. Pilate (again)
4. First civil trial	D. Annas
5. Second civil trial	E. The Sanhedrin
6. Third civil trial	F. Pilate

238. Fill in the blanks: Jesus said, "I am the _____, you are the _____. Those who abide in me and I in them bear much _____" (John 15:5).

239. True or False: The one leper out of ten who returned to thank Jesus for healing him was a Samaritan.

240. Jesus healed what individual who was lowered through the roof of a house? (a) a paralyzed man; (b) a man born blind; (c) a crippled woman; (d) Peter's mother-in-law.

241. What did Jesus do at the Last Supper that Peter initially told the Lord not to do to him?

242. True or False: An angel appeared to Joseph in at least two dreams concerning Jesus.

243. At the Last Supper, which apostle told Jesus to "show us the Father"? (a) Peter; (b) Judas; (c) Philip; (d) Thomas.

244. What did Jesus ask for from the woman at Jacob's well?

245. True or False: Jesus reproached Chorazin and Bethsaida because the people in these towns refused to repent.

246. What does the name *Immanuel* mean? (a) God is with us; (b) bread of life; (c) anointed one; (d) Mighty God.

Answers for this page: **237.** *1D; 2A; 3E; 4F; 5B; 6C* **238.** *vine, branches, fruit* **239.** *True* **240.** *(a) a paralyzed man* **241.** *wash Peter's feet* **242.** *True* **243.** *(c) Philip* **244.** *a drink* **245.** *True* **246.** *(a) God is with us*

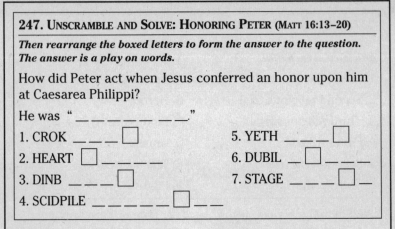

247. UNSCRAMBLE AND **S**OLVE: **H**ONORING **P**ETER (M**ATT** 16:13–20)

Then rearrange the boxed letters to form the answer to the question. The answer is a play on words.

How did Peter act when Jesus conferred an honor upon him at Caesarea Philippi?

He was " __ __ __ __ __ __ __ __."

1. CROK __ __ __ ☐

2. HEART ☐ __ __ __ __

3. DINB __ __ __ ☐

4. SCIDPILE __ __ __ __ __ ☐ __ __

5. YETH __ __ __ ☐

6. DUBIL __ ☐ __ __ __

7. STAGE __ __ __ ☐ __

248. Fill in the blank: Jesus said, "Prophets are not without _____, except in their hometown, and among their own kin, and in their own house" (Mark 6:4).

249. In Jesus' parable of the wise and foolish builders, on what was built the house that did not withstand the rain?

250. True or False: The Gospels reveal few events of Jesus' childhood.

251. What title did the rich young ruler use to address Jesus? (a) Good Teacher; (b) Mighty Prophet; (c) Son of God; (d) Son of Man.

252. Whom did the risen Jesus tell to feed his sheep?

253. Fill in the blank: Jesus asked, "Can any of you by worrying add a single _____ to your span of life?" (Matt 6:27).

254. During his trial, what did Jesus do that amazed Pilate? (a) kept silent; (b) performed a miracle; (c) said he was the Messiah; (d) none of the above.

255. Fill in the blanks: Jesus said, "I am the _____ of the world. Whoever follows me will never walk in _____" (John 8:12).

Answers for this page: **247.** . . . *"keyed up." 1. rock; 2. earth; 3. bind; 4. disciple; 5. they; 6. build; 7. gates* **248.** *honor* **249.** *sand* **250.** *True* **251.** *(a) Good Teacher* **252.** *Peter* **253.** *hour* **254.** *(a) kept silent* **255.** *light, darkness*

256. True or False: Jesus predicted that false messiahs would come as a sign of the end times.

257. What did the centurion who sought healing for his servant say that Jesus has?

258. When accused of "unlawfully" picking grain on the sabbath, Jesus defended his disciples by citing the example of this Old Testament person: (a) David; (b) Moses; (c) Solomon; (d) Isaiah.

259. Fill in the blank: Jesus predicted, "The Son of Man is to be betrayed into human hands, and they will kill him, and _____ days after being killed, he will rise again" (Mark 9:31).

260. True or False: A crowd once tried to throw Jesus off a cliff.

261. In Jesus' parable of the prodigal son, which son squandered away his inheritance?

262. Whom did Jesus say is Lord of the sabbath?

263. True or False: Jesus would not help a Canaanite woman because he told her that he was sent only to the lost sheep of Israel.

264. The New Testament indicates that the people who first visited the baby Jesus were: (a) the wise men; (b) shepherds; (c) soldiers; (d) none of the above.

---

265. MATCHING

The following people had a question or request for Jesus. Match each individual to the request for knowledge or healing.

1. Martha	A. What do I lack?
2. Nicodemus	B. Are you the king of the Jews?
3. John the Baptist	C. How can I be born again?
4. Pilate	D. Are you the Messiah?
5. Rich young ruler	E. Heal my brother.

Answers for this page: **256.** *True* **257.** *authority* **258.** *(a) David* **259.** *three* **260.** *True* **261.** *the younger* **262.** *Jesus* **263.** *False (he helped her)* **264.** *(b) shepherds* **265.** *1E; 2C; 3D; 4B; 5A*

266. CRYPTOGRAM: ALWAYS WITH US

CFRHR ROKS, "OMS UFPFPGFU, K OP BKWI QEH
OXBOQR, WE WIF FMS EN WIF ODF."

267. True or False: Before his resurrection, Jesus did not permit his disciples to baptize because he wanted to baptize people himself.

268. Besides light, Jesus referred to believers as what? (a) honey; (b) floral scent; (c) salt; (d) yeast.

269. True or False: Pilate ordered that soldiers guard Jesus' tomb so that no one could steal his body.

270. What did Jesus say is the second greatest commandment?

271. Jesus told the Pharisees that this Old Testament prophet would be his sign to them: (a) Moses; (b) Isaiah; (c) Jeremiah; (d) Jonah.

272. Fill in the blank: Jesus said, "Blessed are those who are _____ for righteousness' sake, for theirs is the kingdom of heaven" (Matt 5:10).

273. True or False: Jesus told the Apostle Peter to "get behind me, Satan" after Peter rebuked Jesus for predicting his upcoming suffering and death.

274. Fill in the blank: Jesus warned, "Beware of false prophets, who come to you in _____ clothing but inwardly are ravenous wolves" (Matt 7:15).

275. Jesus said not to sound what when you give charity?

276. Jesus told a parable about two men praying at the temple. Whom did the Pharisee scorn? (a) adulterer; (b) thief; (c) tax collector; (d) leper.

277. True or False: People mocked Jesus while he hung from the cross.

278. Jesus said John baptized with water but that his followers will be baptized with what?

Answers for this page: **266.** *Jesus said, "And remember, I am with you always, to the end of the age" (Matt 28:20).* **267.** *False* **268.** *(c) salt* **269.** *True* **270.** *love your neighbor* **271.** *(d) Jonah* **272.** *persecuted* **273.** *True* **274.** *sheep's* **275.** *a trumpet* **276.** *(c) tax collector* **277.** *True* **278.** *the Holy Spirit*

279. After Jesus' resurrection, what woman announced to the apostles that she had seen the Lord? (a) Mary of Bethany; (b) Mary Magdalene; (c) Mary (mother of James); (d) Mary (mother of Jesus).

280. What was written on the sign on Jesus' cross?

281. True or False: The crowd that attempted to arrest Jesus on the Mount of Olives was armed with swords and clubs.

282. What clothing did the soldiers put on Jesus to mock his kingship?

283. During Jesus' trial, Peter was identified by this: (a) his Galilean accent; (b) being seen with Jesus; (c) his clothing; (d) not identified.

284. What is Jesus said to be, which becomes "flesh," at the beginning of John's Gospel?

285. True or False: During Jesus' trial, the high priest was so outraged at Jesus' words that he ripped his own clothes.

286. True or False: Jesus told one of the bandits who was crucified with him that he would be in paradise with him.

287. At the Last Supper, Jesus told his disciples not to have troubled hearts because he will leave them with what?

288. Jesus said he came to fulfill the law and what? (a) people's prayers; (b) the prophets; (c) Jewish tradition; (d) none of the above.

---

289. MATCHING

Match the miracle to what Jesus used or what was mentioned in connection with it.

1. Feeding of 5,000	A. Robe
2. Man born blind	B. Two fish
3. Calming of storm	C. Mud with saliva
4. Woman with blood	D. Spoken word

Answers for this page: **279.** *(b) Mary Magdalene* **280.** *"King of the Jews"* **281.** *True* **282.** *purple robe* **283.** *(a) his Galilean accent* **284.** *Word* **285.** *True* **286.** *True* **287.** *peace* **288.** *(b) the prophets* **289.** *1B; 2C; 3D; 4A*

290. When Jesus was arrested, he said that every day they saw him teaching in this location, yet they did not arrest him: (a) in their homes; (b) by the sea; (c) in the temple courts; (d) in the streets.

291. True or False: Judas was so remorseful after he betrayed Jesus that he killed himself.

292. Fill in the blanks: Jesus said, "Why do you see the _____ in your neighbor's eye, but do not notice the _____ in your own eye?" (Matt 7:3–4).

293. Jesus referred to himself as what part of a building?

294. True or False: When Jesus was in the wilderness, the devil took Jesus to the pinnacle of the temple and told him to jump to prove that he is the Son of God, which Jesus refused to do.

295. Jesus said his followers must daily carry their own what?

296. In an effort to kill the infant Jesus, Herod ordered that all boys under the age of two be slaughtered in this town: (a) Nazareth; (b) Bethlehem; (c) Capernaum; (d) Cana.

297. True or False: Jesus was circumcised on the fourth day after his birth.

---

298. CRISSCROSS PUZZLE: WORDS ABOUT JESUS
Answers on page 37.

Fit each of the following 65 words into the puzzle on page 35. Words are arranged below alphabetically according to the number of letters.

4 letters	**4 letters**	**4 letters**	**4 letters**
acme	earn	love	seed
Amen	*Eloi*	made	sent
dear	head	name	sits
defy	hear	only	vine
doer	Lamb	Rose [of	Word
door		Sharon]	

Answers for this page: **290.** *(c) in the temple courts* **291.** *True* **292.** *speck, log* **293.** *cornerstone* **294.** *True* **295.** *cross* **296.** *(b) Bethlehem* **297.** *False (eighth)*

298. CRISSCROSS PUZZLE: WORDS ABOUT JESUS *continued*

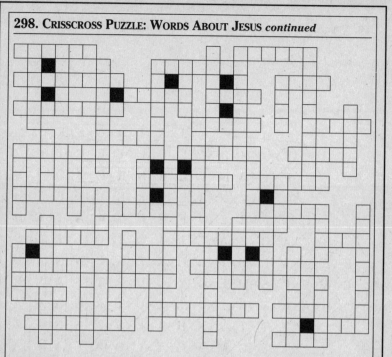

5 letters	5 letters	7 letters	8 letters
above	ruler	believe	shepherd
adore	truth	beloved	"sonlight"
adorn	**6 letters**	eternal	strength
bread	Adonai	highest	**9 letters**
enter	answer	hosanna	ascension
gives	Christ	Messiah	beatitude
ideal	evince	radiant	crucified
image	healer	**8 letters**	firstborn
mercy	living	elevated	**10 letters**
might	manger	marriage	revelation
rabbi	master	Nazareth	
right	ransom	paradise	
	Savior	Redeemer	

156. WORD SEARCH: MIRACLES OF JESUS *Puzzle on page 21.*

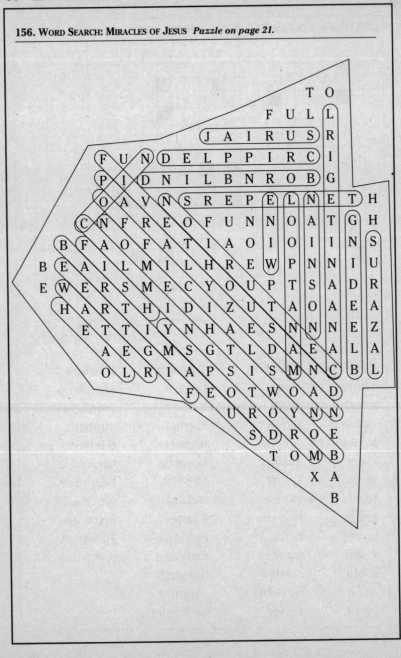

298. CRISSCROSS PUZZLE: WORDS ABOUT JESUS *Puzzle on page 35.*

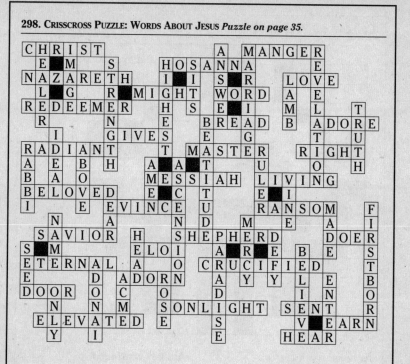

CROSSWORD PUZZLE #1: PRODIGAL SON *Answers on page 278.*

Across

1. David's son (1 Chron 3:5)
*7. Head of the family (Luke 15:12)
12. Sharpen (Ezek 21:10; present tense)
*13. "Bring out a ___" (Luke 15:22).
14. Descendant of Shuthelah (Num 26:36)
15. Son of Manasseh (2 Ki 21:18)
16. The wise __ followed the star (Matt 2:1–2)
*17. Jesus' teaching story.
19. Omega (Rev 21:6)
20. Son of Jacob (Ex 1:4)

Across *continued*

21. Son of Jacob (Ex 1:4)
23. Northwest (abbr)
24. Tellurium (symbol)
25. Large continent (Acts 16:6)
*27. Placed on son's hand (Luke 15:22)
*29. Subject of the parable in Luke 15 (2 wds)
32. Greek letter
*33. "Celebrate and ___!" (Luke 15:32).
36. Used for anointing (Ex 30:25)
*37. Theme of the parable in Luke 15 (4 wds)

CROSSWORD PUZZLE #1: PRODIGAL SON *continued*

Across *continued*

43. One of Noah's sons (Gen 5:32)
*44. Animal fed by 29 across
45. Son of Gad (Num 26:16)
46. "Love __ another" (John 13:34).
47. Cease employment (Num 8:25)
*48. "I have ___ against heaven" (Luke 15:21).

Down

1. Another of Noah's sons (Gen 5:32)
2. Mountain of Go (Ex 3:1)
3. Son of Judah (1 Chron 2:3)
4. Hebrew word for son
*5. 29 across wished to eat some (Luke 15:17)
6. Agreeable (Lev 1:9)
7. Place for herds and plants (Gen 2:20)
8. Singing syllable
*9. 29 across returned ___ (Luke 15)

Down *continued*

10. Fine black wood (Ezek 27:15)
11. Tear (Joel 2:13)
17. Animal foot (1 Sam 17:37)
*18. "Let us __ and celebrate" (Luke 15:23).
20. Growl
22. Emperor during Paul's day
26. ___ facto
28. To the inside of
*30. "Your __ has come" (Luke 15:27).
31. Promised (1 Chron 29:24)
34. Monastic Jewish group
35. Social classes
38. Rabbit (Lev 11:6)
39. Eject
40. "Six days you shall do your ___" (Ex 23:12).
41. How beautiful __ the mountain (Isa 52:7)
42. Number of ungrateful lepers (Luke 17:17)

*From the parable of the Prodigal Son in Luke 15:11–32

How Did You Do?

Many of us like to grade our performances. Whether it's keeping track of our batting average on our church softball team or scoring how well we fared on a word test in a magazine, it's fun to determine how we rate. So for those who want to know how they did in answering the questions in chapter 1, the following chart should give you a good idea of how well you did.

Note that each quotation puzzle, cryptogram, question and answer, multiple choice, fill-in, and true or false is worth 1 point. If a question has more than one answer, divide it accordingly. For example, if one question asks Who were the "Sons of Thunder" and you answer only "John," then you score ½ point. Or, if a fill-in has three blanks and you fill in only one correctly, you score ⅓ point. Matching questions, puzzles, and games are worth as many points as there are answers.

The total number of points possible for this chart includes the questions in chapter 1 and Crossword Puzzle #1:

460 to 512: You are truly a Bible scholar!
384 to 459: You have an excellent grasp of Bible facts.
307 to 383: You have some knowledge of the Bible.
256 to 306: You could brush up on the Bible.
0 to 255: You may want to start studying the Bible.

If you didn't score as well as you wanted to, don't be discouraged. You probably just need to get used to this kind of testing. Incidentally, each chapter is designed to help you do better with each succeeding chapter.

CHAPTER TWO
The Words and Deeds of Men in the Bible

1. True or False: Adam is the first man mentioned in the Bible.

2. Who was thrown into a lion's den but was not harmed?

3. This shepherd saw the burning bush: (a) Ezra; (b) Moses; (c) Joseph; (d) Benjamin.

4. Fill in the blank: Jesus said of Nathanael: "Here is truly an Israelite in whom there is no _____!" (John 1:47).

5. Who tried to run away from God and was swallowed by a large fish?

6. True or False: Abraham's nephew was Lot.

7. Who was called the father of many nations? (a) Adam; (b) Abraham; (c) Jacob; (d) Joseph.

8. To which apostle did Jesus give the keys to the kingdom of heaven?

9. True or False: Esau sold his birthright for food.

---

10. MATCHING

Match married couples.

1. Asenath   A. Er

2. Tamar   B. David

3. Michal   C. Hosea

4. Elizabeth   D. Zacharias

5. Gomer   E. Joseph

Answers for this page: **1.** *True* **2.** *Daniel* **3.** *(b) Moses* **4.** *deceit* **5.** *Jonah* **6.** *True* **7.** *(b) Abraham* **8.** *Peter* **9.** *True* **10.** *1E; 2A; 3B; 4D; 5C*

11. QUOTATION PUZZLE: EVERYTHING IN ITS PLACE?

To find the verse, put the letters that appear in the bottom half of the puzzle into the column of boxes above them. The letters may not be listed in the exact order in which they appear in the quote. Mark off used letters at the bottom. A letter may be used only once. The black boxes represent the space between words.

12. Fill in the blank: John the Baptist declared, "I am the voice of one crying out in the _____" (John 1:23).

13. Who lived 969 years? (a) Cain; (b) Methuselah; (c) Noah; (d) Isaac.

14. True or False: David rejoiced over the death of King Saul.

15. To whom did the Queen of Sheba declare, "Your wisdom and prosperity far surpass the report that I had heard"? (1 Ki 10:7).

16. Who was Abraham's oldest son?

17. Fill in the blanks: "And _____ with his sons and his wife and his sons' wives went into the _____ to escape the waters of the flood" (Gen 7:7).

18. True or False: It was Paul's custom to preach the gospel in the synagogue of each new city he visited.

19. Who was a "good" king? (a) Hezekiah; (b) Jehoshaphat; (c) Joash; (d) all three.

Answers for this page: **11.** *"The Lord God took the man and put him in the garden" (Gen 2:15).* **12.** *wilderness* **13.** *(b) Methuselah* **14.** *False* **15.** *Solomon* **16.** *Ishmael* **17.** *Noah, ark* **18.** *True* **19.** *(d) all three*

20. True or False: Joseph had a silver cup planted in the grain bag of his brother, Judah.

21. Fill in the blank: Job's wife said to him, "Do you still persist in your integrity? Curse _____, and die" (Job 2:9).

22. What was the name, which means "son of encouragement," that the apostles gave to Joseph?

23. What did the Jews call a man who is dedicated to God and who can't cut his hair or drink wine? (a) priest; (b) a Levite; (c) a Nazarite; (d) a prophet.

24. True or False: Ezra told the Hebrew men to stay with their foreign wives.

25. Who was the husband of Sapphira and was killed because he had lied to the Holy Spirit?

26. What did Abraham give Melchizedek? (a) a drink of water; (b) one tenth of all the spoils of battle; (c) his own daughter; (d) a place to sleep.

27. True or False: Moses' older brother was Caleb.

28. Whom did Deborah command to defeat the army of King Jabin? (a) Barak; (b) Gideon; (c) Jephthah; (d) Sisera.

---

29. MATCHING

Match the ruler and the empire or the country.

1. King Cyrus	A. Roman Empire
2. King Belshazzar	B. Persia
3. Tiberius Caesar	C. Egypt
4. Pharaoh Necho	D. Babylon
5. King Asa	E. Judea
6. King Herod	F. Judah

Answers for this page: **20.** *False (Benjamin)* **21.** *God* **22.** *Barnabas* **23.** *(c) a Nazarite* **24.** *False* **25.** *Ananias* **26.** *(b) one tenth of all the spoils of battle* **27.** *False (Aaron)* **28.** *(a) Barak* **29.** *1B; 2D; 3A; 4C; 5F; 6E*

30. Fill in the blanks: "When the donkey saw the angel of the Lord, it lay down under _____; and _____ anger was kindled, and he struck the donkey with his staff" (Num 22:27).

31. Who was married to Rebekah?

32. Fill in the blank: Paul wrote, "Only Luke is with me. Get _____ and bring him with you, for he is useful in my ministry" (2 Tim 4:11).

33. True or False: Boaz was Ruth's second husband.

34. Who anointed the first two kings of Israel? (a) Saul; (b) Samuel; (c) Isaiah; (d) Moses.

35. Fill in the blank: Isaiah prophesied, "Look, the young woman is with child and shall bear a son, and shall name him _____" (Isa 7:14).

36. True or False: Benjamin was Jacob's youngest son.

37. Who was the husband of Queen Jezebel?

38. This judge thrust his sword into the fat belly of King Eglon of Moab: (a) Ehud; (b) Shamgar; (c) Tola; (d) Jair.

39. Fill in the blank: "When Samuel saw _____, the Lord told him, 'Here is the man of whom I spoke to you. He it is who shall rule over my people'" (1 Sam 9:17).

40. True or False: The four Gospel writers were Matthew, Mark, Luke, and John.

41. The Prophet Hananiah broke the wooden yoke from the neck of this prophet to show that God would break the yoke of Nebuchadnezzar from the neck of all nations: (a) Isaiah; (b) Jeremiah; (c) Ezekiel; (d) Micah.

42. True or False: Elisha was the prophet who ascended into heaven in a chariot of fire.

43. Fill in the blanks: Paul said, "We know that all things work together for _____ for those who _____ God" (Rom 8:28).

Answers for this page: **30.** *Balaam, Balaam's* **31.** *Isaac* **32.** *Mark* **33.** *True* **34.** *(b) Samuel* **35.** *Immanuel* **36.** *True* **37.** *Ahab* **38.** *(a) Ehud* **39.** *Saul* **40.** *True* **41.** *(b) Jeremiah* **42.** *False (Elijah in a whirlwind)* **43.** *good, love*

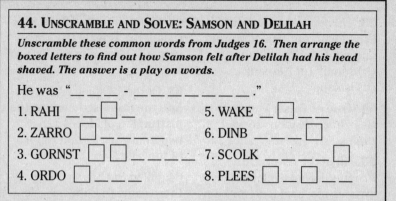

44. UNSCRAMBLE AND SOLVE: SAMSON AND DELILAH

Unscramble these common words from Judges 16. Then arrange the boxed letters to find out how Samson felt after Delilah had his head shaved. The answer is a play on words.

He was "__ __ __ - __ __ __ __ __ __ __ __."

1. RAHI __ __ ☐ __   5. WAKE __ ☐ __ __
2. ZARRO ☐ __ __ __ __   6. DINB __ __ __ ☐
3. GORNST ☐ ☐ __ __ __ __   7. SCOLK __ __ __ __ ☐
4. ORDO ☐ __ __ __   8. PLEES ☐ __ ☐ __ __

45. Besides Jesus, who prayed for God to forgive his murderers?

46. Who saved Jacob and his family from starvation during seven years of famine? (a) Potiphar; (b) Joseph; (c) Jacob; (d) Zephaniah.

47. Fill in the blanks: Moses gave the Israelites the Ten Commandments, which begin: "I am the Lord your God, who brought you out of the land of _____, out of the house of _____" (Ex 20:2).

48. What tax collector wrote a canonical biography of Jesus?

49. Which of the Gospel writers noted that he had acquired his information by research? (a) Matthew; (b) Mark; (c) Luke; (d) John.

50. True or False: The first battle Moses and the Israelites fought after leaving Egypt was with the Amalekites.

51. What cousin of Esther had raised her and helped her become queen of Persia and Media?

52. Fill in the blanks: Paul said, "Do not be deceived: God is not _____, for you reap whatever you _____" (Gal 6:7).

Answers for this page: **44.** . . . "dis-tressed" 1. hair; 2. razor; 3. strong; 4. door; 5. weak; 6. bind; 7. locks; 8. sleep **45.** Stephen **46.** (b) Joseph **47.** Egypt, slavery **48.** Matthew **49.** (c) Luke **50.** True **51.** Mordecai **52.** mocked, sow

53. This prophet confronted David with his sins of murder and adultery: (a) Elijah; (b) Jonah; (c) Nathan; (d) Isaiah.

54. True or False: The apostles chose deacons to wait on tables.

55. Fill in the blank: The Prophet Isaiah exclaimed, "Woe is me! I am lost, for I am a man of unclean _____" (Isa 6:5).

56. Who was the third king of Israel after Saul and David?

57. Who was the first high priest of Israel? (a) Tobias; (b) Eli; (c) Samuel; (d) Aaron.

58. True or False: Because Paul was under house arrest in Rome, the Jewish leaders came to him.

59. Fill in the blank: Peter said to Jesus, "You will never wash my _____" (John 13:8).

60. Who murdered Abel?

61. True or False: Elisha was Elijah's protégé.

62. She was not a wife of King David: (a) Abigail; (b) Ahinoam; (c) Hannah; (d) Bathsheba.

63. Of the 12 spies who went into the Promised Land at the instruction of Moses, what two men gave a good report of the land?

64. Fill in the blank: "Now there came to Ephesus a Jew named _____, a native of Alexandria. He was an eloquent man, well-versed in the scriptures" (Acts 18:24).

65. True or False: The lame son of Jonathan was named Mephibosheth.

66. Who was Jacob's favorite son? (a) Joseph; (b) Reuben; (c) Judah; (d) Levi.

67. Fill in the blank: Agrippa asked Paul, "Are you so quickly persuading me to become a _____?" (Acts 26:28).

68. Which disciple stood beside Jesus' mother at the cross?

Answers for this page: **53.** *(c) Nathan* **54.** *True* **55.** *lips* **56.** *Solomon* **57.** *(d) Aaron* **58.** *True* **59.** *feet* **60.** *Cain* **61.** *True* **62.** *(c) Hannah* **63.** *Joshua, Caleb* **64.** *Apollos* **65.** *True* **66.** *(a) Joseph* **67.** *Christian* **68.** *John*

69. MATCHING

Match the brothers.

1. James	A. Jacob
2. Ephraim	B. Peter
3. Esau	C. John
4. Andrew	D. Levi
5. Reuben	E. Manasseh

70. This prophet had to lie on his left side for 390 days to indicate God's punishment of Israel and then on his right side for 40 days to indicate God's punishment of Judah: (a) Isaiah; (b) Jeremiah; (c) Ezekiel; (d) Nahum.

71. True or False: Both Elijah and Elisha raised a boy from the dead.

72. As a reward for her dancing, the daughter of Herodias asked for whose head?

73. Fill in the blank: "When she got up to glean, _____ instructed his young men, 'Let her glean even among the standing sheaves, and do not reproach her'" (Ruth 2:15).

74. Who was Bathsheba's first husband?

75. Who replaced Judas as an apostle? (a) Barabbas; (b) Matthias; (c) Stephen; (d) Philip.

76. True or False: Solomon built a shrine to the pagan god Chemosh, and 300 years later King Josiah had it destroyed.

77. Who was the father of Rachel and Leah?

78. Fill in the blank: "Her husband _____ said to her, 'Hannah, why do you weep? Why do you not eat? Why is your heart sad? Am I not more to you than ten sons?'" (1 Sam 1:8).

Answers for this page: **69.** *1C; 2E; 3A; 4B; 5D* **70.** *(c) Ezekiel* **71.** *True* **72.** *John the Baptist's* **73.** *Boaz* **74.** *Uriah* **75.** *(b) Matthias* **76.** *True* **77.** *Laban* **78.** *Elkanah*

79. While fleeing from his brother, this man dreamed of angels going up and down a ladder: (a) James; (b) John; (c) Moses; (d) Jacob.

80. True or False: Haman schemed to have Mordecai hanged on a gallows, but he was hanged there instead.

81. Fill in the blanks: Peter said to a lame man, "I have no _____ or _____, but what I have I give you; . . . stand up and _____" (Acts 3:6).

82. When everyone else was afraid of the new convert Paul, who defended him?

83. This judge was the younger brother of Caleb: (a) Ibzan; (b) Elon; (c) Abdon; (d) Othniel.

84. True or False: Ezra and Nehemiah are the two important Jewish leaders associated with the return of the Israelites from Babylonian exile.

85. Who was the ancestor of both the Hebrews and Arabs?

86. Who wrote both letters to the Corinthians? (a) Timothy; (b) Paul; (c) Philemon; (d) Peter.

87. Fill in the blank: The people sang, "Saul has killed his thousands, and _____ his ten thousands" (1 Sam 18:7).

88. Which Jewish king showed all the nation's treasures to the men from Babylon?

89. At whose burial site did Jesus weep?

---

90. CRYPTOGRAM: CREATION OF MAN

Decode the letters in the words of this Bible verse. Each letter corresponds to a different letter in the alphabet.

MJYI MJY RVWB UVB CVWSYB SZI CWVS MJY BQFM
VC MJY UWVQIB, ZIB AWYZMJYB XIMV JXF IVFMWXRF
MJY AWYZMJ VC RXCY.

Answers for this page: **79.** *(d) Jacob* **80.** *True* **81.** *silver, gold, walk*
82. *Barnabas* **83.** *(d) Othniel* **84.** *True* **85.** *Abraham* **86.** *(b) Paul* **87.** *David*
88. *Hezekiah* **89.** *Lazarus's* **90.** *"Then the Lord God formed man from the dust of the ground, and breathed into his nostrils the breath of life" (Gen 2:7).*

91. MATCHING

Match the rulers with their important subject.

1. Pharaoh	A. Nathan
2. Ahasuerus	B. Joseph
3. David	C. Mordecai
4. Nebuchadnezzar	D. Jeremiah
5. Josiah	E. Daniel

92. True or False: Uzzah died because he touched the Ark of the Covenant.

93. Who was the brother of Moses? (a) Aaron; (b) Jacob; (c) Joshua; (d) Jethro.

94. Fill in the blank: David cried out, "My God, my God, why have you _____ me?" (Psa 22:1).

95. True or False: The first Jewish women allowed to inherit land were the daughters of Zelophehad.

96. Fill in the blank: "_____ did more to provoke the anger of the Lord, the God of Israel, than had all the kings of Israel who were before him" (1 Ki 16:33).

97. Who prayed on Mount Carmel for fire to come down and burn up his sacrifice? (a) Enoch; (b) Elijah; (c) Ahab; (d) Hopni.

98. True or False: Ishmael and Isaac, both sons of Abraham, had different mothers.

99. What son of Jacob was left in Egypt until his brothers brought Benjamin to Joseph?

100. Who confronted Cain about the murder he had committed? (a) Adam; (b) God; (c) the devil; (d) Gabriel.

101. True or False: Philip baptized an Ethiopian eunuch.

102. Which son of Isaac was a skillful hunter?

Answers for this page: **91.** *1B; 2C; 3A; 4E; 5D* **92.** *True* **93.** *(a) Aaron* **94.** *forsaken* **95.** *True* **96.** *Ahab* **97.** *(b) Elijah* **98.** *True* **99.** *Simeon* **100.** *(b) God* **101.** *True* **102.** *Esau*

103. Fill in the blanks: David prayed, "Create in me a clean _____, O God, and put a new and right _____ within me" (Psa 51:10).

104. Who succeeded Moses as the leader of the Hebrew nation?

105. God told this prophet to love a woman who has a lover and is an adulteress:
(a) Isaiah; (b) Jeremiah;
(c) Hosea; (d) Ezekiel.

106. Who was the Philistine giant whom David killed with a stone?

---

107. HIDDEN WORDS: MEN OF THE OLD TESTAMENT

Find these names hidden in the sentences below:

Moses	Noah	David	Isaac	Jacob
Abraham	Solomon	Adam	Joseph	

1. Jack will play his violin solo Monday.

2. My father had a midlife crisis.

3. The photographer gave Linda videotapes of her performances.

4. Be sure to fill each thermos, especially the largest one.

5. Louisa accepted the job of president of the science club.

6. The Sabra hampered the enemies of the new state of Israel.

7. The answer is no; a home for the aged will not be built in this town.

8. The city of San Jose phased out its old system of tax collection.

9. Today at the Pentagon, Maj. A. C. O'Brien received a silver star for bravery.

Answers for this page: **103.** *heart, spirit* **104.** *Joshua* **105.** *(c) Hosea*
106. *Goliath* **107.** *1. Solomon; 2. Adam; 3. David; 4. Moses; 5. Isaac; 6. Abraham; 7. Noah; 8. Joseph; 9. Jacob*

108. True or False: Lot refused to give his two virgin daughters to the men of Sodom for their pleasure.

109. This apostle cut off the right ear of the high priest's slave: (a) Peter; (b) John; (c) James; (d) Thomas.

110. True or False: Samson's attraction to Philistine women led to his moral downfall.

111. This son of David raped his half-sister, Tamar: (a) Absalom; (b) Amnon; (c) Adonijah; (d) Nathan.

112. Fill in the blank: Elijah prayed, "I alone am left, and they are seeking my _____, to take it away" (1 Ki 19:14).

113. True or False: Onesimus was a runaway slave who returned to his master, Philemon.

114. What Jew was a cupbearer to the King of Persia?

115. True or False: Moses died before the Israelites entered the Promised Land.

116. He was not an ancestor of Jesus: (a) Abraham; (b) Judah; (c) Moses; (d) David.

117. This king of Judah discovered the Book of the Law in the temple and instituted religious reforms in the Southern Kingdom: (a) Solomon; (b) Jehoshaphat; (c) Hezekiah; (d) Josiah.

118. Fill in the blanks: Paul said, "I will never eat _____, so that I may not cause one of them to _____" (1 Cor 8:13).

119. This son of Jacob plotted with Simeon to kill Shechem for having dishonored their sister: (a) Reuben; (b) Judah; (c) Levi; (d) Issachar.

120. Who betrayed Jesus with a kiss?

121. True or False: Seth was Adam's third son.

122. Who was Moses' father-in-law? (a) Dathan; (b) Jethro; (c) Nadab; (d) Abihu.

Answers for this page: **108.** *False* **109.** *(a) Peter* **110.** *True* **111.** *(b) Amnon* **112.** *life* **113.** *True* **114.** *Nehemiah* **115.** *True* **116.** *(c) Moses* **117.** *(d) Josiah* **118.** *meat, fall* **119.** *(c) Levi* **120.** *Judas Iscariot* **121.** *True* **122.** *(b) Jethro*

123. This minor prophet said Elijah would appear before the coming of the Lord: (a) Obadiah; (b) Nahum; (c) Zechariah; (d) Malachi.

124. After receiving the Holy Spirit, who preached the gospel to the people on the day of Pentecost?

125. True or False: Abraham's wife hated Ishmael, and that's why Abraham banished his son.

126. Fill in the blanks: Just after John baptized Jesus, a voice from heaven said, "This is my _____, the _____, with whom I am well pleased" (Matt 3:17).

127. This son saw Noah's nakedness while he was asleep: (a) Shem; (b) Ham; (c) Japheth; (d) Canaan.

128. True or False: King Rehoboam listened to the advice of his young friends, which cost him half his kingdom.

129. Which judge sought God's assurance by laying a wool fleece on a threshing floor?

130. This apostle was called a "Zealot": (a) Philip; (b) Bartholomew; (c) Simon; (d) Thomas.

---

131. MATCHING

Match the godless son with his godly father.

1. Phinchas	A. Samuel
2. Manasseh	B. Josiah
3. Joel	C. Eli
4. Zedekiah	D. Hezekiah
5. Abimelech	E. David
6. Amnon	F. Gideon

Answers for this page: **123.** *(d) Malachi* **124.** *Peter* **125.** *True* **126.** *Son, Beloved* **127.** *(b) Ham* **128.** *True* **129.** *Gideon* **130.** *(c) Simon* **131.** *1C; 2D; 3A; 4B; 5F; 6E*

132. QUOTATION PUZZLE: A BIG JOB

O	A	E	L	B	T	C	D	E	T	L	F	Y	T	H	M	I	A	A	T
T	H	N	D	M	A	O	A	G	A	O	R		A	A	D	E	S	O	R
T	H	A		L	I	N		T	V	E	E		N	A	N		M	I	L
		E				R		S		V	E			N	E		T		

---

133. True or False: Elijah was taken up to heaven in a whirlwind.

134. What Gentile was Paul's companion and a physician?

135. True or False: Job's friends wondered why God would persecute such a righteous man as Job.

136. What respected Pharisee told the Jewish council to leave the Christians alone for the council could be fighting against God?

137. Fill in the blanks: Job said, "For I know that my _____ lives, and that at the last he will stand upon the _____" (Job 19:25).

138. True or False: Joseph was thrown into prison because he tried to seduce Potiphar's wife.

139. What Hebrew patriarch allowed his wife to be admitted into Pharaoh's harem?

140. This tax collector promised to give half of his possessions to the poor: (a) Zacchaeus; (b) Zechariah; (c) Matthew; (d) no tax collector would do that.

141. True or False: Uriah, the Hittite, committed suicide by swallowing poison when he learned that his wife had been unfaithful.

Answers for this page: **132.** *"The man gave names to all cattle, and to the birds of the air, and to every animal" (Gen 2:20).* **133.** *True* **134.** *Luke* **135.** *False* **136.** *Gamaliel* **137.** *Redeemer, earth* **138.** *False (she fabricated this story)* **139.** *Abraham* **140.** *(a) Zacchaeus* **141.** *False (murdered in battle)*

142. What king ordered a baby to be cut in two in order to determine its true mother?

143. When he couldn't buy a particular vineyard, which king returned home, went to bed, and refused to eat? (a) Hezekiah; (b) Ahab; (c) Herod; (d) Rehoboam.

144. True or False: The Apostle John had a vision of the end times.

145. Fill in the blanks: "The _____ indeed was given through Moses; grace and _____ came through Jesus Christ" (John 1:17).

146. Who formed a golden calf for the Israelites to worship in the wilderness? (a) Moses; (b) Joshua; (c) Dathan; (d) Aaron.

147. Who was stoned to death for proclaiming the gospel to the Jewish council?

148. True or False: Abraham refused to sacrifice his son, Isaac.

149. Who was David's father and Ruth's grandson?

150. Who was not a judge in Israel? (a) Korah; (b) Shamgar; (c) Jephthah; (d) Abdon.

151. True or False: Jonah proclaimed God's judgment against Nineveh.

152. Which of these ordeals did Paul not suffer? (a) stoning; (b) crucifixion; (c) shipwreck; (d) hunger and thirst.

153. Fill in the blanks: Joshua declared, "Choose this day whom you will _____, . . . but as for me and my household, we will _____ the Lord" (Josh 24:15).

154. To whom did God promise to place a rainbow in the clouds as a sign of his covenant with the earth?

155. Although he was chief of David's Thirty, he was not one of David's Three: (a) Josheb-basshebeth; (b) Eleazar; (c) Shammah; (d) Abishai.

156. True or False: After Joshua's death, the children of Israel faithfully obeyed God.

Answers for this page: **142.** *Solomon* **143.** *(b) Ahab* **144.** *True* **145.** *law, truth* **146.** *(d) Aaron* **147.** *Stephen* **148.** *False* **149.** *Jesse* **150.** *(a) Korah* **151.** *True* **152.** *(b) crucifixion* **153.** *serve, serve* **154.** *Noah* **155.** *(d) Abishai* **156.** *False*

157. MATCHING

Match these men with their vocation.

1. Sisera	A. Priest
2. Apollos	B. Prophet
3. Jehoiada	C. King
4. Sennacherib	D. Soldier
5. Habakkuk	E. Evangelist

158. Paul wrote two New Testament letters to this person whom he regarded as a son.

159. Who was the son of Rachel and the brother of Joseph? (a) Naphtali; (b) Dan; (c) Benjamin; (d) Judah.

160. Whose name was changed to "Israel"?

161. Fill in the blank: Joseph told his brothers, "_____ sent me before you to preserve for you a remnant on earth" (Gen 45:7).

162. True or False: Adam persuaded Eve to eat the forbidden fruit.

163. Who heard God call him when he was a young ward of Eli?

164. What man did David love more than he loved any woman? (a) Absalom; (b) Saul; (c) Jonathan; (d) Samuel.

165. True or False: Peter bitterly wept when the cock crowed.

166. What son of Isaac was a gentle young man who preferred to dwell in his tent and was close to his mother?

167. Solomon ordered the execution of this general who had served King David: (a) Abner; (b) Joab; (c) Amasa; (d) Benaiah.

168. True or False: Samson used a donkey's jawbone to slay a thousand Philistines.

Answers for this page: **157.** *1D; 2E; 3A; 4C; 5B* **158.** *Timothy* **159.** *(c) Benjamin* **160.** *Jacob* **161.** *God* **162.** *False* **163.** *Samuel* **164.** *(c) Jonathan* **165.** *True* **166.** *Jacob* **167.** *(b) Joab* **168.** *True*

169. WORD SEARCH: KINGS OF ISRAEL AND JUDAH
Answers on page 70.

In the puzzle below, find the 32 kings of Israel and Judah. You can find words diagonally, vertically, horizontally, backward, and forward. When you find a name in the puzzle, cross it off the list.

Abijah	Hezekiah	Jehu	Omri
Ahab	Hoshea	Jeroboam	Pekah
Amaziah	Jehoahaz	Joash	Rehoboam
Amon	Jehoash	Joram	Saul
Asa	Jehoiachin	Josiah	Solomon
Baasha	Jehoiakim	Jotham	Tibni
David	Jehoram	Manasseh	Zechariah
Elah	Jehoshaphat	Nadab	Zimri

```
J  H  A  I  S  O  J  E  H  O  A  S  H  R  N
E  E  J  E  H  O  I  A  C  H  I  N  A  E  O
H  Z  R  E  Y  U  J  V  E  C  B  S  I  H  M
O  E  M  O  H  I  T  X  T  L  A  Z  R  O  O
I  K  A  U  B  O  D  K  A  N  A  D  A  B  L
A  I  W  A  P  O  S  U  H  E  J  H  H  O  O
K  A  M  A  Z  I  A  H  S  Z  O  O  C  A  S
I  H  J  I  R  M  O  M  A  L  A  S  E  M  M
M  A  N  A  S  S  E  H  A  P  S  H  Z  H  A
E  K  E  Z  E  D  A  T  B  R  H  E  A  U  R
A  E  M  A  I  O  N  U  A  B  O  A  M  B  O
H  P  Y  V  H  M  S  W  L  M  A  H  T  O  J
A  V  A  E  C  O  R  D  R  X  O  S  E  L  K
Z  D  J  S  I  N  B  I  T  H  A  N  O  J  B
```

170. What disciple in Damascus helped Saul of Tarsus regain his sight?

171. Fill in the blanks: "The Lord said to _____, 'Where is your brother _____?' He said, 'I do not know; am I my brother's keeper?'" (Gen 4:9).

172. True or False: On his way to Succoth with his wives and children, Jacob fled from his brother, Esau, who tried to kill him.

173. What prophet cursed a number of boys who were jeering him?

174. This apostle kept the common purse of Jesus' band: (a) Andrew; (b) Philip; (c) Thomas; (d) Judas Iscariot.

175. True or False: Naaman, the Aramean commander, was cured of leprosy after immersing himself seven times in the Jordan.

176. What Hebrew was made governor over Egypt?

177. This Hebrew prophet was assigned the Babylonian name Belteshazzar and informed Nebuchadnezzar that he would go mad: (a) Isaiah; (b) Jeremiah; (c) Ezekiel; (d) Daniel.

178. True or False: Peter and Barnabas went on several missionary journeys together.

179. Fill in the blanks: David wept and cried out, "O my son _____, my son, my son _____! Would I had died instead of you, O _____, my son, my son!" (2 Sam 18:33).

180. This king of Judah was struck with leprosy: (a) Amaziah; (b) Uzziah; (c) Jotham; (d) Ahaz.

181. Who preached a sermon on Mars Hill in Athens?

182. True or False: Ezekiel had a vision of a heavenly chariot bearing the throne of God.

183. Who is known as the great lawgiver among the Jewish people?

Answers for this page: **170.** *Ananias* **171.** *Cain, Abel* **172.** *False (Esau welcomed Jacob)* **173.** *Elisha* **174.** *(d) Judas Iscariot* **175.** *True* **176.** *Joseph* **177.** *(d) Daniel* **178.** *False* **179.** *Absalom, Absalom, Absalom* **180.** *(b) Uzziah* **181.** *Paul* **182.** *True* **183.** *Moses*

184. MATCHING

Match these men with their sisters.

1. Simeon	A. Martha
2. Laban	B. Miriam
3. Lazarus	C. Tamar
4. Absalom	D. Rebekah
5. Aaron	E. Dinah

185. This Jewish poet began one poem with the immortal phrase: "The Lord is my shepherd . . .": (a) Deborah; (b) David; (c) Solomon; (d) Isaiah.

186. Which apostle's name means "the rock"?

187. True or False: Shortly after Aaron entered the Promised Land, he rested with his fathers.

188. Both Abraham and Isaac tried to deceive this king of Gerar: (a) Abimelech; (b) Amraphel; (c) Chedorlaomer; (d) Tidal.

189. True or False: Solomon remained faithful to God throughout his life.

190. Fill in the blanks: Jesus said of Lazarus's sickness, "This illness does not lead to _____; rather it is for God's _____" (John 11:4).

191. True or False: The Bible lists Uriah the Hittite as one of David's renowned warriors.

192. He was the first mighty warrior on the earth and was called "A mighty hunter before the Lord": (a) Cain; (b) Lemech; (c) Nimrod; (d) Jared.

193. True or False: Because his ship sank, Paul was never able to reach Rome.

194. Who were the "Sons of Thunder"?

Answers for this page: **184.** *1E; 2D; 3A; 4C; 5B* **185.** *(b) David* **186.** *Peter* **187.** *False (didn't enter the Promised Land)* **188.** *(a) Abimelech* **189.** *False* **190.** *death, glory* **191.** *True* **192.** *(c) Nimrod* **193.** *False* **194.** *James, John*

195. What judge routed a Midian army with a hundred men by blowing trumpets and smashing jars at night?

196. This son defiled Jacob's bed: (a) Reuben; (b) Simeon; (c) Gad; (d) Asher.

197. Fill in the blank: "Then _____ came to his home at Mizpah; and there was his daughter coming out to meet him with timbrels and with dancing" (Judg 11:34).

198. Name the Israelite whom Pharaoh's daughter raised as her son: (a) Hur; (b) Moses; (c) Joshua; (d) Aaron.

199. True or False: Timothy was never circumcised.

200. Who was exalted when God parted the Jordan in order for the children of Israel to cross?

201. Who ate the holy bread when he fled from King Saul? (a) David; (b) Jonathan; (c) Joab; (d) Samuel.

202. Who told his servant to place his hand under his thigh and thereby promise to find a wife for his son among his kindred?

203. Fill in the blank: "_____ was eight years old when he began to reign; he reigned thirty-one years in Jerusalem" (2 Ki 22:1).

204. True or False: Paul was a Roman citizen by birth.

---

205. MATCHING

Match the person who died with the one who raised that person from the dead.

1. Dorcas	A. Jesus
2. Shunammite woman's son	B. Elijah
3. Jairus's daughter	C. Paul
4. Zarephath widow's son	D. Elisha
5. Eutychus	E. Peter

Answers for this page: **195.** *Gideon* **196.** *(a) Reuben* **197.** *Jephthah* **198.** *(b) Moses* **199.** *False* **200.** *Joshua* **201.** *(a) David* **202.** *Abraham* **203.** *Josiah* **204.** *True* **205.** *1E; 2D; 3A; 4B; 5C*

206. This judge tore a lion apart barehanded: (a) Barak; (b) Gideon; (c) Samson; (d) none of the above.

207. Who commanded the Israelite army on the day the Amorite kings were defeated and the sun stood still at Gibeon?

208. This prophet walked around naked for three years as a sign against Egypt and Ethiopia: (a) Isaiah; (b) Jeremiah; (c) Ezekiel; (d) Amos.

209. True or False: After Noah planted a vineyard, he drank wine and became drunk.

210. What Levite was from Cyprus, sold his field, and laid the money at the apostles' feet?

211. How old was Abraham when Isaac was born? (a) 30; (b) 55; (c) 70; (d) 100.

212. True or False: After Joseph interpreted the dreams of the baker and cupbearer, he was immediately released from prison.

213. Who said he had the power to crucify Jesus?

214. Fill in the blank: "Then _____ was so filled with rage against Shadrach, Meshach, and Abednego that his face was distorted. He ordered the furnace heated up seven times more than was customary" (Dan 3:19).

215. True or False: Adam blamed God for his sin of eating the forbidden fruit.

216. Who rebuked Peter for not eating with Gentile believers?

217. True or False: Abraham tried to dissuade the Lord from destroying Sodom.

---

218. CRYPTOGRAM: A KING OF GOD'S CHOOSING

VCJ PZFS CHQ QZXTCV ZXV H DHK HNVJF CUQ ZRK
CJHFV; HKS VCJ PZFS CHQ HEEZUKVJS CUD VZ AJ FXPJF
ZGJF CUQ EJZEPJ.

Answers for this page: **206.** *(c) Samson* **207.** *Joshua* **208.** *(a) Isaiah* **209.** *True* **210.** *Barnabas* **211.** *(d) 100* **212.** *False* **213.** *Pilate* **214.** *Nebuchadnezzar* **215.** *True* **216.** *Paul* **217.** *True* **218.** *"The Lord has sought out a man after his own heart; and the Lord has appointed him to be ruler over his people" (1 Sam 13:14).*

219. UNSCRAMBLE AND MATCH: WHAT'S MY LINE?

Unscramble the names of the Bible characters, then match each with their occupation.

1. RAZE	_____	A. Carpenter
2. SOMES	_____	B. Tentmaker
3. HAMEHINE	_____	C. Priest
4. TEMWHAT	_____	D. Building supervisor
5. HOPEJS	_____	E. Army commander
6. ANNAMA	_____	F. Tax collector
7. WANDER	_____	G. Physican
8. LUPA	_____	H. Fisherman
9. KLUE	_____	I. Shepherd

220. Who advised Moses not to judge every dispute among the Hebrews? (a) Aaron; (b) Jethro; (c) Joshua; (d) Caleb.

221. He was the first king of the northern kingdom of Israel: (a) Rehoboam; (b) Jeroboam; (c) Abijah; (d) Ahijah.

222. Who was the first person to die in the Bible?

223. Who drove the three sons of Anak out of Hebron? (a) Moses; (b) Joshua; (c) Caleb; (d) no one did.

224. Whom did James say was justified by his works and of whom did Paul say his faith was reckoned to him as righteousness?

225. Fill in the blank: "There he found a Jew named _____, a native of Pontus, who had recently come from Italy with his wife Priscilla, because Claudius had ordered all Jews to leave Rome" (Acts 18:2).

226. Which prophet deciphered God's message written on Belshazzar's palace wall?

Answers for this page: **219.** *1. Ezra/C; 2. Moses/I; 3. Nehemiah/D; 4. Matthew/F; 5. Joseph/A; 6. Namaan/E; 7. Andrew/H; 8. Paul/B; 9. Luke/G* **220.** *(b) Jethro* **221.** *(b) Jeroboam* **222.** *Abel* **223.** *(c) Caleb* **224.** *Abraham* **225.** *Aquila* **226.** *Daniel*

227. MATCHING

Match the son with his godly mother.

1. Samuel	A. Mary
2. John the Baptist	B. Eunice
3. Obed	C. Leah
4. Mark	D. Hannah
5. Judah	E. Elizabeth
6. Timothy	F. Ruth

228. True or False: The descendants of Seth remained faithful to God until the Flood.

229. This Hebrew tribe became responsible for the priestly duties of the nation of Israel: (a) Judah; (b) Benjamin; (c) Ephraim; (d) Levi.

230. True or False: Peter was the first person to speak with Jesus after his resurrection.

231. Fill in the blank: "_____ spoke all the words that the Lord had spoken to Moses, and performed the signs in the sight of the people" (Ex 4:30).

232. What judge was famous for making up riddles?

233. True or False: The Prophet Jeremiah lamented the Babylonian destruction of Jerusalem.

234. What judge had to sacrifice his daughter: (a) Shamgar; (b) Jair; (c) Jephthah; (d) Elon.

235. What sorcerer offered money to the apostles to have the ability to give the Holy Spirit to people?

236. Fill in the blank: "Jude, a servant of Jesus Christ and brother of _____, to those who are called, who are beloved in God the Father and kept safe for Jesus Christ" (Jude 1).

Answers for this page: **227.** *1D; 2E; 3F; 4A; 5C; 6B* **228.** *False* **229.** *(d) Levi* **230.** *False (Mary Magdalene)* **231.** *Aaron* **232.** *Samson* **233.** *True* **234.** *(c) Jephthah* **235.** *Simon* **236.** *James*

237. True or False: Cyrus established the Persian Empire and allowed the Jews to return to Judea.

238. On Mount Horeb Elijah became aware of God in: (a) the wind; (b) the earthquake; (c) the fire; (d) the silence.

239. Who was the father of Manasseh and Ephraim?

240. Fill in the blank: "The Lord said to Joshua, 'This day I will begin to exalt you in the sight of all Israel, so that they may know that I will be with you as I was with _____.'" (Josh 3:7).

241. This son of David rebelled against his father and publicly dishonored him: (a) Absalom; (b) Amnon; (c) Adonijah; (d) Solomon.

242. True or False: Melchizedek was king of Salem and priest of God Most High.

243. Who was the only man not born from a woman?

244. Fill in the blank: "While _____ was sitting at the king's gate, Bigthan and Teresh, two of the king's eunuchs, who guarded the threshold, became angry and conspired to assassinate King Ahasuerus" (Est 2:21).

---

245. QUOTATION PUZZLE: THAT'S THE QUESTION!

T	S	E	I	M	T	N	E	I	I	A	T	W	R	E	N	G
W	O	T	S	I	A	H	O	A	K	E		T	H	P	R	W
I	H	W		O	N		L	F	N	D		E	H	O		K
N	A	O			S					N		T	H	I		E

Answers for this page: **237.** *True* **238.** *(d) the silence* **239.** *Joseph* **240.** *Moses* **241.** *(a) Absalom* **242.** *True* **243.** *Adam* **244.** *Mordecai* **245.** *"Who is like the wise man? And who knows the interpretation of a thing?" (Eccl 8:1).*

246. This believer brought Paul's letter from prison to the Christians in Colossae: (a) Epaphras; (b) Epaphroditus; (c) Tychicus; (d) Archippus.

247. True or False: The Hittites offered their choicest burial places to Abraham to bury Sarah after she passed away.

248. Who walked with God and then was no more because God took him?

249. True or False: Stephen not only spoke with wisdom in defense of the gospel but also performed great wonders and signs.

250. Whose bones were taken out of Egypt when God delivered the children of Israel out of bondage? (a) Abraham; (b) Isaac; (c) Jacob; (d) Joseph.

251. Who used a medium to bring up Samuel from the dead?

252. True or False: Jonah was relieved when God decided not to destroy Nineveh.

253. Paul was a member of this Hebrew tribe: (a) Ephraim; (b) Levi; (c) Benjamin; (d) Judah.

254. Who toppled the temple of Dagon though he was blind?

255. This apostle reclined against Jesus during the Last Supper: (a) Peter; (b) John; (c) Philip; (d) Judas.

256. True or False: Abraham departed from Egypt a wealthy man.

257. What prophet did King Balak of Moab try to entice with riches and honor to curse God's chosen people?

258. This man did not rebel against Moses: (a) Korah; (b) Dathan; (c) Abiram; (d) Phinehas.

259. True or False: Paul and Silas collected money to take to Jerusalem for famine relief.

260. What Babylonian king devastated Jerusalem in the sixth century B.C.?

261. What leader of the Pharisees was Paul's teacher?

Answers for this page: **246.** *(c) Tychicus* **247.** *True* **248.** *Enoch* **249.** *True* **250.** *(d) Joseph* **251.** *Saul* **252.** *False* **253.** *(c) Benjamin* **254.** *Samson* **255.** *(b) John* **256.** *True* **257.** *Balaam* **258.** *(d) Phinehas* **259.** *True* **260.** *Nebuchadnezzar* **261.** *Gamaliel*

262. MATCHING

Match the person with the musical instrument he is associated with.

1. David   A. Pipe

2. Asaph   B. Lyre

3. Joshua   C. Cymbals

4. Jubal   D. Trumpets

263. Fill in the blank: "Then the Lord said to _____ , 'With the three hundred that lapped I will deliver you, and give the Midianites into your hand. Let all the others go to their homes'" (Judg 7:7).

264. True or False: Because Achan sinned against God, the men of Ai defeated the Israelites.

265. Luke wrote his biography of Jesus and history of the early church to this man: (a) Tertius; (b) Theophilus; (c) Philemon; (d) Nereus.

266. Fill in the blank: "Then _____ son of Shealtiel and Jeshua son of Jozadak set out to rebuild the house of God in Jerusalem; and with them were the prophets of God, helping them" (Ezra 5:2).

267. What king made a pact with King Hiram of Tyre in order to acquire materials to build the temple of God?

268. True or False: Amos was a farmer from Tekoa before God called him to prophesy against the injustices of Israel.

269. This son succeeded Aaron as high priest of Israel: (a) Nadab; (b) Abihu; (c) Eleazar; (d) Ithamar.

270. Queen Jezebel plotted to steal the vineyard of this Jezreelite: (a) Naboth; (b) Micaiah; (c) Joram; (d) Elijah.

271. What Roman centurion had a vision in which the angel of God told him to invite Peter to his home?

Answers for this page: **262.** *1B; 2C; 3D; 4A* **263.** *Gideon* **264.** *True* **265.** *(b) Theophilus* **266.** *Zerubbabel* **267.** *Solomon* **268.** *True* **269.** *(c) Eleazar* **270.** *(a) Naboth* **271.** *Cornelius*

272. CRISSCROSS PUZZLE: MALE NAMES AND ROLES

Answers on page 71.

Fit each of the following 66 words into the puzzle below. Words are arranged below alphabetically according to the number of letters.

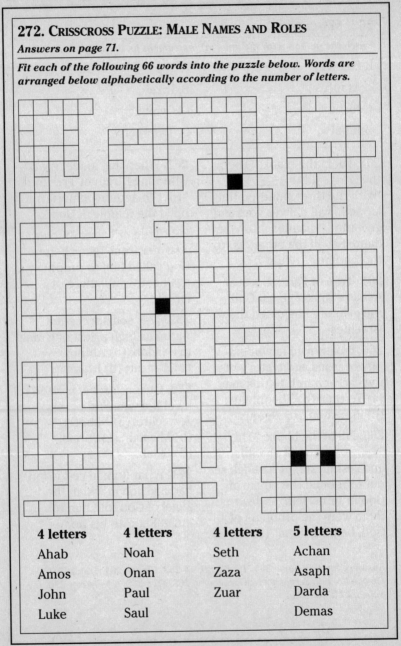

4 letters	**4 letters**	**4 letters**	**5 letters**
Ahab	Noah	Seth	Achan
Amos	Onan	Zaza	Asaph
John	Paul	Zuar	Darda
Luke	Saul		Demas

272. CRISSCROSS PUZZLE: MALE NAMES AND ROLES *continued*

5 letters	6 letters	6 letters	8 Letters
Elder	Carpus	Uzziah	Abiathar
Hegai	Daniel	**7 Letters**	Hezekiah
Hosea	Elisha	Ahaziah	Jeremiah
Isaac	Gideon	Ananias	Onesimus
Jesus	Hezron	Apostle	**9 letters**
Jonah	Hoshea	Bedeiah	Elimelech
Laban	Joseph	Eleazar	Nethanial
Micah	Josiah	Husband	Zechariah
Moses	Nathan	Malchus	Zephaniah
Peter	Philip	Obadiah	**10 letters**
Uriah	Pilate	Prophet	Ishbosheth
Uriel	Samson	Stephen	Zelophehad
6 letters	Samuel	Timaeus	**11 letters**
Bariah	Thomas	Zebulun	Melchizedek

273. True or False: Nabal told Abigail to send supplies to David out of respect for David's father.

274. Fill in the blank: "And Nehemiah, who was the governor, and _____ the priest and scribe, and the Levites who taught the people said to all the people, 'This day is holy to the Lord your God'" (Neh 8:9).

275. The Danites stole the idol and Levite priest from this man before they attacked the people of Laish: (a) Jonathan; (b) Gershom; (c) Nahum; (d) Micah.

276. Which prophet envisioned the Messiah to be "a man of suffering," who would bear the iniquities of many?

277. Who had his name changed from "Abram"?

Answers for this page: **273.** *False (Nabal disrespected David's father)* **274.** *Ezra* **275.** *(d) Micah* **276.** *Isaiah* **277.** *Abraham*

278. True or False: King Herod ordered the Apostle James to be killed by the sword.

279. What judge was mourned by all Israel when he died and was buried at his home in Ramah?

280. True or False: John the Baptist led the Apostle Matthew to Jesus.

281. This friend of Job was younger than Job's other three friends, and yet he still rebuked them for having no answer to Job's self-justification: (a) Eliphaz; (b) Elihu; (c) Bildad; (d) Zophar.

282. Who was the first Hebrew king to have his brother killed?

283. True or False: Adam spoke to God after the Fall.

284. Which apostle asked Jesus to show them their heavenly Father? (a) John; (b) Peter; (c) Thomas; (d) Philip.

285. Fill in the blank: Concerning the Promised Land, "_____ quieted the people before Moses, and said, 'Let us go up at once and occupy it, for we are well able to overcome it'" (Num 13:30).

286. True or False: Laban tricked Jacob into marrying his oldest daughter.

287. What relative of Barnabas did Paul refuse to allow to go on one of his missionary journeys?

288. This son of Jacob became the ancestor of Moses: (a) Joseph; (b) Judah; (c) Levi; (d) Benjamin.

289. True or False: James was a leader of the early Christian church.

290. What prophet did God forbid to marry? (a) Isaiah; (b) Jeremiah; (c) Hosea; (d) God never forbade marriage.

Answers for this page: **278.** *True* **279.** *Samuel* **280.** *False* **281.** *(b) Elihu* **282.** *Solomon* **283.** *True* **284.** *(d) Philip* **285.** *Caleb* **286.** *True* **287.** *Mark* **288.** *(c) Levi* **289.** *True* **290.** *(b) Jeremiah*

291. Fill in the blank: "At Gibeon the Lord appeared to _____ in a dream by night; and God said, 'Ask what I should give you'" (1 Ki 3:5).

292. True or False: The first time Joseph's brothers saw him as governor over the land in Egypt, Joseph wanted them to see how powerful he had become.

293. This Gospel writer was one of the three apostles whom Jesus separated from the others in the Garden of Gethsemane and who fell asleep: (a) Matthew; (b) Mark; (c) Peter; (d) John.

294. Besides Hur, who held up Moses' hands in order for the Israelites to prevail over the Amalekites?

295. True or False: David chose Solomon to succeed him as king of Israel.

296. This prophet asked for a double share of Elijah's spirit: (a) Elisha; (b) Isaiah; (c) Joel; (d) Nathan.

297. Who was inflicted with sores from the soles of his feet to the crown of his head?

298. Fill in the blanks: Paul "fell to the ground and heard a voice saying to him, '_____, _____, why do you persecute me'" (Acts 9:4).

299. This judge was a left-handed Benjaminite, who subdued the mighty Moabites: (a) Barak; (b) Gideon; (c) Samson; (d) Ehud.

300. True or False: King Saul was ashamed of his son, Jonathan, because Jonathan was afraid to fight Israel's enemies.

Answers for this page: **291.** *Solomon* **292.** *False* **293.** *(d) John* **294.** *Aaron* **295.** *True* **296.** *(a) Elisha* **297.** *Job* **298.** *Saul, Saul* **299.** *(d) Ehud* **300.** *False (Jonathan was courageous)*

WORD SEARCH: KINGS OF ISRAEL AND JUDAH *Puzzle on page 56.*

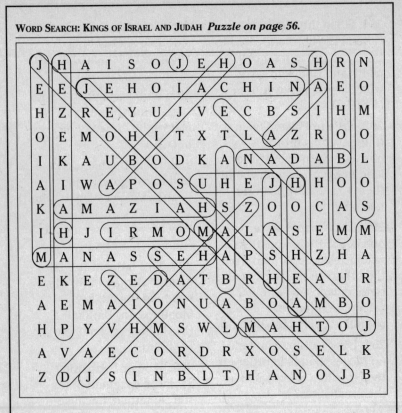

J H A I S O J E H O A S H R N
E E J E H O I A C H I N A E O
H Z R E Y U J V E C B S I H M
O E M O H I T X T L A Z R O O
I K A U B O D K A N A D A B L
A I W A P O S U H E J H H O O
K A M A Z I A H S Z O O C A S
I H J I R M O M A L A S E M M
M A N A S S E H A P S H Z H A
E K E Z E D A T B R H E A U R
A E M A I O N U A B O A M B O
H P Y V H M S W L M A H T O J
A V A E C O R D R X O S E L K
Z D J S I N B I T H A N O J B

CRISSCROSS PUZZLE: MALE NAMES AND ROLES *Puzzle on page 66.*

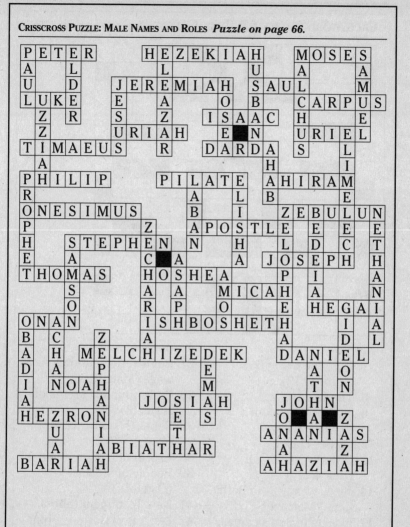

CROSSWORD PUZZLE #2: BIBLE COUPLES *Answers on page 278.*

Across

1. "____ be with you" (John 20:19).
6. The Creator
8. Sister of Absalom (2 Sam 13:1)
12. Comes closer
13. Grandson of Asher (Gen 46:17)
14. Jesus was ____ in Bethlehem. (Matt 2:1)
17. Insects in lion's carcass (Judg 14:8)
19. Bible couple: Parents of Jacob (3 wds)
24. Grassland
25. First woman
26. Violent storm (Psa 55:8)

Across *continued*

27. Coins representing a day's wage (Matt 18:28)
29. Bible couple: Parents of Jesus (3 wds)
37. Rebekah's brother (Gen 24:29)
38. Expression of greeting
39. People of Media (Dan 6:12)
41. New Testament (abbr)
42. "Angels of God ____ him" (Gen 32:1).
43. "God saw that ____ was good" (Gen 1:18).
44. Jewish month
48. Exclamation of joy (Gen 27:27)

Across *continued*

50. Bible couple: Parents of Isaac (3 wds)

56. One who helps

57. Home of Saul's medium (1 Sam 28:7)

58. Nightfall (2 wds) (Josh 2:5)

59. Army commander (2 Ki 5:1)

61. Topic (Psa 45:1)

62. Timothy's _____mother—Lois (2 Tim 1:5)

Down

2. Ancestor of Christ (Luke 3:38)

3. Noteworthy period of time (archaic var.)

4. Site of a wedding (John 2:1)

5. Son of Judah (Gen 38:3)

7. Amorite king (Num 21:33)

8. Tellurium (chem)

9. French clergy

10. They'll inherit the earth (Matt 5:5)

11. Space (Deut 23:12)

14. Jesus "saw a man blind from _____" (John 9:1).

15. "Strain out a _____" (Matt 23:24).

16. Produced offspring (Gen 30:38)

18. Arab clan leader

20. Philippian friend of Paul (Phil 4:3)

Down *continued*

21. Plural of first letter

22. First wife

23. Son of Lot (Gen 19:38)

28. Swell of water (Jas 1:6)

29. Joint account (abbr)

30. Obadiah (abbr)

31. Spanish for "saint"

32. Noah's son (Gen 5:32)

33. Fisherman's equipment (Matt 4:18)

34. Of age (abbr)

35. Road (abbr)

36. "Oh ____ of little faith" (Matt 8:26, KJV).

37. Behold! (Isa 17:14)

40. Egyptian king (2 Ki 17:4)

44. Hebrew measure (Isa 5:10; 2 wds)

45. Newly married woman (Jer 2:32)

46. Dog's sound (Isa 56:10)

47. First home of man (Gen 2:15)

48. Fragrance (2 Cor 2:15)

49. Home of Rachel and Jacob (Gen 28:10)

51. Husband of 22 down

52. "____are my mother and my brothers" (Mark 3:34).

53. Vipers (Isa 11:8; pl.)

54. Catch

55. Jewish month (Ezra 6:15)

58. "____ last" (Gen 2:23).

60. Neodymium (chem)

How Did You Do?

By now you've learned how to answer the questions, puzzles, and games in this book, and your score for chapter 2 has probably improved from chapter 1. You've also noticed that questions are rephrased in different chapters. This is not only to focus on a specific element of a topic but also to help you better learn the subject matter.

The total number of points possible for this chart includes the questions in chapter 2 and Crossword Puzzle #2:

474 to 527: You are truly a Bible scholar!
395 to 473: You have an excellent grasp of Bible facts.
316 to 394: You have some knowledge of the Bible.
263 to 315: You could brush up on the Bible.
0 to 262: You may want to start studying the Bible.

Have you jumped from one level to another? See if you can make that leap in the next chapter.

CHAPTER THREE

The Words and Deeds of Women in the Bible

1. Who was the first woman?

2. True or False: Sarah was Ishmael's biological mother.

3. Fill in the blanks: "Therefore a man leaves his father and his mother and clings to his _____, and they become one _____" (Gen 2:24).

4. This woman was Paul's first convert in Europe and sold purple garments: (a) Priscilla; (b) Eunice; (c) Lydia; (d) Lois.

5. True or False: Delilah was Israel's only female judge.

6. Who was the mother of Esau?

7. This woman drew Moses out of the Nile and raised him like a son: (a) Jochebed; (b) Miriam; (c) Pharaoh's daughter; (d) Pharaoh's wife.

8. True or False: Some women used their financial resources to support Jesus' band during his ministry.

---

9. MATCHING

Match these married couples.

1. David

2. Abraham

3. Lamech

4. Mahlon

5. Felix

A. Keturah

B. Ruth

C. Drusilla

D. Ahinoam

E. Adah

Answers for this page: **1.** *Eve* **2.** *False (Hagar)* **3.** *wife, flesh* **4.** *(c) Lydia* **5.** *False (Deborah)* **6.** *Rebekah* **7.** *(c) Pharaoh's daughter* **8.** *True* **9.** *1D; 2A; 3E; 4B; 5C*

10. QUOTATION PUZZLE: FUTURE SHOCK

To find the verse, put the letters that appear in the bottom half of the puzzle into the column of boxes above them. The letters may not be listed in the exact order in which they appear in the quote. Mark off used letters at the bottom. A letter may be used only once. The black boxes represent the space between words.

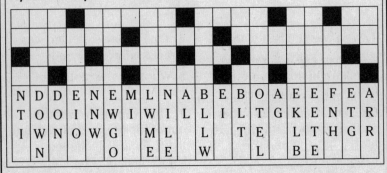

11. Fill in the blanks: An angel told Joseph, "Do not be afraid to take _____ as your wife, for the child conceived in her is from the _____ _____" (Matt 1:20).

12. Who made a little robe for Samuel every year while he was a boy?

13. Who was Jacob's grandmother? (a) Sarah; (b) Eve; (c) Rebekah; (d) Hagar.

14. What did God take out of Adam to form Eve?

15. Fill in the blank: "He who finds a _____ finds a good thing, and obtains favor from the Lord" (Prov 18:22).

16. True or False: Esther's Hebrew name was Hadassah.

17. This wife of David never bore him a child: (a) Abital; (b) Maacah; (c) Abigail; (d) Michal.

18. Fill in the blank: "But _____ said, '. . . your people shall be my people, and your God my God'" (Ruth 1:16).

Answers for this page: **10.** *"Two women will be grinding meal together; one will be taken and one will be left" (Matt 24:41).* **11.** *Mary, Holy Spirit* **12.** *Hannah* **13.** *(a) Sarah* **14.** *a rib* **15.** *wife* **16.** *True* **17.** *(d) Michal* **18.** *Ruth*

19. True or False: Sarah gave her maid Hagar to Abraham to bear a child.

20. This woman corrected Apollos's imperfect teachings about Christ: (a) Priscilla; (b) Lydia; (c) Mary of Bethany; (d) Sapphira.

21. What woman lied about Joseph, the son of Jacob, which caused him to be thrown into prison?

22. True or False: Gomer was faithful to her husband, Hosea.

23. Fill in the blank: "'Honor your father and _____' —this is the first commandment with a promise" (Eph 6:2).

24. What prostitute in Jericho betrayed her people to the Israelites?

25. This woman was set free from seven demons: (a) Joanna; (b) Mary of Bethany; (c) Mary Magdalene; (d) Jezebel.

26. True or False: Jacob married Rachel before marrying Leah.

27. Fill in the blank: "The Lord took note of _____; she conceived and bore three sons and two daughters. And the boy Samuel grew up in the presence of the Lord" (1 Sam 2:21).

28. Who was Timothy's mother? (a) Lois; (b) Lydia; (c) Eunice; (d) Euodia.

29. Who was Jethro's daughter and Moses' wife?

30. True or False: When the men of Sodom knocked on Lot's door, he offered them his two daughters rather than his guests.

31. Fill in the blank: Joel prophesied, "I will pour out my spirit on all flesh; your sons and your _____ shall prophesy" (Joel 2:28).

32. Which of the following women had twins? (a) Leah; (b) Rebekah; (c) Rachel; (d) Sarah.

Answers for this page: **19.** *True* **20.** *(a) Priscilla* **21.** *Potiphar's wife* **22.** *False* **23.** *mother* **24.** *Rahab* **25.** *(c) Mary Magdalene* **26.** *False* **27.** *Hannah* **28.** *(c) Eunice* **29.** *Zipporah* **30.** *True* **31.** *daughters* **32.** *(b) Rebekah*

33. MATCHING

Match these Old Testament women with their nationality.

1. Ruth   A. Egyptian

2. Delilah   B. Sidonian

3. Haggar   C. Philistine

4. Zipporah   D. Moabite

5. Jezebel   E. Midianite

34. Who came up with the plan to steal Naboth's vineyard?

35. Fill in the blank: "At that time _____, a prophetess, wife of Lappidoth, was judging Israel" (Judg 4:4).

36. True or False: Sapphira died because she lied to the Holy Spirit.

37. Of the following, which is *not* something Tamar used to convince Judah that he was the father of her child? (a) a signet; (b) a cord; (c) a staff; (d) a sheep.

38. Fill in the blank: "Learn to do good; seek justice, rescue the oppressed, defend the orphan, plead for the _____" (Isa 1:17).

39. Who was the mother of the world's first murderer?

40. This woman preceded Esther as Ahasuerus's queen: (a) Jezebel; (b) Vashti; (c) Athaliah; (d) Jehosheba.

41. Fill in the blanks: "But _____ stood weeping outside the tomb. As she wept, she bent over to look into the tomb; and she saw two _____ in white, sitting where the body of Jesus had been lying" (John 20:11–12).

42. True or False: God blessed the Hebrew midwives with their own families, even though they had lied to Pharaoh.

Answers for this page: **33.** *1D; 2C; 3A; 4E; 5B* **34.** *Jezebel* **35.** *Deborah* **36.** *True* **37.** *(d) a sheep* **38.** *widow* **39.** *Eve* **40.** *(b) Vashti* **41.** *Mary, angels* **42.** *True*

43. What woman sang about Israel's victory over King Jabin of Canaan and Sisera's death?

44. Fill in the blanks: From the cross Jesus said to his mother, "Woman, here is your _____." Then he said to John, "Here is your _____" (John 19:26–27).

45. True or False: Sarah told the pharaoh of Egypt that she was Abraham's sister to protect her husband's life.

46. In whose field did Ruth glean?

47. What did the queen of Sheba give Solomon, the quantity of which was never again seen? (a) gold; (b) spices; (c) jewels; (d) expensive clothes.

48. True or False: None of the genealogies in Scriptures list women's names.

49. Who named Eve? (a) God; (b) Eve herself; (c) Adam; (d) none of the above.

50. Fill in the blank: "Let your fountain be blessed, and rejoice in the _____ of your youth" (Prov 5:18).

---

51. UNSCRAMBLE AND SOLVE: DORCAS (ACTS 9:36–43)

Then rearrange the boxed letters to form the answer to the question. The answer is a play on words.

How did Dorcas feel just after Peter raised her from the dead? "__ __ __ - __ __ __"

1. KROWS ☐ __ __ __ __
2. TASC __ __ __ ☐
3. PEWNIGE __ ☐ __ __ __ __ __
4. WODWIS __ __ __ __ __ ☐
5. SHADEW ☐ __ __ __ __ __
6. TWEN __ ☐ __ __

Answers for this page: **43.** *Deborah* **44.** *son, mother* **45.** *True* **46.** *Boaz's* **47.** *(b) spices* **48.** *False* **49.** *(c) Adam* **50.** *wife* **51.** *"sew-sew"* 1. *works;* 2. *acts;* 3. *weeping;* 4. *widows;* 5. *washed;* 6. *went*

52. MATCHING

Match these sisters.

1. Oholah	A. Tirzah
2. Mary	B. Merab
3. Leah	C. Martha
4. Mahlah	D. Oholibah
5. Michal	E. Rachel

53. True or False: Eve had only two children.

54. Nathan informed this mother that Adonijah was seeking David's throne: (a) Maacah; (b) Bathsheba; (c) Abital; (d) Haggith.

55. What woman was known for being beautiful and clever and saved the life of her husband, was known for being surly and mean?

56. Fill in the blank: The Lord said to Abraham, "Why did _____ laugh, and say, 'Shall I indeed bear a child, now that I am old?'" (Gen 18:13).

57. The Jewish festival of Purim was begun as a result of the actions of what queen?

58. True or False: Mary chose the better part when she decided to listen to Jesus' words.

59. This was not true of Jehoshabeth: (a) devoted follower of Athaliah, who sought Joash's death; (b) wife of the priest Jehoiada, who had Athaliah killed; (c) the mother of Zechariah, who prophesied against Judah; (d) saved Joash, who became king of Judah.

60. Fill in the blank: "They blessed _____ and said to her, 'May you, our sister, become thousands of myriads; may your offspring gain possession of the gates of their foes'" (Gen 24:60).

Answers for this page: **52.** *1D; 2C; 3E; 4A; 5B* **53.** *False (at least three)* **54.** *(b) Bathsheba* **55.** *Abigail* **56.** *Sarah* **57.** *Esther* **58.** *True* **59.** *(a) devoted follower of Athaliah, who sought Joash's death* **60.** *Rebekah*

61. What woman returned to Judah after her husband, Elimelech, and her two sons had died?

62. This servant of Leah bore two of Jacob's sons: (a) Huldah; (b) Dinah; (c) Zilpah; (d) Bilhah.

63. Fill in the blank: As Jesus was led to his crucifixion, he said, "_____ of Jerusalem, do not weep for me, but weep for yourselves and for your children" (Luke 23:28).

64. Whom did Saul consult in order to raise the spirit of Samuel?

65. True or False: Naomi's next-of-kin wanted both her land and Ruth.

66. How many Hebrew spies did Rahab hide?

67. Fill in the blank: Jacob told his sons, "I am about to be gathered to my people. Bury me with my ancestors … there I buried _____" (Gen 49:29, 31).

68. What friend of Paul had to leave Rome because she was a Jew? (a) Lois; (b) Lydia; (c) Priscilla; (d) Paula.

69. True or False: Elisheba was the wife of Aaron and from the tribe of Judah.

70. Mary treasured many facts about Jesus in: (a) her mind; (b) her heart; (c) her soul; (d) her diary.

71. True or False: Tamar, King David's daughter, was Absalom's half sister.

72. What woman was the mother of a hairy son and a smooth son?

---

73. CRYPTOGRAM: CAPABLE WIFE

Decode the letters in the words of this Bible verse. Each letter corresponds to a different letter in the alphabet.

Z BZOZAKD VHED VGN BZM EHMC? RGD HR EZQ LNQD
OQDBHNTR SGZM IDVDKR. SGD GDZQS NE GDQ
GTRAZMC SQTRSR HM GDQ.

Answers for this page: **61.** *Naomi* **62.** *(c) Zilpah* **63.** *Daughters* **64.** *the witch of Endor* **65.** *False (not Ruth)* **66.** *two* **67.** *Leah* **68.** *(c) Priscilla* **69.** *True* **70.** *(b) her heart* **71.** *False (full sister)* **72.** *Rebekah* **73.** *"A capable wife who can find? She is far more precious than jewels. The heart of her husband trusts in her"* *(Prov 31:10–11).*

74. WORD SEARCH: A WORLD OF WOMEN Answers on page 100.

Find the 18 pairs and 1 trio of women in the puzzle below. Look for the names in bold. You can find names linked together diagonally, vertically, horizontally, backward, and forward. When you find a name in the puzzle below, cross it off the list on this and the next page.

```
E  U  N  I  C  E  L  O  I  S  L  O  L  S  I  A
V  U  Q  A  B  E  D  I  T  H  Z  K  E  W  U  X
E  J  O  C  H  V  E  D  A  R  Y  A  B  E  L  O
M  O  D  D  X  E  V  I  E  R  B  A  E  Q  U  M
A  C  U  S  I  H  T  H  A  B  N  O  Z  J  M  I
R  A  G  A  H  A  N  M  I  N  U  S  E  H  A  R
Y  O  U  R  X  R  S  E  A  H  C  O  J  U  R  I
A  N  E  A  M  A  R  Y  M  A  R  T  H  A  Y  A
A  N  X  H  C  S  R  U  N  C  H  Y  A  E  E  M
C  E  N  R  X  A  T  R  A  T  V  O  I  Q  L  J
S  I  O  A  M  E  R  U  B  A  Y  W  L  T  I  O
I  D  U  C  H  A  E  L  L  E  H  C  A  R  Z  C
R  O  R  H  A  U  P  H  A  R  P  I  H  S  A  H
P  H  O  E  B  E  L  Y  D  I  A  N  T  E  B  E
A  U  L  L  Y  D  I  D  A  N  C  E  A  A  E  B
D  R  A  C  H  E  L  H  A  N  N  A  H  C  T  E
O  U  B  A  R  E  M  L  A  H  C  I  M  T  H  D
H  O  R  P  A  H  N  A  O  M  I  R  U  T  H  O
R  B  I  L  H  A  H  Z  I  L  P  A  H  V  W  X
```

Anna & **Huldah** (prophetesses)

Athaliah & **Jezebel** (evil queens)

Bilhah & **Zilpah** (Jacob's concubines)

Dorcas & **Mary** of Bethany (charitable women)

Eunice & Lois (Timothy's mother and grandmother respectively)

Euodia & Syntyche (combatants within the church)

Eve & Mary, mother of Jesus (the mothers of the "offspring" that would crush the serpent)

Mary & Anna (met in the temple)

Mary & Elizabeth (cousins)

Mary & Martha (sisters)

Michal & Merab (daughters of Saul)

Miriam & Jochebed (mother and daughter)

Orpah, Naomi & Ruth (two sisters-in-law with their mother-in-law)

Phoebe & Lydia (church leaders)

Rachel & Hannah (favored wives)

Rachel & Leah (sisters)

Rhoda & Prisca (Priscilla) (church members)

Sarah & Eve (mothers of nations)

Sarah & Rachel (barren women turned mothers)

75. Fill in the blanks: "Each of you, however, should _____ his wife as himself, and a wife should _____ her husband" (Eph 5:33).

76. True or False: Leah bore Jacob his first son.

77. When Paul cast a spirit out of a slave girl, she could no longer do this: (a) see or speak; (b) predict the future; (c) bear children; (d) walk.

78. Which of David's wives despised him when she saw him dancing with joy at the return of the ark to Jerusalem?

79. Fill in the blank: Judah was told, "Your daughter-in-law _____ has played the whore; moreover she is pregnant as a result of whoredom" (Gen 38:24).

Answers for this page: **75.** *love, respect* **76.** *True* **77.** *(b) predict the future* **78.** *Michal* **79.** *Tamar*

80. MATCHING

Match mothers with their kingly offspring.

1. Mary
2. Namaah
3. Abijah
4. Jezebel
5. Athaliah

A. Hezekiah
B. Ahaziah
C. Joram
D. Rehoboam
E. Jesus

81. This woman killed Sisera, the Canaanite army commander: (a) Deborah; (b) Huldah; (c) Jael; (d) Rahab.

82. True or False: There were three women in Noah's ark.

83. Fill in the blank: "A good wife is the _____ of her husband" (Prov 12:4).

84. With what did God punish Miriam for criticizing Moses' marrying a Cushite? (a) instant death; (b) deafness; (c) blindness; (d) leprosy.

85. What woman could say this about her man: "A fool and his hair are soon parted"?

86. True or False: Ruth was part of Jesus' family line.

87. Fill in the blanks: The Lord answered her, "_____, _____, you are worried and distracted by many things; there is need of only one thing" (Luke 10:42–43).

88. What did Rachel steal from her father's household that enraged him?

89. Joseph left this item in the hand of Potiphar's wife when he fled from her: (a) his garment; (b) his ring; (c) his shoe; (d) his headband.

90. Fill in the blank: David demanded from her brother: "Give me my wife _____, to whom I became engaged at the price of one hundred foreskins of the Philistines" (2 Sam 3:14).

Answers for this page: **80.** *1E; 2D; 3A; 4C; 5B* **81.** *(c) Jael* **82.** *False (four)* **83.** *crown* **84.** *(d) leprosy* **85.** *Delilah* **86.** *True* **87.** *Martha, Martha* **88.** *household idols* **89.** *(a) his garment* **90.** *Michal*

91. Fill in the blanks: The Apostle Peter had this advice for women: "Let your adornment be the inner self with the lasting beauty of a _____ and _____ spirit, which is very precious in God's sight" (1 Pet 3:4).

92. What Midianite woman was the mother of two Hebrew sons, Gershom and Eliezer?

93. What Jewish woman became the queen of Persia? (a) Ruth; (b) Miriam; (c) Deborah; (d) Esther.

94. True or False: Pharaoh gave Joseph (son of Jacob) a Jewish wife.

95. Whose wife had a dream warning her husband not to condemn an innocent man?

96. True or False: Leah gave Jacob more than half of his children.

97. Fill in the blanks: God said, "It is not good that the man should be _____; I will make him a helper as his _____" (Gen 2:18).

98. Peter raised this kind woman from the dead: (a) Deborah; (b) Delilah; (c) Dorcas; (d) Dinah.

99. True or False: Orpah went with Ruth and Naomi back to Bethlehem.

100. Who was Rebekah's beloved wet nurse?

101. Which of these women was not an ancestor of Jesus? (a) Tamar; (b) Bathsheba; (c) Rahab; (d) Abigail.

102. True or False: The New Testament tells us that the wife of the Apostle Peter was a devout follower of Jesus.

103. While on his rooftop, whom did David see bathing?

104. Fill in the blank: Jacob said to Laban, "I will serve you seven years for your younger daughter _____" (Gen 29:18).

105. True or False: One of Job's afflictions was the death of his wife.

106. Who was the wife of Nabal, a man who foolishly insulted David?

Answers for this page: **91.** *gentle, quiet* **92.** *Zipporah* **93.** *(d) Esther* **94.** *False (Egyptian)* **95.** *Pilate's* **96.** *True* **97.** *alone, partner* **98.** *(c) Dorcas* **99.** *False* **100.** *Deborah* **101.** *(d) Abigail* **102.** *False (it does not say)* **103.** *Bathsheba* **104.** *Rachel* **105.** *False* **106.** *Abigail*

107. Matching

Match these daughters with their fathers.

1. Leah   A. Saul

2. Merab   B. Hosea

3. Tamar   C. Ethbaal

4. Lo-ruhamah   D. Laban

5. Jezebel   E. Absalom

108. "Grandmother of the Year" is an award that definitely would not go to this woman: (a) Naomi; (b) Lois; (c) Hagar; (d) Athaliah.

109. True or False: The angel of the Lord told Mary in a dream to take the infant Jesus to Egypt.

110. She was the unloved wife of Jacob: (a) Leah; (b) Rebekah; (c) Rachel; (d) Dinah.

111. Amnon pretended to be ill in order to lure his half-sister into his house to rape her. What was her name?

112. True or False: Because of Sarah's beauty, Abraham told Abimilech that she was his sister.

113. Fill in the blank: Part of the Ten Commandments admonishes: "You shall not covet your neighbor's house; you shall not covet your neighbor's _____" (Ex 20:17).

114. Who was the mother of John the Baptist?

115. Rebekah claimed that she did not want Jacob to marry this kind of woman: (a) Hittite; (b) Israelite; (c) Ammonite; (d) Philistine.

116. True or False: Simeon and Levi considered themselves "avengers" of Dinah's honor.

117. Who told Ruth to stay with her own people, the Moabites?

Answers for this page: **107.** *1D; 2A; 3E; 4B; 5C* **108.** *(d) Athaliah* **109.** *False (told Joseph)* **110.** *(a) Leah* **111.** *Tamar* **112.** *True* **113.** *wife* **114.** *Elizabeth* **115.** *(a) Hittite* **116.** *True* **117.** *Naomi*

118. This consort and sister of King Agrippa II came to pay her respects to Festus: (a) Drusilla; (b) Bernice; (c) Damaris; (d) Beryl.

119. Fill in the blank: "Paul said farewell to the believers and sailed for Syria, accompanied by _____ and Aquila" (Acts 18:18).

120. Who was the sister of Moses and Aaron?

121. The grisly death of this woman led to a civil war that nearly wiped out the Benjamites: (a) Dinah; (b) Lot's daughter; (c) a Levite's concubine; (d) Tamar.

122. True or False: The Canaanite (Syrophoenician) woman stopped calling out to Jesus when the disciples told her to leave.

123. Who was the first woman Jacob met upon arriving in Haran and with whom he fell in love?

124. What virgin slept with David to keep him warm in his old age? (a) Ahinoam; (b) Abishag; (c) Abigail; (d) Aretha.

125. True or False: Abraham personally chose Rebekah to marry Isaac.

---

126. QUOTATION PUZZLE: HANNAH'S SONG

L	E	S	E	D	C	H	E	L	O	K	E	D	H	U	R	E	G	I	D
N	E	E	R	O	T	I	S	Y	I	O	R	T	O	L	R		O	O	E
T	O	K	R	E	E	K			N	U		H	O	E	Y		O	N	S
B	I		I		S	S			L					N	O			N	E

Answers for this page: **118.** *(b) Bernice* **119.** *Priscilla* **120.** *Miriam* **121.** *(c) a Levite's concubine* **122.** *False (she kept calling)* **123.** *Rachel* **124.** *(b) Abishag* **125.** *False (Abraham's servant chose Rebekah)* **126.** *"There is no Holy One like the Lord, no one besides you; there is no Rock like our God" (1 Sam 2:2).*

127. HIDDEN WORDS: GODLY WOMEN

Find the names of eight godly women hidden in the sentences below.

Hannah	Rebekah	Elizabeth	Esther
Ruth	Sarah	Lydia	Mary

1. Nehru, the former prime minister of India, was the father of Indira Gandhi.

2. Omar, your favorite poet, was also a mathematician.

3. As she traveled west, her car continued to lose oil.

4. "Give us a rah, rah," shouted the cheerleaders.

5. There are few books in the Bible shorter than Nahum.

6. One type of loon is a grebe. Kahunas, native medicine men, collect their feathers.

7. Rick made Liz a bet her car couldn't beat his in a race.

8. Sally dialed 911 when she smelled smoke.

128. Fill in the blanks: Paul told Timothy to speak "to older women as _____, to younger women as _____ —with absolute purity" (1 Tim 5:1–2).

129. Paul tried to persuade these two "pillars" of the Philippian church to agree: (a) Lois and Eunice; (b) Euodia and Syntyche; (c) Priscilla and Mary; (d) Dorcas and Lydia.

130. True or False: Hosea bought back his wife, Gomer.

131. What cousin did Mordecai adopt as his own daughter?

132. When Barak was told to go to battle against Sisera and his troops, he refused to go unless this person went with him: (a) Esther; (b) Miriam; (c) Abigail; (d) Deborah.

133. True or False: God changed Sarah's name to Sarai.

Answers for this page: **127.** *1. Ruth; 2. Mary; 3. Esther; 4. Sarah; 5. Hannah; 6. Rebekah; 7. Elizabeth; 8. Lydia* **128.** *mothers, sisters* **129.** *(b) Euodia and Syntyche* **130.** *True* **131.** *Esther* **132.** *(d) Deborah* **133.** *False (Sarai to Sarah)*

134. What woman betrayed Samson and caused him to lose his strength?

135. Fill in the blank: "By faith _____ the prostitute did not perish with those who were disobedient, because she had received the spies in peace" (Heb 11:31).

136. True or False: Mary, mother of Jesus, saw her son die on the cross.

137. Who was the mother of Moses?

138. Before her vow to the Lord, this wife of Elkanah was barren: (a) Hannah; (b) Peninnah; (c) neither wife was barren; (d) both wives were barren.

139. What woman conspired to have John the Baptist killed?

140. True or False: Athaliah was the only woman to reign over Judah.

141. With what woman did Reuben sleep, which cost him his rights as Jacob's firstborn? (a) Zilpah; (b) Bilhah; (c) Huldah; (d) Dinah.

142. What woman from Jericho has a place in King David's genealogy?

143. Fill in the blanks: After crossing the Red Sea, Miriam sang, "Sing to the Lord, for he has triumphed gloriously; _____ and _____ he has thrown into the sea" (Ex 15:21).

---

144. MATCHING

Match the woman with her vocation or responsibility.

1. Phoebe   A. Shepherdess

2. Zipporah   B. Queen

3. Candace   C. Deaconess

4. Miriam   D. Merchant

5. Lydia   E. Prophetess

Answers for this page: **134.** *Delilah* **135.** *Rahab* **136.** *True* **137.** *Jochebed* **138.** *(a) Hannah* **139.** *Herodias* **140.** *True* **141.** *(b) Bilhah* **142.** *Rahab* **143.** *horse, rider* **144.** *1C; 2A; 3B; 4E; 5D*

145. True or False: Eve told the serpent that God had warned her not to eat nor touch the fruit from the tree of the knowledge of good and evil.

146. Who turned into a pillar of salt while fleeing the destruction of Sodom?

147. She was Joseph's Egyptian wife: (a) Potiphera; (b) Asenath; (c) Nefertiti; (d) Hapshepsut.

148. True or False: Lydia wanted to be baptized after her conversion, but the members of her household refused.

149. Who uncovered the feet of her future husband on the threshing floor?

150. How was the mother of the young man who warned the tribune about the plot to murder Paul related to Paul? (a) mother; (b) sister; (c) aunt; (d) none of the above.

151. True or False: Peter raised Tabitha from the dead.

152. Fill in the blank: "Then David consoled his wife _____, and went to her, and lay with her; and she bore a son, and he named him Solomon" (2 Sam 12:24).

153. Who insisted that Zechariah's son not be named "Zechariah" but "John"?

154. True or False: Dogs ate the carcass of Jezebel.

155. She was the wife of Haman, an official in King Ahasuerus's court: (a) Zeresh; (b) Azubah; (c) Ephrath; (d) Abijah.

156. This woman died giving birth to one of Jacob's sons: (a) Leah; (b) Rachel; (c) Bilhah; (d) Zilpah.

157. Fill in the blank: "Charm is deceitful, and beauty is vain, but a woman who fears the Lord is to be _____" (Prov 31:30).

158. True or False: Jephthah's daughter tried to flee to the mountains when she learned that her father intended to sacrifice her.

Answers for this page: *145. True 146. Lot's wife 147. (b) Asenath 148. False (all were baptized) 149. Ruth 150. (b) sister 151. True 152. Bathsheba 153. Elizabeth 154. True 155. (a) Zeresh 156. (b) Rachel 157. praised 158. False (she was willing)*

159. MATCHING

Match these women with their brothers.

1. Michal	A. Jezreel
2. Lo-ruhamah	B. Tubal-cain
3. Jehosheba	C. Nahshon
4. Naamah	D. Jonathan
5. Elisheba	E. Ahaziah

160. In Jesus' parable of the ten bridesmaids, what did the five "foolish" bridesmaids lack? (a) lamps; (b) oil; (c) water; (d) direction.

161. What did Rahab put in the window to show that her household should be spared?

162. True or False: Hagar ran away from her mistress twice.

163. This grandmother was deposed from her position as queen mother because she put up an Asherah pole: (a) Jezebel; (b) Athaliah; (c) Maacah; (d) Bathsheba.

164. What prophetess was the daughter of Phanuel and spoke about the child Jesus in the temple in Jerusalem?

165. Fill in the blank: She said, "If you have judged me to be faithful to the Lord, come and stay at my home." . . . "After leaving the prison they went to _____ home" (Acts 16:15, 40).

166. True or False: Shiphrah and Puah were Hebrew midwives who disobeyed Pharaoh's order to kill male Hebrew babies.

167. Who was more to Naomi "than seven sons"?

168. What was Mary doing that irked her sister, Martha? (a) sleeping; (b) sitting at Jesus' feet; (c) chatting with the disciples; (d) visiting neighbors.

Answers for this page: **159.** *1D; 2A; 3E; 4B; 5C* **160.** *(b) oil* **161.** *crimson cord* **162.** *False (once)* **163.** *(c) Maacah* **164.** *Anna* **165.** *Lydia's* **166.** *True* **167.** *Ruth* **168.** *(b) sitting at Jesus' feet*

169. CRYPTOGRAM: BONE AND FLESH

NXWG ON TOGN WG PCAS CZ BI PCASG OAR ZTSGX
CZ BI ZTSGX; NXWG CAS GXOTT PS QOTTSR KCBOA,
ZCF CMN CZ BOA NXWG CAS KOG NOUSA.

170. True or False: David had Abigail's husband killed so he could marry her.

171. Who told Barak that a woman would slay Sisera?

172. This queen mother killed almost all of the royal family in the house of Judah to usurp the throne for herself: (a) Jezebel; (b) Athaliah; (c) Jehosheba; (d) Bathsheba.

173. True or False: Sapphira did not know that her husband kept part of the money from the sale of their land.

174. Whom did Abraham's servant find near a spring of water, which indicated to him that she was the one he was looking for?

175. How many coins did the poor widow put into the treasury while Jesus watched? (a) 1; (b) 2; (c) 3; (d) 4.

176. Fill in the blank: "The unmarried woman and the virgin are anxious about the affairs of the Lord, so that they may be _____ in body and spirit" (1 Cor 7:34).

177. What woman did Palti follow, weeping after her, because his wife was being taken away from him?

178. True or False: Shechem defiled Dinah, the daughter of Jacob, and he also wanted to marry her.

179. These two nations came from Lot and his two daughters: (a) Ammonites and Philistines; (b) Moabites and Hittites; (c) Moabites and Ammonites; (d) Edomites and Philistines.

180. Who declared that all generations will call her "blessed" because "the Mighty One" had looked on her with favor?

Answers for this page: **169.** *"This at last is bone of my bones and flesh of my flesh; this one shall be called Woman, for out of Man this one was taken" (Gen 2:23).* **170.** *False* **171.** *Deborah* **172.** *(b) Athaliah* **173.** *False (she knew)* **174.** *Rebekah* **175.** *(b) 2* **176.** *holy* **177.** *Michal* **178.** *True* **179.** *(c) Moabites and Ammonites* **180.** *Mary*

181. True or False: Other than Isaac, the Bible mentions only Abraham's son with Hagar.

182. Queen Vashti refused to do this at the king's banquet: (a) eat unclean food; (b) display herself; (c) drink wine; (d) dance before the men.

183. Fill in the blank: "When he knocked at the outer gate, a maid named _____ came to answer. On recognizing Peter's voice, she was so overjoyed that, instead of opening the gate, she ran in and announced that Peter was standing at the gate" (Acts 12:13–14).

184. True or False: The mother of Jephthah, one of Israel's judges, was a prostitute.

185. What woman pretended to be a temple prostitute in order to bear Jacob a grandson?

186. The slave girl who had a spirit of divination and who followed Paul and Silas declared that they were: (a) gods; (b) demons; (c) slaves of God; (d) impostors.

187. Who let David down through the window so he could escape from King Saul?

---

188. UNSCRAMBLE AND MATCH: WOMEN AT WORK

Unscramble the names of the Bible women on the left, then match each woman with her occupation.

1. CARDOS	_ _ _ _ _ _	A. SELLER OF PURPLE
2. TERSHE	_ _ _ _ _ _	B. JUDGE
3. DIALY	_ _ _ _ _	C. TENTMAKER
4. HABORED	_ _ _ _ _ _ _	D. SEAMSTRESS
5. ALPLISCIR	_ _ _ _ _ _ _ _ _	E. QUEEN
6. NAAN	_ _ _ _	F. FIELD WORKER
7. HURT	_ _ _ _	G. PROPHETESS

Answers for this page: **181.** *False (other sons are named)* **182.** *(b) display herself* **183.** *Rhoda* **184.** *True* **185.** *Tamar* **186.** *(c) slaves of God* **187.** *Michal* **188.** *1. Dorcas/D; 2. Esther/E; 3. Lydia/A; 4. Deborah/B; 5. Priscilla/C; 6. Anna/G; 7. Ruth/F*

189. MATCHING

Match these women with the Bible book they appear in.

1. Naomi
2. Priscilla
3. Deborah
4. Leah
5. Anna

A. Acts
B. Genesis
C. Luke
D. Ruth
E. Judges

190. True or False: Rebekah helped Jacob trick his father into giving him the blessing, which belonged to Esau.

191. In Zechariah's vision, he saw a woman sitting in a basket. What did this woman represent? (a) adultery; (b) wisdom; (c) wickedness; (d) folly.

192. Fill in the blank: Paul wrote, "To the unmarried and the _____ I say that it is well for them to remain unmarried as I am" (1 Cor 7:8).

193. True or False: The foreign wives of Solomon worshiped pagan gods, but they could not persuade Solomon to do likewise.

194. At what wicked queen's table did 450 prophets of Baal and 400 prophets of Asherah eat?

195. True or False: Jochebed named her second son Moses.

196. Zipporah did this to prevent God from killing her husband: (a) circumcised their son; (b) prayed for forgiveness; (c) fasted for a week; (d) sacrificed a lamb.

197. What group of Hellenist women did the early church neglect in the daily distribution of food, which caused the Hellenist Christians to complain against the Hebrew Christians?

Answers for this page: **189.** *1D; 2A; 3E; 4B; 5C* **190.** *True* **191.** *(c) wickedness* **192.** *widows* **193.** *False (they did persuade him)* **194.** *Jezebel's* **195.** *False (Pharaoh's daughter named him)* **196.** *(a) circumcised their son* **197.** *widows*

198. True or False: Because of the manner in which Hannah prayed, Eli the priest mistakenly thought she was drunk.

199. The widow of Zarephath was angry at Elijah for this reason: (a) he ate her food; (b) her son died; (c) she was starving; (d) he refused to marry her.

200. Fill in the blank: "Then _____ said in reply to Mordecai, '. . . I will go to the king, though it is against the law; and if I perish, I perish'" (Est 4:15–16).

201. What spiritual gift did Philip's four unmarried daughters have?

202. Hilkiah the priest consulted with this prophetess, on behalf of King Josiah, concerning the book of the law: (a) Miriam; (b) Deborah; (c) Anna; (d) Huldah.

203. True or False: After the men of Gibeah raped and murdered his concubine, the Levite cut her body into 12 pieces, sending them throughout the territory of Israel.

204. This barren woman demanded of her husband, "Give me children, or I shall die!" (a) Sarah; (b) Rachel; (c) Hannah; (d) Elizabeth.

---

205. QUOTATION PUZZLE: A GOOD GIFT

				■			■						■		
■							■				■				
		■		■		■								■	
	■														■
F	I	S	H	B	U	F	T	O	M	W	R	U	O	M	L	T	A	D	E
H	T	U	I	E	R	A	R	D	D	P	T	H	L	E	N	O	R	R	I
N	O	N	S	E		I	N	E			F	A	E	T	H	P	A	W	E
	E		S			T		A			E	R	D					R	

Answers for this page: **198.** *True* **199.** *(b) her son died* **200.** *Esther* **201.** *prophecy* **202.** *(d) Huldah* **203.** *True* **204.** *(b) Rachel* **205.** *"House and wealth are inherited from parents, but a prudent wife is from the Lord"* *(Prov 19:14).*

206. MATCHING

Match these daughters with their mothers.

1. Athaliah   A. Athaliah

2. Lo-ruhamah   B. Jezebel

3. Dinah   C. Maacah

4. Jehosheba   D. Gomer

5. Tamar   E. Leah

207. Who was the wife of Uriah the Hittite?

208. Fill in the blank: Paul said, "There is no longer Jew or Greek, there is no longer slave or free, there is no longer male and _____; for all of you are one in Christ Jesus" (Gal 3:28).

209. True or False: After Hagar and her son ran out of water in the wilderness of Beer-sheba, God showed her a well of water.

210. She gave birth to Zebulun: (a) Rachel; (b) Bilhah; (c) Zilpah; (d) Leah.

211. True or False: The Book of Hebrews does not include Eve in its list of people of faith.

212. Who used a tent peg to fulfill Deborah's prophecy to Barak?

213. Adonijah made a request to Solomon that he marry this woman: (a) Bathsheba; (b) Tamar; (c) Abishag; (d) Abital.

214. Who journeyed from Haran to Canaan to marry a future patriarch?

215. Fill in the blank: "When _____ came where Jesus was and saw him, she knelt at his feet and said to him, 'Lord, if you had been here, my brother would not have died'" (John 11:32).

216. True or False: Sarah was 127 years old when she died.

Answers for this page: **206.** *1B; 2D; 3E; 4A; 5C* **207.** *Bathsheba* **208.** *female* **209.** *True* **210.** *(d) Leah* **211.** *True* **212.** *Jael* **213.** *(c) Abishag* **214.** *Rebekah* **215.** *Mary* **216.** *True*

217. What evil queen wanted to kill Elijah?

218. Whose people reported to Paul that quarrels were occurring in the church in Corinth? (a) Lydia's; (b) Priscilla's; (c) Chloe's; (d) Claudia's.

219. True or False: Leah praised the Lord after she gave birth to her fourth son.

220. What woman did Saul promise to give to David, but instead gave her to another man, and later David handed over her five sons to the Gibeonites to slay?

221. What woman became a Christian after hearing Paul speak in Athens? (a) Damaris; (b) Julia; (c) Junia; (d) Prisca.

222. Fill in the blanks: According to the law of Moses: "You shall not uncover the nakedness of a _____ and her _____" (Lev 18:17).

223. What Egyptian slave was told by an angel to return to her mistress and that she would bear a son who would be a "wild ass of a man"?

224. True or False: Paul would not accept any provisions from women during his public ministry.

225. She was the sister of David and the mother of Joab, Asahel, and Abishai: (a) Zeruiah; (b) Tamar; (c) Maacah; (d) Eglah.

---

226. MATCHING

Match the woman with the food or drink associated with her.

1. Esther	A. Wine
2. Rebekah	B. Honey
3. Ruth	C. Milk
4. Samson's wife	D. Savory meal
5. Jael	E. Barley

Answers for this page: **217.** *Jezebel* **218.** *(c) Chloe's* **219.** *True* **220.** *Merab* **221.** *(a) Damaris* **222.** *woman, daughter* **223.** *Hagar* **224.** *False* **225.** *(a) Zeruiah* **226.** *1A; 2D; 3E; 4B; 5C*

227. CRISSCROSS PUZZLE: NAMES OF WOMEN

Answers on page 101.

Fit each of the following 51 words into the puzzle below. Words are arranged below alphabetically according to the number of letters.

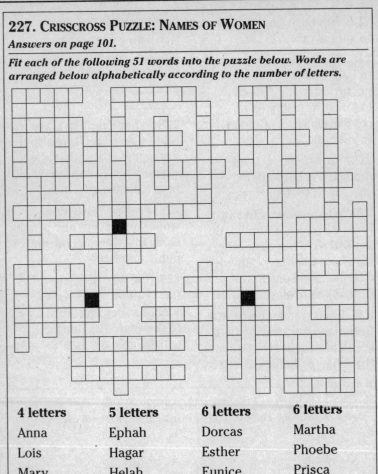

4 letters	5 letters	6 letters	6 letters
Anna	Ephah	Dorcas	Martha
Lois	Hagar	Esther	Phoebe
Mary	Helah	Eunice	Prisca
Noah	Lydia	Hannah	Reumah
Puah	Naomi	Hoglah	Salome
Ruth	Orpah	Huldah	Tirzah
5 letters	Rhoda	Joanna	Zeresh
Cozbi	Sarah	Judith	Zilpah
Dinah	Tamar	Keziah	**7 letters**
Eglah	Timna	Maacah	Abigail

227. CRISSCROSS PUZZLE: NAMES OF WOMEN *continued*

7 letters	8 letters	8 letters	9 letters
Abishag	Athaliah	Sapphira	Elizabeth
Damaris	Basemath	Shimrith	Hephzibah
Ephrath	Herodias	Tryphosa	
Haggith	Peninnah		

228. These brotherless sisters set a legal precedent by asking Moses to allow them to inherit their father's property: (a) Aaron's daughters; (b) Zelophehad's daughters; (c) Caleb's daughters; (d) Joshua's daughters.

229. Who was the first woman to be given the title "prophetess" in the Bible?

230. True or False: Some of the descendants of Keturah became bitter enemies of the Israelites.

231. This was not true of Joanna: (a) Jesus' sister; (b) wife of Chuza, Herod's steward; (c) healed of an affliction by Jesus; (d) visited Jesus' tomb.

232. Who was the mother of Ishmael?

233. Fill in the blank: "David said to _____, 'Blessed be the Lord, the God of Israel, who sent you to meet me today! Blessed be your good sense'" (1 Sam 25:32–33).

234. True or False: Naomi always praised the Lord for her circumstances.

235. Phinehas killed this Midianite woman with a spear in order to stop a plague among the people of Israel: (a) Serah; (b) Hoglah; (c) Cozbi; (d) Milcah.

236. What woman did Jehu command some eunuchs to throw out of a window?

237. True or False: Prior to Jesus' birth, Joseph planned to quietly dismiss Mary, but he didn't do it.

Answers for this page: **228.** *(b) Zelophehad's daughters* **229.** *Miriam* **230.** *True* **231.** *(a) Jesus' sister* **232.** *Hagar* **233.** *Abigail* **234.** *False* **235.** *(c) Cozbi* **236.** *Jezebel* **237.** *True*

74. Word Search: A World of Women *Puzzle on page 82.*

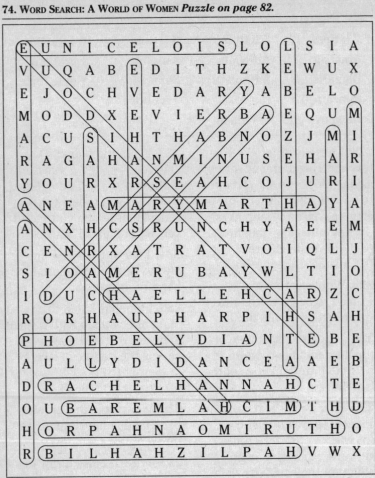

227. CRISSCROSS PUZZLE: NAMES OF WOMEN *Puzzle on page 98.*

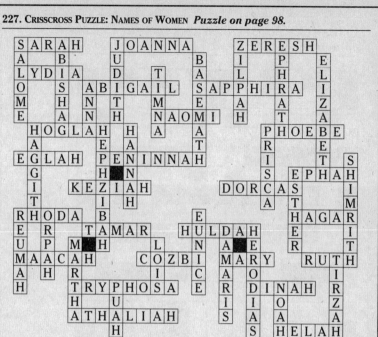

How Did You Do?

How was your knowledge of women in the Bible? By now, you must realize that many of them played vital roles in the history of Israel and the life of Jesus.

The total number of points possible for this chart includes the questions in chapter 3 and Crossword Puzzle #3:

426 to 474: You are truly a Bible scholar!
355 to 425: You have an excellent grasp of Bible facts.
284 to 354: You have some knowledge of the Bible.
237 to 283: You could brush up on the Bible.
0 to 236: You may want to start studying the Bible.

CROSSWORD PUZZLE #3: WHERE ARE THE CHILDREN?
Answers on page 279.

Across

7. Baby Moses was placed in it (Ex 2:3)
10. Israelites did it for 40 years (present tense)
14. "Put _____ _____ him" (Mark 15:17; 2 wds).
16. "Wash in the _____ of Siloam" (John 9:7).
18. Where was the baby Moses found? (4 wds)
21. Genesis (abbr)
22. Mother of Samuel
25. Sister of Moses

Across *continued*

28. Where would one find young Samuel? (4 wds)
32. Egyptian sun god (Joseph's wife's cult)
33. Tree cutter (Deut 19:5)
34. Religious hermit
37. "_____ _____ entered into me" (Ezek 2:2; 2 wds).
39. What kind of horns were used outside Jericho? (Josh 6:5)
41. Baby Jesus was found in what state? (4 wds)

CROSSWORD PUZZLE #3: WHERE ARE THE CHILDREN?
continued

Across *continued*

48. "He _____ up the people" (Luke 23:5).
49. What is done to rams' skins? (Ex 25:5)
50. Long for (Isa 26:9)
51. Sacred bull of Egypt (Jer 46:15)
52. 7th letter of Greek alphabet
53. Earth (Ger.)

Down

1. 11th Jewish month
2. "The race _____ not _____ the swift" (Eccl 9:11; 2 wds).
3. Abraham's dwelling (Gen 12:8)
4. 11th Hebrew letter
5. Hebrew root word for "Lord"
6. Abraham's hometown (Gen 11:31)
8. Be ill (Luke 13:12)
9. Among the invaders of Judah (Ezek 23:23)
11. Noah (alt. spelling)
12. Samuel's temple priest (1 Sam 3:1)
13. "...a light to my _____" (Psa 119:105).
15. "Sing to the Lord _____ _____ song" (Psa 149:1; 2 wds).

Down *continued*

17. Log (Matt 7:4, KJV trans.)
19. King of Bashan (Num 21:33)
20. Ton (abbr)
23. Worship site
24. Prophet and Bible book (abbr)
26. Outer edge (Ex 25:25)
27. Father of David's overseer (1 Chron 27:29)
28. Governor of Damascus (2 Cor 11:32)
29. "Neither cold nor _____" (Rev 3:16).
30. It is
31. Nonresident
35. In actual existence (2 wds)
36. Clan of Gad (Num 26:16)
37. Mountain (Sol 4:8)
38. "For this child I _____" (1 Sam 1:27).
40. Father of Shamgar (Judg 3:31)
42. Led the wise men to Jesus (Matt 2:10)
43. "Cover his upper _____" (Lev 13:45).
44. Son of Gad (Gen 46:16)
45. Grandfather of Saul (1 Chron 8:33)
46. Leah's son (Gen 30:11)
47. Day before Jewish sabbath or holiday

CHAPTER FOUR

Children: Young and Old

1. Who was the first child to be born of a woman?

2. Fill in the blanks: The angel said to Joseph, "She will bear a son, and you are to name him _____, for he will save his people from their _____" (Matt 1:21).

3. Which of Isaac's sons was supposed to receive the family birthright? (a) Esau; (b) Jacob; (c) Abraham; (d) Joseph.

4. True or False: During Bible times, children were seen as a blessing from God.

5. What was the occupation of John the Baptist's father? (a) a carpenter; (b) a priest; (c) a scribe; (d) a Sadducee.

6. Fill in the blanks: Jesus said, "Let the little _____ come to me, and do not stop them; for it is to such as these that the kingdom of _____ belongs" (Matt 19:14).

---

7. MATCHING

Match these Old Testament mothers and sons.

1. Eve	A. Moses
2. Leah	B. Solomon
3. Rebekah	C. Seth
4. Jochebed	D. Judah
5. Bathsheba	E. Esau

Answers for this page: **1.** *Cain* **2.** *Jesus, sins* **3.** *(a) Esau* **4.** *True* **5.** *(b) a priest* **6.** *children, heaven* **7.** *1C; 2D; 3E; 4A; 5B*

8. QUOTATION PUZZLE: A SMALL REMINDER

To find the verse, put the letters that appear in the bottom half of the puzzle into the column of boxes above them. The letters may not be listed in the exact order in which they appear in the quote. Mark off used letters at the bottom. A letter may be used only once. The black boxes represent the space between words.

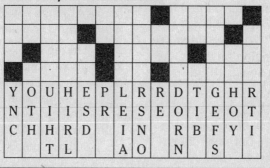

9. Who had seven sons and three daughters twice?

10. Who was Jacob and Esau's mother? (a) Sarah; (b) Rachel; (c) Rahab; (d) Rebekah.

11. What young man was mentored by Paul, who regarded him as a son?

12. Who nursed Moses when he was a baby? (a) his sister, Miriam; (b) an Egyptian midwife; (c) the Egyptian princess; (d) his mother.

13. True or False: David's best friend was the son of his enemy, King Saul.

14. Fill in the blank: "For a _____ has been born for us, a son given to us; authority rests upon his shoulders; and he is named Wonderful Counselor, Mighty God, Everlasting Father, Prince of Peace" (Isa 9:6).

15. True or False: Ruth was the grandmother of King David.

Answers for this page: **8.** *"Children, obey your parents in the Lord, for this is right" (Eph 6:1).* **9.** *Job* **10.** *(d) Rebekah* **11.** *Timothy* **12.** *(d) his mother* **13.** *True (Jonathan)* **14.** *child* **15.** *False (great-grandmother)*

16. Fill in the blank: "Like _____ in the hand of a warrior are the sons of one's youth" (Psa 127:4).

17. What happened to Zechariah after Gabriel told him that he was going to be a father? (a) he couldn't see; (b) he couldn't hear; (c) he couldn't speak; (d) he couldn't walk.

18. True or False: Naomi traveled back to her home-town with both her daughters-in-law.

19. Fill in the blank: "In Christ Jesus you are all children of God through _____" (Gal 3:26).

20. What son of Terah did God have a covenant with?

21. True or False: Jacob's wife, Rachel, was the daughter of Laban.

22. What judge never cut his hair from his childhood?

23. Fill in the blanks: "Adam knew his wife again, and she bore a son and named him _____, for she said, 'God has appointed for me another child instead of Abel, because _____ killed him'" (Gen 4:25).

24. True or False: According to the Old Testament, Molech was a pagan god who required child sacrifices.

---

25. MATCHING

Match these children with what they are known for.

1. Moses	A. Sold into slavery by his brothers
2. Jesus	B. Wrestled with his twin brother in the womb
3. Jacob	C. Born in a stable
4. Isaac	D. Hidden in a floating basket
5. Joseph	E. Almost sacrificed by his own father

Answers for this page: **16.** *arrows* **17.** *(c) he couldn't speak* **18.** *False (only one of them)* **19.** *faith* **20.** *Abraham* **21.** *True* **22.** *Samson* **23.** *Seth, Cain* **24.** *True* **25.** *1D; 2C; 3B; 4E; 5A*

26. This king forced his son to pass through fire: (a) Solomon; (b) Jehoshaphat; (c) Hezekiah; (d) Manasseh.

27. Fill in the blanks: Jesus declared, "Blessed are the peacemakers, for they will be called _____ of _____ " (Matt 5:9).

28. How many sons did Noah have?

29. What is the meaning for the Hebrew word *bath*: (a) father; (b) mother; (c) son; (d) daughter.

30. True or False: The New Testament says that God's children will be known by their love for one another.

31. Fill in the blanks: "My child, give me your _____, and let your _____ observe my ways" (Prov 23:26).

32. What king began his reign in Judah when he was seven years old after being hidden in the house of God for six years?

33. True or False: According to the writer of Hebrews, we are not God's children if he does not discipline us.

34. As a child, Joshua was known as the son of what man? (a) Moses; (b) Amram; (c) Nun; (d) Manee.

35. What son of King David died when he was hung by his hair on a tree?

36. True or False: Lot was the father of two of his grandchildren.

37. Fill in the blanks: "'Look, the _____ shall conceive and bear a son, and they shall name him _____,' which means, 'God is with us'" (Matt 1:23).

38. Which prophet had a wife who had "children of whoredom"?

39. What did God substitute for Isaac when Abraham was about to sacrifice his son? (a) another child; (b) a dove; (c) a sheep; (d) a ram.

Answers for this page: **26.** *(d) Manasseh* **27.** *children, God* **28.** *three* **29.** *(d) daughter* **30.** *True* **31.** *heart, eyes* **32.** *Jehoash (Joash)* **33.** *True* **34.** *(c) Nun* **35.** *Absalom* **36.** *True* **37.** *virgin, Emmanuel* **38.** *Hosea* **39.** *(d) ram*

40. UNSCRAMBLE AND SOLVE: HANNAH'S HARDSHIP (1 SAM 1)

Then rearrange the boxed letters to form the answer to the question.

What was life like for Hannah without children?

" _ _ _ _ _ _ _ _ _ _ "

1. LEAM _ ☐ _ _

2. BOWM _ _ _ ☐

3. PEWE _ ☐ _ _

4. ANEW _ _ ☐ _

5. DILCH _ _ _ ☐ _

6. RUNES _ _ _ _ _ ☐

7. REPARY _ ☐ _ _ _ _

8. SHANBUD _ ☐ _ ☐ _ ☐ _

41. True or False: Solomon was the son of King David and Queen Jezebel.

42. Fill in the blanks: "The parents have eaten sour _____, and the children's _____ are set on edge" (Ezek 18:2).

43. Who was Abraham's oldest son?

44. True or False: Paul wrote that young Timothy was influenced spiritually by his mother and grandmother.

45. Fill in the blanks: "Folly is bound up in the _____ of a boy, but the _____ of discipline drives it far away" (Prov 22:15).

46. What giant did King David kill when he was a young shepherd?

47. Jacob and Esau's first conflict happened when? (a) when they were 12 years old; (b) when they were teenagers; (c) when they were preschoolers; (d) during birth.

48. Fill in the blanks: "For all who are led by the _____ of God are _____ of God" (Rom 8:14).

49. What boy was called by God in the temple and later would become a judge over Israel?

Answers for this page: **40.** *"unbearable" 1. male; 2. womb; 3. weep; 4. wean; 5. child; 6. nurse; 7. prayer; 8. husband* **41.** *False (Bathsheba)* **42.** *grapes, teeth* **43.** *Ishmael* **44.** *True* **45.** *heart, rod* **46.** *Goliath* **47.** *(d) during birth* **48.** *Spirit, children* **49.** *Samuel*

50. True or False: Queen Athaliah, daughter of King Ahab, killed her sons so they wouldn't succeed her.

51. Who brought gifts of gold, frankincense, and myrrh to the infant Jesus? (a) the shepherds; (b) Herod; (c) the wise men; (d) no one.

52. True or False: David's first wife, Michal, never had any children.

53. Where did Cain kill Abel? (a) in the garden; (b) in a field; (c) in the temple; (d) in a stream.

54. True or False: An angel appeared to Samson's parents to tell them how to raise their child.

55. Who was the youngest son of Jacob?

56. Fill in the blanks: Elizabeth said to Mary with a loud voice, "Blessed are you among _____, and blessed is the _____ of your womb" (Luke 1:42).

57. Who helped Jacob trick his father into giving him the family blessing? (a) his wife; (b) his sister; (c) his mother; (d) his brother.

58. Fill in the blank: "Out of the mouths of _____ and infants you have founded a bulwark because of your foes, to silence the enemy and the avenger" (Psa 8:2).

---

59. MATCHING

Match these women who struggled with being barren with their firstborn children.

1. Hannah   A. Isaac

2. Sarah   B. John

3. Elizabeth   C. Joseph

4. Rachel   D. Esau

5. Rebekah   E. Samuel

Answers for this page: **50.** *True* **51.** *(c) the wise men* **52.** *True* **53.** *(b) in a field* **54.** *True* **55.** *Benjamin* **56.** *women, fruit* **57.** *(c) his mother* **58.** *babes* **59.** *1E; 2A; 3B; 4C; 5D*

60. How old was Jesus when he was left behind at the temple?

61. True or False: The child that came from David's adulterous relationship with Bathsheba went on to become a king of Israel.

62. How did the Hebrew midwives respond to Pharoah's command to kill all the Hebrew baby boys? (a) they carried it out; (b) they ignored it; (c) they threw the edict in his face; (d) they talked him out of it.

63. Fill in the blanks: "Fathers, do not provoke your children to _____, but bring them up in the discipline and instruction of the _____" (Eph 6:4).

64. True or False: Jephthah had only one child— a daughter.

65. What ruler ordered Hebrew baby boys killed when Jesus was a toddler?

66. What was the name of Judah's daughter-in-law, who gave birth to his twins? (a) Rahab; (b) Tamar; (c) Ruth; (d) Mary.

67. Fill in the blank: "Do not withhold _____ from your children" (Prov 23:13).

68. What baby leaped for joy in Elizabeth's womb in the presence of Mary?

69. True or False: David had three sons.

---

70. CRYPTOGRAM: A YOUNG LEADER

Decode the letters in the words of this Bible verse. Each letter corresponds to a different letter in the alphabet.

NPX UXYLVMS GPVUU UWX SYDO DWNP NPX EWS, NPX KVUR VOS NPX UWYO VOS NPX RVNUWOA NYAXNPXM, VOS V UWNNUX KPWUS GPVUU UXVS NPXC.

Answers for this page: **60.** *12 years old* **61.** *False (died as an infant)* **62.** *(b) they ignored it* **63.** *anger, Lord* **64.** *True* **65.** *Herod* **66.** *(b) Tamar* **67.** *discipline* **68.** *John the Baptist* **69.** *False (more than three)* **70.** *"The leopard shall lie down with the kid, the calf and the lion and the fatling together, and a little child shall lead them" (Isa 11:6).*

71. MATCHING

Match these people to the Bible book they appear in as children.

1. Miriam	A. 1 Samuel
2. David	B. Mark
3. Benjamin	C. 2 Kings
4. Jesus	D. Exodus
5. Josiah	E. Genesis

72. What killed the children who taunted Elisha? (a) a lion; (b) a pair of wolves; (c) two she-bears; (d) an earthquake.

73. Whose heel did Jacob grab during his birth?

74. What country was Joseph taken to when his brothers sold him as a youth? (a) Edom; (b) Egypt; (c) Canaan; (d) Babylon.

75. Fill in the blank: "Fathers, do not provoke your children, or they may lose _____" (Col 3:21).

76. True or False: Anna was the prophetess at the temple who recognized the infant Jesus as the Messiah.

77. What was Sarah's response to the news that she would bear a child in her old age? (a) she fell down and worshiped God; (b) she laughed; (c) she prayed; (d) she fainted.

78. Fill in the blanks: "Her children rise up and call her _____; her husband too, and he praises her" (Prov 31:28).

79. What did Ruth and Boaz name their firstborn?

80. True or False: Isaac's wife, Rebekah, was the daughter of Lot.

81. Who was not a son of Noah? (a) Ham; (b) Shem; (c) Canaan; (d) Japheth.

Answers for this page: **71.** *1D; 2A; 3E; 4B; 5C* **72.** *(c) two she-bears* **73.** *Esau's* **74.** *(b) Egypt* **75.** *heart* **76.** *True* **77.** *(b) she laughed* **78.** *happy* **79.** *Obed* **80.** *False (Bethuel)* **81.** *(c) Canaan*

82. How many children of Jacob are named in the Bible?

83. Fill in the blanks: "An angel of the Lord appeared to Joseph in a dream and said, 'Get up, take the _____ and his mother, and flee to _____'" (Matt 2:13).

84. True or False: The Book of Proverbs teaches that the children of a godly woman will speak well of her.

85. Who was Ruth's mother-in-law? (a) Sarah; (b) Esther; (c) Deborah; (d) Naomi.

86. What was the Apostle Paul's name when he was a boy?

87. Fill in the blanks: "As a father has compassion for his _____, so the Lord has compassion for those who _____ him" (Psa 103:13).

---

88. WORD SEARCH: BIBLE-TIME CHILDREN *Answers on page 131.*

Children were a blessing to Bible-time parents. The Bible mentions many parents and their offspring. Find the 31 children below in the puzzle on page 115. You can find words diagonally, vertically, horizontally, backward, and forward. When you find a word in the puzzle, cross it off the list.

Abel	Ishmael	Maher-Shalal-Hash-Baz
Absalom	Jacob	Manasseh
Adonijah	Jairus['s] daughter	Miriam
Cain	Jesus	Moses
[Children] of God	Jezreel	Obed
David	Joash	Samson
Dinah	John	Samuel
Esau	Joseph	Seth
Gershom	Josiah	Tamar
Ichabod	Lo-Ammi	
Isaac	Lo-Ruhamah	

Answers for this page: **82.** *13* **83.** *child, Egypt* **84.** *True* **85.** *(d) Naomi* **86.** *Saul* **87.** *children, fear*

88. WORD SEARCH: BIBLE-TIME CHILDREN *continued*

```
S   E   T   H   E   S   S   A   N   A   M

Z   B   E   A   D   O   N   I   J   A   H

A   E   J   M   O   M   O   B   E   T   K

B   O   C   A   J   O   S   H   U   L   L

H   F   O   H   R   E   M   A   H   E   R

S   G   B   U   A   S   A   L   A   L   E

A   O   W   R   M   E   S   N   L   C   T

H   D   J   O   A   S   H   E   A   C   H

L   L   W   L   T   O   A   I   N   E   G

A   E   E   S   J   M   N   E   N   L   U

L   B   U   E   H   Q   I   T   O   A   A

A   Y   S   S   R   E   D   A   V   I   D

H   U   I   A   A   Z   M   U   C   C   S

S   A   M   U   L   M   E   B   J   H   U

R   J   C   K   I   O   U   J   O   A   R

E   C   O   R   O   O   M   E   N   B   I

H   A   I   S   O   J   M   Q   L   O   A

A   A   G   E   E   D   E   B   O   D   J

M   S   A   M   U   P   H   I   L   L   P

A   I   G   E   R   S   H   O   M   E   R
```

89. MATCHING

Match these grandparents with their grandchildren.

1. Eve	A. Rehoboam
2. Jesse	B. Dinah
3. Sarah	C. Obed
4. Rebekah	D. Enosh
5. Jethro	E. Esau
6. Bathsheba	F. Tamar
7. Naomi	G. Gershom

90. True or False: A great wind killed Job's sons and daughters.

91. What special article of clothing did Jacob make for his son, Joseph? (a) sandals; (b) a hat; (c) a coat; (d) a belt.

92. True or False: Jesus was born in an inn in the village of Bethlehem.

93. Fill in the blank: Paul said to Timothy, "Let no one despise your _____, but set the believers an example in speech and conduct, in love, in faith, in purity" (1 Tim 4:12).

94. Rachel died when she gave birth to whom?

95. True or False: Ichabod, Phinehas's son, was born just after the Ark of the Covenant was taken from Israel.

96. What great-grandson of Abraham was sold to descendants of his oldest son?

97. In what city was Jesus born? (a) Capernaum; (b) Nazareth; (c) Bethlehem; (d) Jerusalem.

98. Fill in the blank: "_____ was eight years old when he began to reign; he reigned thirty-one years in Jerusalem" (2 Ki 22:1).

Answers for this page: **89.** *1D; 2F; 3E; 4B; 5G; 6A; 7C* **90.** *True* **91.** *(c) a coat* **92.** *False (stable)* **93.** *youth* **94.** *Benjamin* **95.** *True* **96.** *Joseph* **97.** *(c) Bethlehem* **98.** *Josiah*

99. True or False: Eli's sons did not respect the Lord.

100. Whom did Mordecai adopt and raise as his own daughter? (a) Deborah; (b) Esther; (c) Ruth; (d) Judith.

101. Fill in the blank: Jesus asked, "Is there anyone among you who, if your child asks for bread, will give a _____?" (Matt 7:9).

102. How many daughters did Lot have?

103. Who was David's first-born son? (a) Solomon; (b) Absalom; (c) Amnon; (d) Adonijah.

104. True or False: Moses was in danger of being murdered even as a baby.

105. What family member did Jairus beg Jesus to heal?

106. Fill in the blanks: "I have been _____, and now am old, yet I have not seen the righteous forsaken or their _____ begging bread" (Psa 37:25).

107. True or False: Abel was Adam and Eve's third son.

108. Who saw Hannah praying for a child? (a) Samuel; (b) Elkanah; (c) Nadab; (d) Eli.

---

109. QUOTATION PUZZLE: A PARENT'S PURPOSE

Y	N	W	H	W	L	E	N	G	T	T	S	W	R	H	E
N	R	D	I	N	H	C	H	O	L	L	D	E	N	A	Y
A		T		L		R	I	I	O	D	R		A	Y	I
		A		E			N	H					T		

Answers for this page: **99.** *True* **100.** *(b) Esther* **101.** *stone* **102.** *two* **103.** *(c) Amnon* **104.** *True* **105.** *his daughter* **106.** *young, children* **107.** *False (Abel was their second)* **108.** *(d) Eli* **109.** "Train children in the right way, and when old, they will not stray" (Prov 22:6).

110. Which son of Zebedee was martyred by King Herod?

111. True or False: Jacob favored his oldest son, Reuben.

112. What members of Lot's family survived the destruction of Sodom and Gomorrah? (a) his wives; (b) his daughters; (c) his sons; (d) his sisters.

113. Who was Boaz and Ruth's royal great-grandson?

114. Fill in the blanks: Jesus said, "I thank you, Father, Lord of heaven and earth, because you have hidden these things from the _____ and the intelligent and have revealed them to _____ " (Matt 11:25).

115. This son of Jacob is described by Jacob on his deathbed as "a haven for ships": (a) Zebulun; (b) Issachar; (c) Asher; (d) Naphtali.

116. True or False: Azariah was 16 when he began to reign in Judah.

117. When Jesus was a youngster, his parents found him at the temple asking questions of whom?

118. Noah cursed this grandson: (a) Gomer; (b) Canaan; (c) Cush; (d) Aram.

119. True or False: Jephthah had to sacrifice his own daughter because of an oath made in order to win a battle.

120. When Jesus was a youngster, what trade did he learn from his earthly father?

121. Fill in the blank: "Even _____ make themselves known by their acts, by whether what they do is pure and right" (Prov 20:11).

122. True or False: After the Flood, Ham, Noah's son, sinned by murdering his children.

123. What did Jesus' disciples do when the children ran up to Jesus? (a) put them on their own shoulders so they could see Jesus; (b) brought them to Jesus; (c) stopped them; (d) chased them away.

Answers for this page: **110.** *James* **111.** *False (Joseph)* **112.** *(b) his daughters* **113.** *David* **114.** *wise, infants* **115.** *(a) Zebulun* **116.** *True* **117.** *teachers* **118.** *(b) Canaan* **119.** *True* **120.** *carpentry* **121.** *children* **122.** *False* **123.** *(c) stopped them*

124. MATCHING

Match these mentors with their young apprentices.

1. Paul	A. Samuel
2. Eli	B. Joshua
3. Elijah	C. Elisha
4. Moses	D. John
5. Jesus	E. Timothy

125. During the last plague on Egypt, who were killed?

126. True or False: Isaiah was the prophet who fathered three children with "a wife of whoredom," whose name was Gomer.

127. Where did Hannah promise to have her first son raised? (a) at home; (b) at the temple; (c) at the home of her mother-in-law; (d) at her uncle's religious school.

128. Who were Joseph's sons who received Jacob's blessing?

129. Fill in the blank: "_____ your father and mother"—this is the first commandment with a promise" (Eph 6:2).

130. When Isaac gave his blessing, which son did he think he was giving it to? (a) Jacob; (b) Esau; (c) Laban; (d) Joseph.

131. What child did God command to be sacrificed on a mountain in the land of Moriah?

132. True or False: The Prophet Isaiah was the son of King Solomon.

133. Where was Joseph in the birth order of Jacob's sons? (a) youngest; (b) oldest; (c) next to the youngest; (d) next to the oldest.

134. Which of David's sons was known for his wisdom?

Answers for this page: **124.** *1E; 2A; 3C; 4B; 5D* **125.** *the firstborn* **126.** *False (Hosea)* **127.** *(b) at the temple* **128.** *Ephraim, Manasseh* **129.** *Honor* **130.** *(b) Esau* **131.** *Isaac* **132.** *False* **133.** *(c) next to the youngest* **134.** *Solomon*

135. HIDDEN WORDS: JACOB'S OFFSPRING

Within the following sentences, find the names of eight of Jacob's children:

Dinah	Reuben	Naphtali	Asher	Judah
Issachar	Zebulun	Joseph	Gad	Dan
	Levi	Benjamin	Simeon	

1. The frog had to kiss a charming young lady to turn into a prince.

2. Tomorrow the owner will evict the troublesome tenants.

3. The boy's dirty clothes landed in a heap on the bedroom floor.

4. Mother gave Jud a helping of mashed potatoes.

5. "Folks, I'm eons away from discovering a cure for this disease," admitted the scientist.

6. "Jose, phone home as soon as you can."

7. I saw Ben jam in between the buildings with his truck.

8. Jennifer's doll collection is not as large as her sister's.

136. True or False: Jesus raised a 12-year-old girl from the dead.

137. Fill in the blanks: The elders of Israel said to Samuel, "You are old and your _____ do not follow in your ways; appoint for us, then, a king to govern us, like other _____" (1 Sam 8:4).

138. What young king of Judah commanded the people to obey the book of the law?

139. True or False: Jacob and Esau were identical twins.

140. Moses was the son of this man? (a) Putnam; (b) Amram; (c) Isram; (d) Ophram.

Answers for this page: **135.** *1. Issachar; 2. Levi; 3. Dinah; 4. Judah; 5. Simeon; 6. Joseph; 7. Benjamin; 8. Asher* **136.** *True* **137.** *sons, nations* **138.** *Josiah* **139.** *False (fraternal)* **140.** *(b) Amram*

141. Which son of Adam and Eve was given a mark so that he would not be killed?

142. True or False: The Hebrews never took part in child sacrifices.

143. In Jesus' parable of the prodigal son, which brother became angry during the homecoming celebration? (a) the older brother; (b) the younger brother; (c) both brothers; (d) stepbrother.

144. Fill in the blank: "Therefore be _____ of God, as beloved children" (Eph 5:1).

145. True or False: The 12 tribes of Israel are descendants of the 12 sons of Abraham.

146. Noah was the grandson of this man: (a) Enoch; (b) Lamech; (c) Jared; (d) Methuselah.

147. Which daughter of King David was raped by her half-brother?

148. Which of Isaac's sons was known as a deceiver?

149. True or False: Paul adopted Timothy when Timothy was just a toddler.

150. Who was the oldest child of Moses and Zipporah? (a) Eliezer; (b) Gershom; (c) Kohath; (d) Merari.

151. What ceremony was performed on Jewish baby boys to set them apart from Gentiles?

152. Fill in the blank: King David said to the whole assembly, "My son _____, whom alone God has chosen, is young and inexperienced, and the work is great; for the temple will not be for mortals but for the Lord God" (1 Chron 29:1).

153. When Paul wrote to Philemon, whom did he call his "child"? (a) Onesimus; (b) Philemon; (c) Timothy; (d) Silas.

154. Fill in the blank: "By faith _____ was hidden by his parents for three months after his birth" (Heb 11:23).

Answers for this page: *141. Cain 142. False 143. (a) the older brother 144. imitators 145. False (Jacob) 146. (d) Methuselah 147. Tamar 148. Jacob 149. False (did not adopt) 150. (b) Gershom 151. circumcision 152. Solomon 153. (a) Onesimus 154. Moses*

155. MATCHING

Match these mothers and daughters-in-law.

1. Naomi	A. Naamah
2. Bathsheba	B. Judith
3. Rebekah	C. Maacah
4. Rachel	D. Orpah
5. Naamah	E. Asenath

156. True or False: Naomi did not have any grandchildren through her own seed.

157. Who made King Herod aware of the birth of the Messiah? (a) chief priests; (b) scribes; (c) wise men; (d) John the Baptist.

158. True or False: Part of Eve's punishment for her sin was increased pain during childbirth.

159. Who was the Jewish orphan girl who later became queen of Persia?

160. True or False: Uzziah was 16 when he succeeded his father, Amaziah, as king of Judah.

161. What two people never were children?

162. When Samuel was a boy, God called out to him in the temple. Whom did Samuel think he heard? (a) Eli; (b) Moses; (c) Jesus; (d) Elkanah.

163. True or False: Herod's step-daughter requested that John the Baptist be beheaded.

164. Whose sons did Abimelech kill in order to be his only heir?

165. Which son of David raped his sister? (a) Solomon; (b) Absalom; (c) Adonijah; (d) Amnon.

166. What great-grandson of Noah became known in ancient times as a "mighty warrior"?

Answers for this page: **155.** *1D; 2A; 3B; 4E; 5C* **156.** *True* **157.** *(c) wise men* **158.** *True* **159.** *Esther* **160.** *True* **161.** *Adam, Eve* **162.** *(a) Eli* **163.** *True* **164.** *Gideon's (or Jerubbaal's)* **165.** *(d) Amnon* **166.** *Nimrod*

167. Fill in the blanks: Judah said to Joseph, "We have a father, an old man, and a young brother, the _____ of his old age. His _____ is dead; he alone is left of his mother's children, and his father loves him" (Gen 44:20).

168. True or False: Elisha promised the Shunammite woman that she would have a son though her husband was old.

169. In Jesus' parable, what did the prodigal son ask for before he left home? (a) horses; (b) cattle; (c) his inheritance; (d) father's blessing.

170. Who was Isaac's older half-brother?

171. Who was Paul's teacher while he was growing up in Tarsus?

172. True or False: The infant Joash was hidden from Athaliah because she would have crowned him king of Judah too young.

173. As a boy, David used this weapon to slay the Philistine champion: (a) sword; (b) sling and stone; (c) bow and arrow; (d) bazooka.

174. True or False: In the days of the Hebrew patriarchs, barren women often offered their maidservants to their husbands to bear children for them.

175. Rebekah was the daughter of this man: (a) Bethuel; (b) Laban; (c) Nahor; (d) Lot.

176. True or False: The law of Moses teaches that a father's sins often hold consequences for his children and grandchildren.

---

177. CRYPTOGRAM: BE LIKE CHILDREN

YWZQD N YJQQ DTZ, ZSQJXX DTZ HMFSLJ FSI GJHTRJ QNPJ HMNQIWJS, DTZ BNQQ SJAJW JSYJW YMJ PNSLITR TK MJFAJS.

Answers for this page: **167.** *child, brother* **168.** *True* **169.** *(c) his inheritance* **170.** *Ishmael* **171.** *Gamaliel* **172.** *False (she wanted to kill him)* **173.** *(b) sling and stone* **174.** *True* **175.** *(a) Bethuel* **176.** *True* **177.** *"Truly I tell you, unless you change and become like children, you will never enter the kingdom of heaven" (Matt 18:3).*

178. Fill in the blanks: Jesus said, "Whoever becomes _____ like this child is the greatest in the kingdom of heaven. Whoever welcomes one such child in my _____ welcomes me" (Matt 18:4–5).

179. Who told Mary that she will conceive and bear a son, who will be called the "Son of the Most High"? (a) Michael; (b) Gabriel; (c) Elizabeth; (d) Simeon.

180. Who told his young son that God would provide the lamb for a burnt offering, while the boy carried the wood and he brought the fire and the knife?

181. As a child, Samson was known as the son of what man? (a) Zorah; (b) Zebulon; (c) Elijah; (d) Manoah.

182. Who was the mother of an infant who died because of the moral failure of a king?

---

183. UNSCRAMBLE AND MATCH: MOTHER AND CHILD

Unscramble the names of these Bible children and match them with their mothers.

1. BODE	__ __ __ __	A. EUNICE
2. MAULES	__ __ __ __ __ __	B. MARY
3. MOYTITH	__ __ __ __ __ __ __	C. RUTH
4. CASIA	__ __ __ __ __	D. ELIZABETH
5. USJES	__ __ __ __ __	E. HAGAR
6. CABOJ	__ __ __ __ __	F. SARAH
7. HETS	__ __ __ __	G. EVE
8. HONJ	__ __ __ __	H. REBEKAH
9. ESHPOJ	__ __ __ __ __ __	I. HANNAH
10. LAMISHE	__ __ __ __ __ __ __	J. RACHEL

Answers for this page: **178.** humble, name **179.** *(b) Gabriel* **180.** *Abraham* **181.** *(d) Manoah* **182.** *Bathsheba* **183.** *1. Obed/C; 2. Samuel/I; 3. Timothy/A; 4. Isaac/F; 5. Jesus/B; 6. Jacob/H; 7. Seth/G; 8. John/D; 9. Joseph/J; 10. Ishmael/E*

184. MATCHING

Match these Old Testament fathers and daughters.

1. Jacob	A. Tamar
2. David	B. Michal
3. Saul	C. Dinah
4. Amram	D. Leah
5. Laban	E. Miriam

185. True or False: Although David was the youngest and still a lad, Samuel anointed him as God's chosen in the presence of his brothers.

186. Fill in the blanks: "In all the land there were no _____ so beautiful as Job's _____; and their father gave them an inheritance along with their brothers" (Job 42:15).

187. True or False: Herod tried to convince the wise men to report Jesus' location under the guise that he wanted to worship the child.

188. What did two prostitutes argue over, bringing their claim before King Solomon?

189. How many children does the Bible record Leah's giving birth to? (a) 2; (b) 4; (c) 6; (d) 7.

190. True or False: Timothy was the son of a Jewish mother and a Greek father, and he became a dedicated follower of Christ.

191. What prophet from the Hebrew nobility was deported to Babylon as a youth and was taught the literature and language of the Chaldeans?

192. This man became a wicked king of Judah at the age of 12: (a) Josiah; (b) Manasseh; (c) Joash (d) Uzziah.

Answers for this page: **184.** *1C; 2A; 3B; 4E; 5D* **185.** *True* **186.** *women, daughters* **187.** *True* **188.** *a baby* **189.** *(d) 7* **190.** *True* **191.** *Daniel* **192.** *(b) Manasseh*

193. MATCHING

Match these New Testament sons and fathers.

1. Apostle John   A. Alphaeus
2. James   B. James
3. John the Baptist   C. John
4. Judas   D. Zechariah
5. Peter   E. Zebedee

194. Fill in the blanks: "When I was a child, I _____ like a child, I _____ like a child, I _____ like a child; when I became an adult, I put an end to childish ways" (1 Cor 13:11).

195. Who was the mother of Boaz?

196. True or False: The children of Joseph became two of the 12 tribes of Israel.

197. How many small boys were mauled after Elisha cursed them? (a) 8; (b) 17; (c) 28; (d) 42.

198. True or False: Jesus healed the young son of a royal official without even seeing the child.

199. Who boasted to his two wives that he had killed "a young man" for striking him, while comparing himself to Cain, his great-great-great grandfather?

200. What was Jeremiah's response when God called him to prophesy? (a) I am just a child; (b) I am just a man; (c) I don't speak well; (d) I have to bury my father.

201. Fill in the blanks: "Therefore the Lord himself will give you a sign. Look, the young woman is with _____ and shall bear a _____, and shall name him Immanuel" (Isa 7:14).

202. True or False: All the Hebrew firstborn belonged to God.

Answers for this page: **193.** *1E; 2A; 3D; 4B; 5C* **194.** *spoke, thought, reasoned* **195.** *Rahab* **196.** *True* **197.** *(d) 42* **198.** *True* **199.** *Lamech* **200.** *(a) I am just a child* **201.** *child, son* **202.** *True*

203. He was not a son of Terah: (a) Abram; (b) Nahor; (c) Haran; (d) Lot.

204. What did Gabriel tell Zechariah to name his son?

205. True or False: When Samuel was a youngster, God told him that he would bless Eli's family forever.

206. What son of Isaiah means "a remnant shall return"? (a) Ahaz; (b) Maher-shalal-hash-baz; (c) Shear-jashub; (d) Rezin.

207. What son of David tried to usurp his throne?

208. Fill in the blanks: "I will pour out my Spirit upon all flesh, and your sons and your daughters shall _____, and your young men shall see _____" (Acts 2:17).

209. What made it difficult for Sarah and Abraham to believe God's promise that they'd have a child? (a) God's previous broken promises; (b) their age; (c) their health; (d) their belief in pagan gods.

210. True or False: Jesus cast a demon out of the daughter of a Gentile woman.

---

211. QUOTATION PUZZLE: A SIGN OF FAVOR

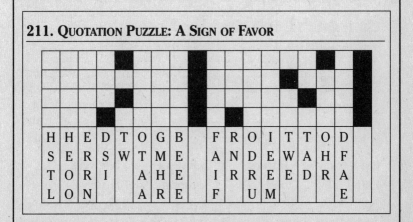

Answers for this page: **203.** *(d) Lot* **204.** *John* **205.** *False* **206.** *(c) Shear-jashub* **207.** *Absalom* **208.** *prophesy, visions* **209.** *(b) their age* **210.** *True* **211.** *"Sons are indeed a heritage from the Lord, the fruit of the womb a reward" (Psa 127:3).*

212. CRISSCROSS PUZZLE: CHILDREN *Answers on page 130.*

Fit each of the 60 words on pages 128–129 into the puzzle below. Words are arranged below alphabetically according to the number of letters.

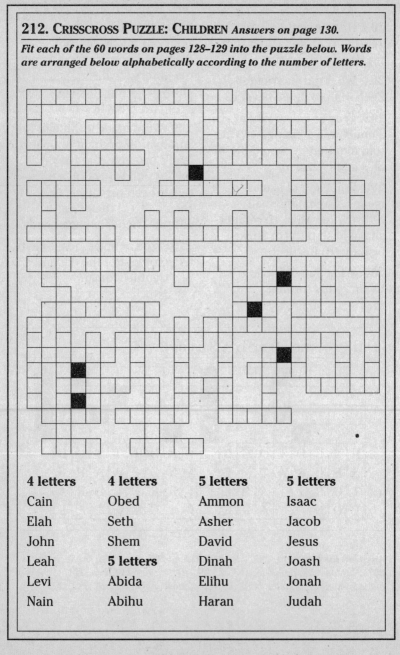

4 letters	4 letters	5 letters	5 letters
Cain	Obed	Ammon	Isaac
Elah	Seth	Asher	Jacob
John	Shem	David	Jesus
Leah	**5 letters**	Dinah	Joash
Levi	Abida	Elihu	Jonah
Nain	Abihu	Haran	Judah

212. CRISSCROSS PUZZLE: CHILDREN *continued*

5 letters	6 letters	7 letters	8 letters
Moses	Jairus	Absalom	Hasadiah
Nadab	Joseph	Eliphaz	Issachar
Pekah	Josiah	Ephraim	Manasseh
Perez	Lo-Ammi	Gershom	Naphtali
Shuah	Miriam	Ishmael	Sharezer
Tamar	Reuben	Japheth	**9 letters**
Terah	Salome	Zebulun	Lo-Ruhamah
Zabdi	Samson	**8 letters**	**11 letters**
Zerah	Samuel	Adonijah	Adrammelech
	Shelah	Benjamin	**12 letters**
	Simeon		Mephibosheth

213. What young boy was thrown into a pit by his brothers because of their jealousy?

214. This king produced children from only one wife: (a) David; (b) Solomon; (c) Rehoboam; (d) none of the above.

215. True or False: When Samson was a boy, God would not bless him because he was too self-centered.

216. Who was Eve talking about when she said, "I have produced a man with the help of the Lord"?

217. Fill in the blanks: "Better is a poor but wise _____ than an old but foolish _____, who will no longer take advice" (Eccl 4:13).

218. True or False: As a youth, Jesus was worshiped by his family and neighbors in Nazareth.

219. He took his grandson, Lot, from Ur of the Chaldeans to Haran: (a) Terah; (b) Abram; (c) Nahor; (d) Haran.

Answers for this page: **213.** *Joseph* **214.** *(d) none of the above* **215.** *False (God blessed him)* **216.** *Cain* **217.** *youth, king* **218.** *False* **219.** *(a) Terah*

220. MATCHING

Match these young people with the relative who intended to harm them.

1. Abel   A. Brothers

2. Joseph   B. Grandmother

3. Jacob   C. Brother

4. Isaac   D. Twin

5. Joash   E. Father

221. Who announced the birth of Jesus to the shepherds?

222. True or False: Elijah raised the son of the widow from Zarephath from the dead by stretching himself on the child three times.

223. He angrily upbraided the youthful David for leaving the sheep unattended in order to see Israel's battle with the Philistines: (a) Jesse; (b) Eliab; (c) Samuel; (d) Saul.

224. What young man refused to eat the royal rations of King Nebuchadnezzar yet appeared more healthy than those who ate the royal rations?

225. Fill in the blanks: "For God so loved the world that he gave his only _____, so that everyone who believes in him may not perish but may have eternal _____" (John 3:16).

226. What is the meaning for the Hebrew word *ben*: (a) father; (b) mother; (c) son; (d) daughter.

227. True or False: All the kings of Judah who were crowned before adulthood became godly rulers.

228. God heard the voice of what boy in the wilderness of Beer-sheba and saved him and his mother?

Answers for this page: **220.** *1C; 2A; 3D; 4E; 5B* **221.** *angels* **222.** *True* **223.** *(b) Eliab* **224.** *Daniel* **225.** *Son, life* **226.** *(c) son* **227.** *False (Manasseh was wicked)* **228.** *Ishmael*

229. As a boy, David was known for playing this musical instrument: (a) lyre; (b) cymbal; (c) trumpet; (d) flute.

230. True or False: According to John's vision of the future, a dragon will be unsuccessful in its attempt to devour "a male child, who is to rule all the nations with a rod of iron."

231. What grandson of King David listened to the advice of the friends of his youth and did not heed the wisdom of his elders, which caused Israel to be split into two kingdoms?

232. Fill in the blanks: God said to the serpent, "I will put enmity between you and the woman, and between your offspring and hers; he will strike your _____, and you will strike his _____" (Gen 3:15).

233. True or False: All the descendants of Abraham belong to the Hebrew race.

234. What righteous and devout man in Jerusalem was told by the Holy Spirit that he would not see death before he had seen the Messiah and who later did see and bless the infant Jesus?

235. This son of Jacob is described by Jacob on his deathbed as having rich food and providing "royal delicacies": (a) Zebulun; (b) Issachar; (c) Asher; (d) Naphtali.

236. True or False: Samuel made his sons, Joel and Abijah, judges over Israel, but they perverted justice.

237. What son of Amittai told mariners to throw him overboard because his presence was the cause for God to send a mighty storm to sink their ship?

238. The Bible says that children are what from God? (a) a reward; (b) a burden; (c) a mixed blessing; (d) a trial.

Answers for this page: **229.** *(a) lyre* **230.** *True* **231.** *Rehoboam* **232.** *head, heel* **233.** *False (descendants of Jacob)* **234.** *Simeon* **235.** *(c) Asher* **236.** *True* **237.** *Jonah* **238.** *(a) a reward*

239. This youthful king followed the godly instructions of the priest Jehoiada:
(a) Josiah; (b) Manasseh;
(c) Jehoash; (d) Uzziah.

240. Fill in the blanks.
"_____ are the crown of the aged, and the glory of children is their _____"
(Prov 17:6).

241. True or False: Paul never referred to his Jewish upbringing as a youngster.

242. What newborn baby was red and very hairy?

243. Jacob said to this son that the scepter will never depart from him: (a) Reuben;
(b) Judah; (c) Joseph;
(d) Levi.

244. What sister watched to see who would discover her baby brother in a basket among the reeds on an Egyptian river?

---

212. CRISSCROSS PUZZLE: CHILDREN *Puzzle on page 126.*

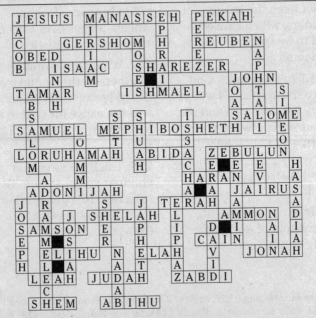

Answers for this page: **239.** *(c) Jehoash* **240.** *Grandchildren, parents*
241. *False* **242.** *Esau* **243.** *(b) Judah* **244.** *Miriam*

88. WORD SEARCH: BIBLE–TIME CHILDREN *Puzzle on page 113.*

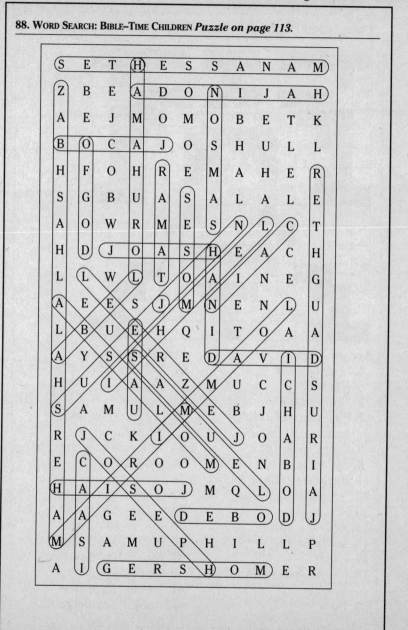

CROSSWORD PUZZLE #4: BIBLE FACTS *Answers on page 279.*

Across

4. "Let there be _____"
   (Gen 1:3).
5. Temple lights
7. Birthplace of Terah,
   father of Abraham
8. Egyptian sun god
9. Father of Isaac
11. Registered Nurse (abbr)
12. "I _ WHO I AM" (Ex
    3:14).
14. Ask for charity
16. Sea in Arabia and Africa
17. Exist
18. United States of America
    (abbr)
20. Bone

Across *continued*

21. Mother of John the
    Baptist
22. Listens
25. Ancient river near
    Ninevah
26. Women's quarters
30. Prophetess
31. Minor prophet
32. Musical passage
33. _____ ark (poss)
35. Cut sheep's wool
36. North Dakota (abbr)
37. One of David's wives
40. Right (abbr)
41. Genus of macaws
42. Book of Samuel (abbr)

CROSSWORD PUZZLE #4: BIBLE FACTS *continued*

Across *continued*

44. Jewish religious festival
46. Chief of Edom (Gen 36:40)
47. Noah's son
48. Form of verb "to be"

Down

1. Jezebel's husband
2. Site of a miracle
3. Mother of Timothy
6. Wife of Jacob
9. God's messengers
10. Town near Jerusalem (Mic 1:12)
11. Issac's wife
13. Was tossed into a furnace (Dan 3:19–20)
15. Rebekah's husband

Down *continued*

18. Priest in post-exilic period (Neh 12:19)
19. Father (Mark 14:36)
22. Mother of Samuel
23. A slight bow (2 wds)
24. Cell chemical
27. Fish eggs
28. Near Jacob's tent (Gen 35:21, KJV)
29. Sister of Lazarus
34. Wife of Abraham
35. Bond servant
38. Foundation
39. Small island
41. plural of "a"
43. Adam was the first
45. Thulium (chem.)
46. Jewish month

How Did You Do?

You should be quite familiar with the many families in the Bible by now, knowing how those people related to one another and how they got along. Retain what you've learned, for such knowledge will not only aid you in the following chapters but will also impress your fellow Bible readers.

The total number of points possible for this chart includes the questions in chapter 4 and Crossword Puzzle #4:

406 to 452: You are truly a Bible scholar!
339 to 405: You have an excellent grasp of Bible facts.
271 to 338: You have some knowledge of the Bible.
226 to 270: You could brush up on the Bible.
0 to 225: You may want to start studying the Bible.

Now you will be moving into more difficult areas of the Bible, such as places, animals, and customs. But first, a good transition into the second half of this book is a chapter on "extraordinary events"—many you will probably know, and some will be quite challenging.

CHAPTER FIVE

Extraordinary Events of the Bible

1. At Creation, what did God name the darkness?

2. Peter reminded the Council at Jerusalem that God had already accepted the Gentiles as believers because he had given them: (a) visions; (b) miraculous signs; (c) the Holy Spirit; (d) disciples.

3. Fill in the blank: After Satan walked up and down the earth, the Lord said to him, "Have you considered my _____ Job?" (Job 1:8).

4. True or False: The tower that people made upon a plain in the land of Shinar to reach heaven was called Babel because God confused their language.

5. After the great Flood, what sign did God promise Noah that he would give to indicate his covenant with every living creature? (a) thunder and lightning; (b) a dove; (c) a rainbow; (d) the blooming of a lily.

---

6. MATCHING

Match the days and creation events.

1. Day One   A. Land animals and human life

2. Day Three   B. Light and darkness

3. Day Five   C. Rest

4. Day Six   D. Vegetation

5. Day Seven   E. Sea creatures and birds

Answers for this page: **1.** *night* **2.** *(c) the Holy Spirit* **3.** *servant* **4.** *True* **5.** *(c) a rainbow* **6.** *1B; 2D; 3E; 4A; 5C*

7. QUOTATION PUZZLE: QUICK AS A FLASH

To find the verse, put the letters that appear in the bottom half of the puzzle into the column of boxes above them. The letters may not be listed in the exact order in which they appear in the quote. Mark off used letters at the bottom. A letter may be used only once. The black boxes represent the space between words.

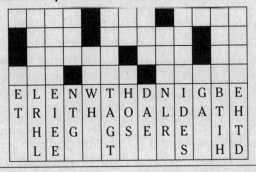

8. How many days and nights was Jonah in the belly of a large fish?

9. True or False: The disciples were first called Christians at Antioch.

10. What strange sight did Moses see on Mount Horeb? (a) a burning bush; (b) a radiant angel; (c) a column of fire; (d) a flaming chariot.

11. Fill in the blanks: Moses and Aaron said to Pharaoh, "Thus says the Lord, the God of _____, 'Let my people _____'" (Ex 5:1).

12. True or False: Samuel anointed Saul as the first king over Israel.

13. One of Jesus' most famous miracles was when he fed over 5,000 people. What did he feed them?

14. Fill in the blanks: "In the beginning when _____ created the _____ and the earth" (Gen 1:1).

15. What was the name given to "the heroes that were of old, warriors of renown"? (a) Cherub; (b) Sanhedrin; (c) Seraphim; (d) Nephilim.

Answers for this page: **7.** *"Then God said, 'Let there be light'; and there was light" (Gen 1:3).* **8.** *three* **9.** *True* **10.** *(a) a burning bush* **11.** *Israel, go* **12.** *True* **13.** *bread, fish* **14.** *God, heavens* **15.** *(d) Nephilim*

16. True or False: God took the great prophet Elisha up to heaven in a fiery chariot.

17. Fill in the blanks: There has been no day like it before or since when God heeded the voice of Joshua; that is, when "the _____ stood still, and the _____ stopped" (Josh 10:13).

18. Whom did Melchizedek bless?

19. Saul of Tarsus encountered him on the road to Damascus: (a) Peter; (b) Paul; (c) Jesus; (d) Barnabas.

20. True or False: The Assyrians conquered the northern kingdom of Israel and deported its people.

21. Fill in the blank: After God told Cain that he would be a fugitive for having murdered his brother, Cain cried out, "My _____ is greater than I can bear!" (Gen 4:13).

22. True or False: Joshua led the Israelites across the Jordan, whose water the Lord had parted for them.

23. Besides Eve, whom did Adam blame for his sin?

24. Which disciple preached at Pentecost, as recorded in the Bible? (a) James; (b) John; (c) Paul; (d) Peter.

25. True or False: Abraham bound Isaac on the altar and killed him.

26. How was Elijah taken up to heaven?

27. Fill in the blank: "Now the _____ was more crafty than any other wild animal that the Lord God had made" (Gen 3:1).

28. Where did the Apostle John receive "the revelation of Jesus Christ"? (a) Rome; (b) island of Patmos; (c) Jerusalem; (d) Mount Horeb.

29. True or False: God was never sorry that he had created humankind.

30. Where did Moses receive the Ten Commandments? (a) Midian; (b) Jerusalem; (c) Bethel; (d) Mount Sinai.

Answers for this page: **16.** *False* **17.** *sun, moon* **18.** *Abraham* **19.** *(c) Jesus* **20.** *True* **21.** *punishment* **22.** *True* **23.** *God* **24.** *(d) Peter* **25.** *False* **26.** *in a whirlwind* **27.** *serpent* **28.** *(b) island of Patmos* **29.** *False* **30.** *(d) Mount Sinai*

31. MATCHING

Match the killer with the one killed.

1. Cain	A. Goliath
2. Jael	B. Abel
3. David	C. Agag
4. Samuel	D. Eglon
5. Ehud	E. Sisera

32. Fill in the blanks: When the Prophet Isaiah described the coming of the Messiah, he said, "A shoot shall come out from the stump of _____, and a _____ shall grow out of his roots" (Isa 11:1).

33. What tribe of Israel was nearly wiped out at the end of the Book of Judges?

34. Fill in the blank: After the Israelites destroyed this city, Joshua pronounced this oath: "Cursed before the Lord be anyone who tries to build this city—this _____!" (Josh 6:26).

35. True or False: Jesus was crucified between two religious martyrs.

36. What musical instrument was used to flatten the walls of Jericho?

37. Joseph did not serve this man: (a) jailer; (b) Potiphar; (c) baker; (d) Pharaoh.

38. True or False: Pharaoh commanded the midwives to kill all Hebrew babies.

39. Fill in the blanks: A loud voice said to John in his vision, "God himself will be with them; he will wipe every _____ from their eyes. _____ will be no more" (Rev 21:3–4).

40. How many years did the Israelites wander in the Sinai wilderness before they entered the Promised Land?

Answers for this page: **31.** *1B; 2E; 3A; 4C; 5D* **32.** *Jesse, branch* **33.** *the Benjaminites* **34.** *Jericho* **35.** *False (two bandits)* **36.** *trumpet* **37.** *(c) baker* **38.** *False (not baby girls)* **39.** *tear, Death* **40.** *40*

41. He was not present at Jesus' transfiguration: (a) Peter; (b) Moses; (c) Abraham; (d) Elijah.

42. True or False: Daniel was martyred in the lion's den.

43. Fill in the blank: God told Noah, "Of every living thing, of all flesh, you shall bring _____ of every kind into the ark" (Gen 6:19).

44. Whose daughter danced before Herod and then requested the head of John the Baptist?

45. When Jesus died on the cross, what happened to the temple curtain?

46. Who was 365 years old when God took him? (a) Methuselah; (b) Enoch; (c) Elijah; (d) Abraham.

47. Fill in the blanks: At the end of his career as their leader, Joshua told the Hebrews to decide between serving God or pagan gods. Then he declared, "As for me and my _____, we will serve the _____" (Josh 24:15).

48. True or False: At the burning bush, God was angry with Moses because he made excuses not to speak to Pharaoh.

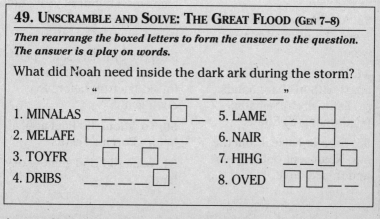

49. UNSCRAMBLE AND SOLVE: THE GREAT FLOOD (GEN 7–8)

Then rearrange the boxed letters to form the answer to the question. The answer is a play on words.

What did Noah need inside the dark ark during the storm?

" _ _ _ _ _ _ _ _ _ _ _ "

1. MINALAS _ _ _ _ _ _ □ _
2. MELAFE □ _ _ _ _ _
3. TOYFR _ □ _ □ _
4. DRIBS _ _ _ _ □

5. LAME _ _ □ _
6. NAIR _ _ □ _
7. HIHG _ _ □ □
8. OVED □ □ _ _

50. MATCHING

Match the judges with what is noted about them.

1. Ehud
2. Deborah
3. Gideon
4. Samuel
5. Jephthah

A. Put out the fleece
B. Was left handed
C. Was an anointing judge
D. Made a rash vow
E. Sang a victory song

51. Elijah defeated the priests of this pagan god on Mount Carmel: (a) Baal; (b) Molech; (c) Chemosh; (d) Satan.

52. Fill in the blank: He was the first mighty warrior on earth. In fact, the Bible says, "Like _____ a mighty hunter before the Lord" (Gen 10:9).

53. At what ceremony did Jesus change water into wine?

54. This judge tore a lion apart with his bare hands: (a) Samuel; (b) Samson; (c) Gideon; (d) Ehud.

55. True or False: From the ark, Noah sent out a raven and then a dove.

56. David was first crowned king of Judah and then crowned king of what nation?

57. Joseph's brothers sold him to these people: (a) Egyptians; (b) Edomites; (c) Midianites; (d) Ishmaelites.

58. Fill in the blank: "Abraham was a hundred years old when his son _____ was born to him" (Gen 21:5).

59. True or False: Satan persuaded Adam to eat the forbidden fruit before Eve could eat it.

60. To whom did Paul appeal before Porcius Festus?

61. What did God call the dry land?

Answers for this page: **50.** *1B; 2E; 3A; 4C; 5D* **51.** *(a) Baal* **52.** *Nimrod* **53.** *wedding* **54.** *(b) Samson* **55.** *True* **56.** *Israel* **57.** *(d) Ishmaelites* **58.** *Isaac* **59.** *False (Satan persuaded Eve)* **60.** *the emperor (or Caesar)* **61.** *Earth*

62. True or False: After Pharaoh permitted the Hebrews to leave Egypt, he still sent his soldiers to pursue and slay them.

63. Fill in the blanks: After the high priest ordered Peter and the apostles not to teach in Jesus' name, they answered, "We must obey _____ rather than any _____ authority" (Acts 5:29).

64. Nebuchadnezzar did not command that this man be thrown into the furnace of blazing fire: (a) Daniel; (b) Meshach; (c) Abednego; (d) Shadrach.

65. True or False: It took Solomon longer to build his palaces than God's temple.

66. Fill in the blanks: When God told Abraham to leave Ur of the Chaldeans, he promised Abraham, "I will make of you a great _____, and I will bless you, and make your _____ great" (Gen 12:2).

67. This judge and his men defeated the Midianite army using trumpets and jars: (a) Samson; (b) Joshua; (c) Gideon; (d) Barak.

68. What was the name of the angel who visited Zechariah and Mary?

69. Fill in the blanks: After Satan inflicted Job with loathsome sores, his wife said to him, "Do you still persist in your integrity? Curse _____, and _____" (Job 1:9).

---

70. CRYPTOGRAM: GOOD NEWS

Decode the letters in the words of this Bible verse. Each letter corresponds to a different letter in the alphabet.

E MA LVEZXEZX OYS XYYJ ZIQT YH XVIMU DYO HYV MBB UFI GIYGBI: UY OYS ET LYVZ UFET JMO EZ UFI KEUO YH JMREJ M TMREYV.

Answers for this page: **62.** *True* **63.** *God, human* **64.** *(a) Daniel* **65.** *True* **66.** *nation, name* **67.** *(c) Gideon* **68.** *Gabriel* **69.** *God, die* **70.** *"I am bringing you good news of great joy for all the people: to you is born this day in the city of David a savior" (Luke 2:10–11).*

71. True or False: God told Ezekiel to eat a scroll before speaking to Israel.

72. He became the first king of the northern kingdom of Israel: (a) Jeroboam; (b) Saul; (c) Rehoboam; (d) Solomon.

73. Who dreamed of a ladder on which angels were ascending and descending from the earth to heaven?

74. True or False: God did not permit Jeremiah to marry and have children.

75. Fill in the blank: Eli told young Samuel to answer God by saying, "Speak, Lord, for your _____ is listening" (1 Sam 3:9).

76. Who baptized the Ethiopian eunuch?

77. True or False: God told Isaiah to walk naked and barefoot for three years.

78. God commanded Adam and Eve not to: (a) eat the fruit from the tree of the knowledge of good and evil; (b) venture outside the Garden of Eden; (c) talk to the serpent; (4) eat the fruit from the tree of life.

79. Fill in the blank: The angel of the Lord said to Gideon, "The Lord is with you, you mighty _____" (Judg 6:12).

80. After Adam and Eve sinned, what was God's first question to them? (a) "Where are you?" (b) "Why are you hiding?" (c) "What is wrong?" (d) "What have you done?"

81. MATCHING

Match the central character and the event.

1. Adam	A. Surviving the flood
2. Joshua	B. Sacrificing his daughter
3. Noah	C. Causing ten plagues
4. Moses	D. Being expelled from Eden
5. Jephthah	E. Entering Canaan

Answers for this page: **71.** *True* **72.** *(a) Jeroboam* **73.** *Jacob* **74.** *True* **75.** *servant* **76.** *Philip* **77.** *True* **78.** *(a) eat the fruit from the tree of the knowledge of good and evil* **79.** *warrior* **80.** *(a) "Where are you?"* **81.** *1D; 2E; 3A; 4C; 5B*

82. For how many days did Jesus appear to his disciples after his suffering and before his ascension into heaven?

83. True or False: Judah was the father of his daughter-in-law's twins.

84. Fill in the blanks: When two women disputed over an infant, Solomon ordered, "_____ the living boy in _____; then give _____ to the one, and _____ to the other" (1 Ki 3:25).

85. When the two estranged brothers met again, Esau (a) beat up Jacob; (b) cursed Jacob; (c) kissed and embraced Jacob; (d) told Jacob to run for his life.

86. Before the Israelites had a king, what nation stole the ark of the covenant from them?

87. Fill in the blanks: When John was baptizing people in the Jordan, he declared, "I am the _____ of one crying out in the _____" (John 1:23).

88. True or False: During Moses' journey back to Egypt, God tried to kill him.

89. What did Rachel steal from her father? (a) jewels; (b) gold; (c) his tunic; (d) household idols.

90. An angel told Zacharias that he would have a son who would have the power of what prophet?

91. Fill in the blank: Then the Lord opened the mouth of the donkey, and it said to Balaam, "What have I done to you, that you have struck me these _____ times?" (Num 22:28).

92. True or False: If the Israelites had not preserved some of the Benjaminites after the battle of Gibeah, Saul would not have been their first king.

93. Who raped his half-sister, which brought division within the house of David?

94. True or False: A Jewish woman became a queen in the Persian Empire.

Answers for this page: **82.** *40* **83.** *True* **84.** *Divide, two, half, half* **85.** *(c) kissed and embraced Jacob* **86.** *the Philistines* **87.** *voice, wilderness* **88.** *True* **89.** *(d) household idols* **90.** *Elijah* **91.** *three* **92.** *True* **93.** *Amnon* **94.** *True*

95. MATCHING

Who had whom killed.

1. David   A. Amnon

2. Absalom   B. Uriah

3. Jezebel   C. Haman

4. Solomon   D. Naboth

5. Ahasuerus   E. Adonijah

96. What did Esau despise? (a) his father's blessing; (b) hunting; (c) his birthright; (d) home-cooked meal.

97. Fill in the blanks: When Amos conveyed God's message to Israel, he stated, "Let _____ roll down like waters, and _____ like an ever-flowing stream" (Amos 5:24).

98. What happened to Uzzah when he touched the Ark of the Covenant?

99. The discovery of this thing caused King Josiah to bring Judah back to God: (a) the book of the law; (b) Moses' staff; (c) the ark of the covenant; (d) Elijah's talisman.

100. Fill in the blanks: After Jesus washed the feet of his disciples, he said to them, "So if I, your _____ and ____, have washed your feet, you also ought to wash one another's feet" (John 13:14).

101. How was Stephen martyred for his faith in Christ?

102. What was the name of David and Bathsheba's second child who succeeded David to the throne?

103. True or False: Jonah begged the men not to throw him overboard when a storm threatened to sink their ship.

104. What did Elijah pour over his Mt. Carmel altar three times? (a) oil; (b) blood; (c) water; (d) dust.

Answers for this page: **95.** *1B; 2A; 3D; 4E; 5C* **96.** *(c) his birthright* **97.** *justice, righteousness* **98.** *he died* **99.** *(a) the book of the law* **100.** *Lord, Teacher* **101.** *stoned* **102.** *Solomon* **103.** *False (Jonah told them to)* **104.** *(c) water*

105. Fill in the blanks: "When morning came, it was _____! And Jacob said to Laban, 'What is this you have done to me? Did I not serve with you for _____?'" (Gen 29:25).

106. This was placed into the Ark of the Covenant: (a) Ten Commandments; (b) the ashes of Moses; (c) Urim and Thummim; (d) gold and silver.

107. True or False: During Jehoshaphat's reign Israel was divided into two kingdoms, Israel and Judah.

108. What Pharisee came to Jesus at night and learned that he had to be born again?

109. King Nebuchadnezzar ruled over what empire, which eventually destroyed the temple in Jerusalem? (a) Persian; (b) Babylonian; (c) Egyptian; (d) Greek.

110. Fill in the blanks: "For you yourselves know very well that the day of the Lord will come like a _____ in the _____" (1 Thes 5:2).

111. Who immersed himself seven times in the Jordan so his flesh would be restored like the flesh of a young boy?

112. True or False: In order to reach the Promised Land, the Israelites had to cross only one body of water.

---

113. QUOTATION PUZZLE: HOPE FLOATS?

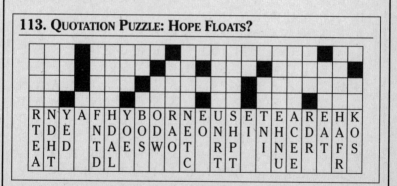

Answers for this page: **105.** *Leah, Rachel* **106.** *(a) Ten Commandments* **107.** *False (during Rehoboam's reign)* **108.** *Nicodemus* **109.** *(b) Babylonian* **110.** *thief, night* **111.** *Naaman* **112.** *False (Red Sea, Jordan River)* **113.** *"The flood continued forty days on the earth, and the waters increased, and bore up the ark" (Gen 7:17).*

114. WORD SEARCH: EVENTS OF A NATION *Answers on page 162.*

Find the 56 events in the puzzle below. You can find words diagonally, vertically, horizontally, backward, and forward. When you find a word in the puzzle, cross it off the list. Words or parts of words in brackets or parentheses are not in the puzzle.

```
R E T A W K C O R R U P T I O N K A H S D
E X W H O D O Y O U S A Y T H A T I A M S
K D O D E A T H O F A G I A N T N I N G S
A I P A I C W J A E L L A F E H T O T G H
T H E F L O O D E A D N O M O R E N O G S
R E N U M B E R I N G L S V E A R G P J H
A R N E W E A R D Q L B A D K U Q Z U L L
V O Y A G E T O R O M E S O B N O A O E P
E A I E N H O A W S T E H P O R P A W L L
L T N I A T N A H C A A S I R O F E F I W
S E C N O R S D E V O L T O N O T M Y S E
R N I G H T S O F P R A Y E R O L E E H S
O D D N A M E O F H E B R E W S O N A A E
U O E R A A N N F R O M E X O D U S H E N
N R N I N D R O C S O M E I R O Y S Q L E
D O T A U W E E I O I M B L D Y U S E I V
A P A N A A D S N X M L E E E B L Z L J R
B A R L E Y L M I O I M E R G E N E S A E
O A E I O M I E S W H F A N M I A O P H T
U H B E E S W S P I E S I N C A N A A N N
T U C E S S O N G S O N S C D E N N M O I
E R O I L Y T M O U R Z Y E U M A N I A D
G A N E R E S S J U D G E S S R E A A N O
Y G Q L T E S E B H C R U H C O C N O A G
P B I R T H J O H N O I T A T P M E T I Y
T J E S U S B O R N R O B S I L E A R S I
```

Achan taint	Beginning (Genesis)	Burning bush
Babel (tower of)	Birth [of] John	Burnt [offerings]

114. WORD SEARCH: EVENTS OF A NATION *continued*

Church beset (persecution)

Corruption (of Israel; of priestly office)

Creation

Crucifixion (the)

Dead no more (Lazarus; widow of Nain's son; widow of Zarephath's son)

Death of a giant (Goliath)

Dinah['s] trial

Elisha [&] Elijah (acts of)

Exile (the)

Exodus (the)

Follow a star (Magi)

God intervenes

Hero at Endor (Gideon)

Israel is born

Jael

Jericho (Fall of)

Jesus [is] born

Jesus rose (from the dead)

Job waits

Judges

Kings (acts of Israel's kings)

Moon missing (day sun stood still)

Moses shone (Moses' face reflects God's glory)

New ear (for Malchus)

Nights of prayer

Not loved (*Lo-ruhamah*—a sign for Israel)

Odd name of [a] Hebrew son (Gomer; Isaiah's wife; wife of Phinehas)

Omer [of] manna (Manna given; daily amount each Israelite received)

Priests (priesthood is established)

Prophets

Red Sea [crossing]

Renege (Jacob's sons renege on promise at Shechem)

Renumbering (the tribes of Israel while in the wilderness)

Rock water (Moses gets water from rock)

Spies in Canaan

Temptation (Jesus')

Ten Commandments

Tenants of Rome (Israel)

The cord (crimson cord used by Rahab)

The Fall

The Flood

The Law [is given]

Travels round-about Egypt (Israel in the wilderness; Abraham/Jacob flee there; Jesus was there as a child)

Two-penny incident (widow in the temple)

Voyage to Rome (Paul is ship-wrecked)

Who do you say that I am? (Jesus declared the Messiah)

Wife for Isaac

Wilderness

Wise Daniel

Years of silence (400 years between the Testaments)

115. MATCHING

Match these people to the significant events in King David's life.

1. Bathsheba A. Prophet who confronted David about his sins

2. Nathan B. Woman with whom he committed adultery

3. Solomon C. Son who hung by his hair

4. Absalom D. Son who became king

5. Samuel E. Judge who crowned him as king

116. What cousin of Esther was instrumental in saving the Jews from destruction? (a) Haman; (b) Hadassah; (c) Nehemiah; (d) Mordecai.

117. Fill in the blanks: "The Lord went in front of them in a pillar of _____ by day, to lead them along the way, and in a pillar of _____ by night, to give them light, so that they might travel by day and by night" (Ex 13:21).

118. This prophet helped Haggai and the Jews rebuild the temple during Cyrus's reign: (a) Nehemiah; (b) Isaiah; (c) Zechariah; (d) Jonah.

119. Who led the Israelites into the Promised Land?

120. True or False: The devil offered Jesus authority over all the kingdoms of the world if Jesus worshiped him.

121. On his deathbed in Egypt, who told his 12 sons what would happen to them?

122. True or False: The tower of Babel was built after the Great Flood.

123. Fill in the blanks: "The disagreement became so sharp that they parted company; Barnabas took _____ with him and sailed away to Cyprus. But Paul chose _____ and set out, the believers commending him to the grace of the Lord" (Acts 15:39–40).

Answers for this page: **115.** *1B; 2A; 3D; 4C; 5E* **116.** *(d) Mordecai* **117.** *cloud, fire* **118.** *(c) Zechariah* **119.** *Joshua* **120.** *True* **121.** *Jacob* **122.** *True* **123.** *Mark, Silas*

124. The Prophet Isaiah told what king of Judah that King Sennacherib of Assyria would fail in his seige against Jerusalem?

125. True or False: After Cain became angry with God, God warned him not to allow sin to master him.

126. What was Solomon able to accomplish that God did not allow David to do because David was engaged in warfare? (a) build a palace; (b) build the house for the Lord; (c) build a fleet of ships; (d) build a statue of Moses.

127. Who confronted Ananias and Sapphira with their lying to God?

128. True or False: Gideon needed to make only one trial of laying out a fleece of wool in order to be assured that God would deliver Israel.

129. What did the dove bring back to Noah to indicate that the waters had subsided? (a) worm; (b) oak twig; (c) olive leaf; (d) note from God.

130. Fill in the blanks: "Then the Lord rained on _____ and _____ sulfur and fire from the Lord out of heaven" (Gen 19:24).

131. True or False: Jesus never performed a miracle on a sabbath day.

132. He persuaded his brothers to sell Joseph into slavery: (a) Reuben; (b) Simeon; (c) Levi; (d) Judah.

133. True or False: Abraham left Ur of the Chaldeans in search of a wife among the Canaanites.

134. Who observed the killing of Stephen and approved of it while guarding the coats of the witnesses?

135. This was *not* a plague God sent against Egypt to let His people go: (a) earthquake; (b) boils; (c) hail; (d) darkness.

136. True or False: The marriage of David and the daughter of Pharaoh formed an alliance that lasted 20 years until David's death.

Answers for this page: **124.** *Hezekiah* **125.** *True* **126.** *(b) build the house for the Lord* **127.** *Peter* **128.** *False (twice)* **129.** *(c) olive leaf* **130.** *Sodom, Gomorrah* **131.** *False* **132.** *(d) Judah* **133.** *False* **134.** *Paul (Saul)* **135.** *(a) earthquake* **136.** *False (David did not marry Pharaoh's daughter)*

137. HIDDEN WORDS: THE CRUCIFIXION (MATT 27:27–61)

Within the following sentences, find the following ten people who were associated with or present at the crucifixion of Jesus:

Judas	Bandits	Simon	Barabbas	Pilate
Soldier	Priest	Centurion	Governor	Mary

1. A hungry pupil ate my lunch.

2. The "King of the Jab" Arab basked in their applause after winning his boxing match.

3. The plane was traveling over northern cities when it hit turbulence.

4. The award went to Jud, a second-year medical student.

5. Deneb and its neighboring stars make up the constellation Cygnus.

6. The Isle of Capri, established as a resort town in Roman times, is near the Bay of Naples.

7. "Sorry, you don't get a cent, Uri. Only family members are mentioned in the will."

8. When my building was sold, I erected a new one to house my growing business.

9. Once I get my diploma, Ryswick, near the Hague, is the town I'm heading for.

10. My employee gets no work done unless I monitor his every move.

---

138. In Lystra the people called Paul this Greek god: (a) Zeus; (b) Apollo; (c) Hermes; (d) Ares.

139. True or False: The queen of Sheba came to Jerusalem to test the wisdom of Solomon.

Answers for this page: 137. 1. Pilate; 2. Barabbas; 3. Governor; 4. Judas; 5. Bandits; 6. Priest; 7. Centurion; 8. Soldier; 9. Mary; 10. Simon **138.** *(c) Hermes* **139.** *True*

140. Fill in the blanks: Paul wrote, "For the Lord himself, with a cry of command, with the archangel's call and with the sound of God's trumpet, will descend from _____, and the _____ in Christ will rise first" (1 Thes 4:16).

141. Who molded the golden calf for the Israelites to worship in the wilderness?

142. What did Elisha use to part the Jordan River? (a) salt; (b) the mantle of Elijah; (c) the staff of Isaiah; (d) the ark of God.

143. How many days and nights did rain fall on the earth when Noah and his family were lodged in the ark during the Flood?

144. Fill in the blanks: "And the ____ that the Lord God had taken from the man he made into a _____ and brought her to the man" (Gen 2:22).

145. True or False: A witch was able to call up the ghost of Samuel.

146. Whom did Ishmael and Isaac bury in the cave of Machpelah?

147. Fill in the blanks: "When the day of _____ had come, they were all together in one place. . . . All of them were filled with the _____ _____ and began to speak in other languages" (Acts 2:1, 4).

148. Who was the first person to die?

---

149. MATCHING

Match the people in Esther's life with the event.

1. Hegai
2. Mordecai
3. Vashti
4. Haman
5. Ahaseurus

A. Informed her of the edict
B. Chose her to be queen
C. Plotted against the Jews
D. Took custody of her
E. Refused to appear

Answers for this page: **140.** *heaven, dead* **141.** *Aaron* **142.** *(b) the mantle of Elijah* **143.** *40* **144.** *rib, woman* **145.** *True* **146.** *Abraham* **147.** *Pentecost, Holy Spirit* **148.** *Abel* **149.** *1D; 2A; 3E; 4C; 5B*

150. Cryptogram: Raised!

UB ABL XS ZQHZKU; K GABR LMZL VBN ZHS EBBGKAO
QBH ISJNJ RMB RZJ WHNWKQKSU. MS KJ ABL MSHS;
QBH MS MZJ XSSA HZKJSU, ZJ MS JZKU.

151. Samson used this weapon to slay a thousand Philistines in Ramath-lehi: (a) nine-foot spear; (b) donkey's jawbone; (c) bronze sword; (d) English crossbow.

152. True or False: The sons of God and the daughters of men mated before the great Flood.

153. Jesus saw this apostle under a fig tree and told him that he was an Israelite in whom there is no deceit: (a) Philip; (b) Andrew; (c) Nathanael; (d) Judas Iscariot.

154. Fill in the blanks: "And the women sang to one another as they made merry, '_____ has killed his thousands, and _____ his ten thousands'" (1 Sam 18:7).

155. True or False: Jesus died on the same day he was crucified.

156. What new name did God give Jacob?

157. Jair, the Gileadite judge, had sons who rode on how many donkeys and had how many towns? (a) 12; (b) 20; (c) 30; (d) 40.

158. True or False: God promised Hagar, the Egyptian slave, that her son Ishmael would have innumerable offspring.

159. What prophet brooded under a bush waiting for God to smite Nineveh?

160. Uriah the Hittite was murdered in this manner: (a) poison; (b) drowned; (c) in battle; (d) stabbed.

161. What judge died of a broken neck when he heard that the Philistines had captured the ark of God and killed his two sons?

Answers for this page: **150.** *"Do not be afraid; I know that you are looking for Jesus who was crucified. He is not here; for he has been raised, as he said" (Matt 28:5–6).* **151.** *(b) donkey's jawbone* **152.** *True* **153.** *(c) Nathanael* **154.** *Saul, David* **155.** *True* **156.** *Israel* **157.** *(c) 30* **158.** *True* **159.** *Jonah* **160.** *(c) in battle* **161.** *Eli*

162. Fill in the blanks: Two men in white robes said to the disciples, "Men of _____, why do you stand looking up toward heaven? This _____, who has been taken up from you into heaven, will come in the same way as you saw him go into heaven" (Acts 1:11).

163. True or False: At Jabbok, Jacob wrestled with a man who put out his hip joint.

164. Fill in the blanks: The people settled in Shinar and said, "Come, let us build ourselves a _____, and a _____ with its top in the heavens, and let us make a name for ourselves" (Gen 11:4).

165. He offered the apostles silver to have the power of the Holy Spirit after he saw the Spirit was given through the laying on of the apostles' hands: (a) Ananias; (b) Simon; (c) Aquila; (d) Demetrius.

166. When Nathan told King David a story about a poor man and rich man, what did David say the rich man deserves?

167. True or False: In order to protect Cain, God placed a mark on him.

168. This Ethiopian courtier saved Jeremiah from a slimy cistern: (a) Shephatiah; (b) Pashur; (c) Ebed-melech; (d) Jucal.

---

169. MATCHING

Match these New Testament men with their visions.

1. Ananias	A. Unclean animals
2. John	B. The angel Gabriel
3. Paul	C. Directions to Judas's house
4. Zechariah	D. The Second Coming
5. Peter	E. A Macedonian man

Answers for this page: **162.** *Galilee, Jesus* **163.** *True* **164.** *city, tower* **165.** *(b) Simon* **166.** *to die* **167.** *True* **168.** *(c) Ebed-melech* **169.** *1C; 2D; 3E; 4B; 5A*

170. True or False: Paul and Barnabas went to Rome together, where they preached the gospel to the household of Caesar.

171. Who killed thousands of Philistines by toppling two pillars though he was blind?

172. After the Babylonians destroyed Jerusalem, what king was blinded and taken in chains to Babylon?
(a) Jehoahaz; (b) Jehoiakim;
(c) Jehoiachin; (d) Zedekiah.

173. True or False: After each of the first nine plagues, God hardened the heart of Pharaoh so that he would not let the Israelites depart from Egypt.

174. In the Apostle John's vision of the future, how many churches did he see?

175. This king of Judah forced his sons to pass through fire:
(a) Jotham; (b) Ahaz;
(c) Hezekiah; (d) Uzziah.

176. True or False: All Israel assembled and mourned for Samuel when he died.

177. Fill in the blanks: "So Abraham rose early in the morning, and took bread and a skin of water, and gave it to _____, putting it on her shoulder, along with the _____, and sent her away" (Gen 21:14).

178. This apostle refused to believe Jesus had been raised from the dead until he actually saw Jesus' wounds:
(a) Peter; (b) Philip;
(c) Thomas; (d) Nathanael.

179. When Obed was born, the women in Bethlehem said a son was born to whom?

180. True or False: Noah became drunk after he survived the Flood.

181. How many Assyrians under the command of King Sennacherib did the angel of the Lord strike down outside Jerusalem? (a) 55,000;
(b) 110,000; (c) 185,000;
(d) 225,000.

182. Fill in the blank: When Moses was born, "a new king arose over Egypt, who did not know _____" (Ex 1:8).

Answers for this page: **170.** *False (not Barnabas)* **171.** *Samson* **172.** *(d) Zedekiah* **173.** *True* **174.** *seven* **175.** *(b) Ahaz* **176.** *True* **177.** *Hagar, child* **178.** *(c) Thomas* **179.** *Naomi* **180.** *True* **181.** *(c) 185,000* **182.** *Joseph*

183. UNSCRAMBLE AND MATCH: NOTABLE EVENTS

Unscramble the names of these Bible characters and match the person with the event.

1. HONJA _ _ _ _ _

   A. He tried to walk on water but became afraid.

2. MUSALE _ _ _ _ _ _

   B. He came down from a mountain, carrying two stone tablets.

3. REPTE _ _ _ _ _

   C. He was tossed from a ship during a storm at sea.

4. SEMOS _ _ _ _ _

   D. He interpreted handwriting that mysteriously appeared on a wall.

5. HOJAUS _ _ _ _ _ _

   E. He washed his hands to absolve himself from the guilt of crucifying Jesus.

6. MEANHIEH _ _ _ _ _ _ _ _

   F. At his signal, trumpeting and shouting brought down the walls of Jericho.

7. RADIUS _ _ _ _ _ _

   G. He took on the responsibility of rebuilding the walls of Jerusalem.

8. LENIAD _ _ _ _ _ _

   H. He secretly anointed David king.

9. SEJUS _ _ _ _ _

   I. At his command, a prophet was thrown into the lion's den.

10. LIEAPT _ _ _ _ _ _

   J. A great earthquake occurred when he died on a cross.

Answers for this page: **183.** *1. Jonah/C; 2. Samuel/H; 3. Peter/A; 4. Moses/B; 5. Joshua/F; 6. Nehemiah/G; 7. Darius/I; 8. Daniel/D; 9. Jesus/J; 10. Pilate/E*

184. What Greek goddess was the subject of Demetrius's outcry against the teachings of Paul, which caused a riot in Ephesus?

185. This oldest son of Jesse rebuked David, accusing him of abandoning his duties in order to see a battle: (a) Asahel; (b) Abinadab; (c) Shammah; (d) Eliab.

186. True or False: Before he died, Joshua expelled all the Canaanites from the Promised Land after the battle of Megiddo.

187. Who received a double share of Elijah's spirit when the Lord took Elijah?

188. Why did David recall Uriah from battle? (a) to honor him for heroism; (b) to rebuke him for cowardice; (c) to have him sleep with his wife; (d) to plead for forgiveness.

189. True or False: The Jewish exiles who returned to Jerusalem pledged to Ezra to separate themselves from their foreign wives.

190. What judge sang of a mother anxiously waiting for the return of her son from war?

191. Fill in the blanks: "Then _____ entered the _____ and drove out all who were selling and buying in the _____, and he overturned the tables of the money changers and the seats of those who sold doves" (Matt 21:12).

192. True or False: Ezekiel's wife perished during the Babylonian seige of Jerusalem.

193. This king of Tyre supplied Solomon with cedar and cypress timber to build the temple and his palace: (a) Ethan; (b) Heman; (c) Darda; (d) Hiram.

194. What did the water of the Nile become when Pharaoh refused to let the Israelites leave Egypt?

195. True or False: Shortly before Jesus raised Lazarus from the dead, he wept.

Answers for this page: **184.** *Artemis* **185.** *(d) Eliab* **186.** *False (many remained)* **187.** *Elisha* **188.** *(c) to sleep with his wife* **189.** *True* **190.** *Deborah* **191.** *Jesus, temple, temple* **192.** *True* **193.** *(d) Hiram* **194.** *blood* **195.** *True*

196. MATCHING

Match these Old Testament men with their dreams.

1. Pharaoh's chief baker	A. Sun, moon, and stars bowing
2. Daniel	B. Three branches of grapes
3. Joseph	C. Three cake baskets
4. Pharoah's chief cupbearer	D. A tree great in height
5. King Nebuchadnezzar	E. Four winds of heaven

197. How many stones did the Israelites take out of the Jordan when Joshua led them across it? (a) 1; (b) 3; (c) 7; (d) 12.

198. What two-day commemoration celebrates the rescue of the Jews from destruction because of Esther and Mordecai?

199. Fill in the blanks: "On the third day, when they were still in pain, two of the sons of Jacob, _____ and _____, Dinah's brothers, took their swords and came against the city unawares, and killed all the males" (Gen 34:25).

200. True or False: Moses persuaded God not to utterly destroy the Israelites.

201. After God banished Adam and Eve from the garden of Eden, he placed the cherubim to guard what?

202. True or False: Among the 12 rods representing the tribes of Israel, Levi's rod miraculously produced buds, blossoms, and almonds, which established the Aaronic priesthood.

203. This person did not see Jesus after his resurrection and before his ascension: (a) Mary Magdalene; (b) Judas Iscariot; (c) Thomas; (d) John.

204. Who struck a rock twice at the waters of Meribah, which demonstrated a lack of obedience to God.

Answers for this page: **196.** *1C; 2E; 3A; 4B; 5D* **197.** *(d) 12* **198.** *Purim* **199.** *Simeon, Levi* **200.** *True* **201.** *tree of life* **202.** *True* **203.** *(b) Judas Iscariot* **204.** *Moses*

205. QUOTATION PUZZLE: A SIGHT TO BEHOLD

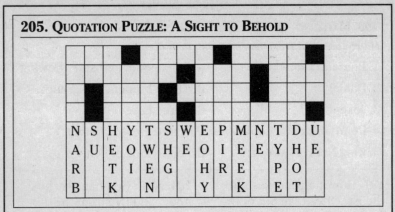

N	S	H	Y	T	S	W	E	P	M	N	T	D	U
A	U	E	O	W	H	E	O	I	E	E	Y	H	E
R		T	I	E	G		H	R	E		P	O	
B		K	N				Y		K		E	T	

206. True or False: Jesus was executed by the Jews.

207. Fill in the blanks: "There he found a man named _____, who had been bedridden for eight years, for he was paralyzed. Peter said to him, '_____, Jesus Christ heals you; get up and make your bed!' And immediately he got up" (Acts 9:33–34).

208. True or False: While Rehoboam was king of Judah, King Shishak of Egypt pillaged Jerusalem and took the treasures in the Lord's temple and the king's palace.

209. This woman's extraordinary act of graciousness appeased David, who otherwise would have killed her husband: (a) Michal; (b) Ahinoam; (c) Abigail; (d) Bathsheba.

210. In John's vision of the end times, the people whose names are not found in what book are thrown into the lake of fire?

211. This number of soldiers lapped water with their tongues as a dog laps and composed the army Gideon led against the Midianites: (a) 100; (b) 200; (c) 300; (d) 400.

Answers for this page: **205.** *"But they kept asking him, 'Then how were your eyes opened?'" (John 9:10).* **206.** *False (Romans)* **207.** *Aeneas, Aeneas* **208.** *True* **209.** *(c) Abigail* **210.** *book of life* **211.** *(c) 300*

212. On the day of Pentecost when the disciples were filled with the Holy Spirit and spoke in different languages, what were they accused of being?

213. How often did the year of Jubilee occur? (a) every year; (b) every seventh year; (c) every fortieth year; (d) every fiftieth year.

214. Fill in the blanks: "The _____ went into the sea on dry ground, the _____ forming a wall for them on their right and on their left" (Ex 14:22).

215. This king of Israel disguised himself at the battle of Ramoth-gilead, but an arrow still killed him: (a) Asa; (b) Ahab; (c) Ahaziah; (d) Jehoshaphat.

216. True or False: Only Peter, John, and James saw Jesus' ascension into heaven.

217. Lot's wife became a pillar of what when she looked back at Sodom?

218. What was the one thing God did not allow Satan to do to Job? (a) afflict his body; (b) kill his wife; (c) kill his friends; (d) take his life.

219. True or False: After the Flood, God promised that he would never destroy every living creature as he had done with the Flood.

220. When John the Baptist was preaching repentance in the Judean wilderness, what kingdom did he say had come near to his listeners?

221. Fill in the blank: "The people refused to listen to the voice of Samuel; they said, 'No! but we are determined to have a _____ over us'" (1 Sam 8:19).

222. True or False: Abram and Lot parted from each other because of strife between their herders.

223. Before the queen of Sheba met King Solomon, she heard that he had great what? (a) courage; (b) beauty; (c) wisdom; (d) humility.

Answers for this page: **212.** *drunk* **213.** *(d) every fiftieth year* **214.** *Israelites, waters* **215.** *(b) Ahab* **216.** *False* **217.** *salt* **218.** *(d) take his life* **219.** *True* **220.** *heaven* **221.** *king* **222.** *False* **223.** *(c) wisdom*

224. Crisscross Puzzle: Events *Answers on page 163.*

Fit each of the following 53 words into the puzzle below. Words are arranged below alphabetically according to the number of letters.

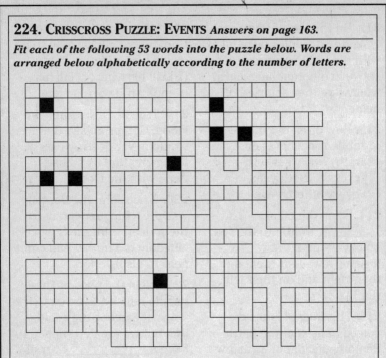

4 letters	5 letters	5 letters	6 letters	8 letters
Fall (the)	anger	tithe	sorrow	prophets
fate	atone	tower	temple	resettle
foes	Exile (the)	trial	**7 letters**	**9 letters**
gate	feast	tribe	Genesis	authority
land	Flood (the)	**6 letters**	opposed	incarnate
lend	gifts	altars	silence	testament
life	light	church	slavery	**10 letters**
name	night	famine	tracing	Tabernacle
save	omers	nation	waiting	**11 letters**
sent	renew	number	**8 letters**	Crucifixion
sins	Roman	prayer	Creation	
star	sleep	priest	offering	
	spies			

225. How long did the sun stop in midheaven when Joshua led the Israelites against the Amorites in battle?

226. True or False: God provided manna as food for the Hebrews during their exodus from Egypt.

227. Who stretched himself upon a dead child in Zarephath three times and brought him back to life?

228. Fill in the blank: God said to Moses, "Come no closer! Remove the sandals from your feet, for the place on which you are standing is _____ ground" (Ex 3:5).

229. This was not a miracle of Jesus: (a) calmed a storm; (b) fed thousands; (c) healed a leper; (d) he did all three.

230. On what day did God create the first human being?

231. True or False: Paul witnessed the crucifixion of Jesus and approved of it.

232. How many days did the Hebrews march around Jericho before its walls collapsed? (a) 3; (b) 5; (c) 7; (d) 10.

233. Whose sin caused a pestilence on Israel that was halted at the threshing floor of Araunah the Jebusite?

---

234. MATCHING

Match the events in chronological order.

1. First	A. Resurrection
2. Second	B. Dispersion of Jews
3. Third	C. Tower of Babel
4. Fourth	D. Second Coming
5. Fifth	E. Great Flood
6. Sixth	F. Pentecost
7. Seventh	G. Exodus

Answers for this page: **225.** *a day* **226.** *True* **227.** *Elijah* **228.** *holy* **229.** *(d) he did all three* **230.** *sixth* **231.** *False (he was not a witness)* **232.** *(c) 7* **233.** *David's* **234.** *1E; 2C; 3G; 4B; 5A; 6F; 7D*

114. WORD SEARCH: EVENTS OF A NATION *Puzzle on page 146.*

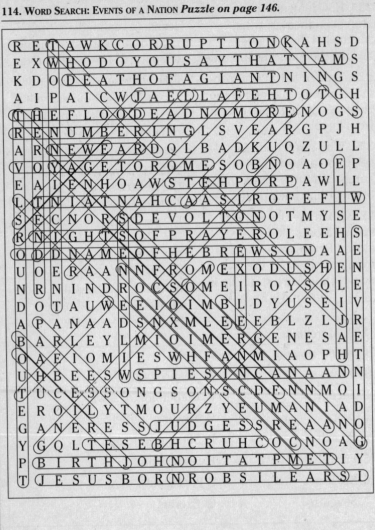

224. Crisscross Puzzle: Events *Puzzle on page 160.*

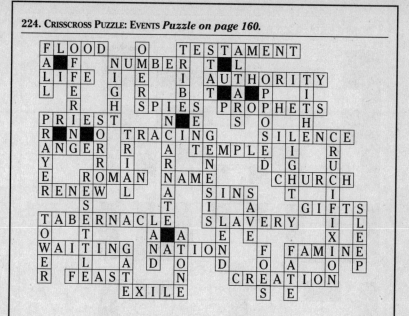

How Did You Do?

The Bible has recorded many amazing events that have occurred in the ancient past. Yet books and films have retold these events, often altering the facts. Study this chapter well for it corrects the numerous misconceptions that have sprung from those books and films.

The total number of points possible for this chart includes the questions in chapter 5 and Crossword Puzzle #5:

398 to 442: You are truly a Bible scholar!
331 to 397: You have an excellent grasp of Bible facts.
265 to 330: You have some knowledge of the Bible.
221 to 264: You could brush up on the Bible.
0 to 220: You may want to start studying the Bible.

CROSSWORD PUZZLE #5: BIBLE PLACES *Answers on page 280.*

Across

1. Southern kingdom
3. Mountain in Sinai
5. Ancient Greek city (Site of Oracle)
6. A city in northern Palestine
7. Town of Jesus' birth
11. Mound of ancient ruins
15. Ancient Greek city
16. Home of Zacchaeus (Luke 19:1–2)
18. Chastizer of Job (Job 35:1)
21. Kidneys (L.)
22. Village on Mount Olivet

Across *continued*

25. Ancient capital on Euphrates
28. Rodent
29. Samuel's mentor
30. Save (Psa 35:17)
31. Site of watery miracle (2 wds)

Down

1. Slayer of Sisera (Judg 4:21)
2. Altitude (Ezek 17:23)
3. Father of Abdon (Judg 12:15)
4. Wilderness stopping place

CROSSWORD PUZZLE #5: BIBLE PLACES *continued*

Down *continued*

7. Town in Manasseh
   (1 Chron 6:70)
8. Leviticus (abbr)
9. Where Abraham took
   Isaac (Gen 22:2)
10. Puerto Rican city
12. Brother of Abraham
    (Gen 11:26)
13. Jesus' home on Sea of
    Galilee (Matt 4:13)

Down *continued*

14. David's royal city
17. Wilderness area
    (Num 13:21)
19. Island in the Philippines
20. Husband of 1 down
    (Judg 4:17)
23. Work for (Hag 1:6)
24. Curve
26. Offer (Job 15:25)
27. Son of Judah (Gen 38:4)

CHAPTER SIX

Places in the Bible

1. What was the name of the place where Adam and Eve first dwelt?

2. True or False: Joseph was reunited with his father and brothers in Egypt.

3. Lot and his two daughters fled this city before it was destroyed: (a) Gomorrah; (b) Zoar; (c) Zebolim; (d) Sodom.

4. Where did God confuse the human language?

5. Fill in the blank: "They came to a place called _____ (which means Place of a Skull)" (Matt 27:33).

6. True or False: God did not allow Moses to cross the Jordan into the Promised Land.

7. In what city did Rahab hide the Hebrew spies? (a) Jericho; (b) Zoar; (c) Bethel; (d) Shechem.

---

8. MATCHING

Match the king with his nation.

1. Darius	A. Israel
2. Jeroboam	B. Babylon
3. Belshazzar	C. Assyria
4. Hezekiah	D. Media
5. Sennacherib	E. Judah

Answers for this page: **1.** *Eden* **2.** *True* **3.** *(d) Sodom* **4.** *Babel* **5.** *Golgotha* **6.** *True* **7.** *(a) Jericho* **8.** *1D; 2A; 3B; 4E; 5C*

9. QUOTATION PUZZLE: WHO OWNS WHAT?

To find the verse, put the letters that appear in the bottom half of the puzzle into the column of boxes above them. The letters may not be listed in the exact order in which they appear in the quote. Mark off used letters at the bottom. A letter may be used only once. The black boxes represent the space between words. In this puzzle, keep in mind that this quotation contains an apostrophe.

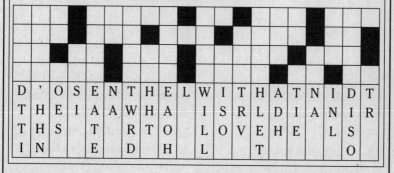

10. Fill in the blank: "I saw the holy city, the new _____, coming down out of heaven from God, prepared as a bride adorned for her husband" (Rev 21:2).

11. The crossing of this body of water coincided with the manna ceasing to appear: (a) Red Sea; (b) Jordan River; (c) Dead Sea; (d) Sea of Galilee.

12. Pharaoh ruled over what nation?

13. True or False: The land flowing with milk and honey is a description of the land of Egypt.

14. This city had a church that was neither cold nor hot in John's vision: (a) Sardis; (b) Philadelphia; (c) Pergamum; (d) Laodicea.

15. Fill in the blank: "There came to Ephesus a Jew named Apollos, a native of _____. He was an eloquent man, well-versed in the scriptures" (Acts 18:24).

Answers for this page: **9.** *"The earth is the Lord's and all that is in it, the world, and those who live in it" (Psa 24:1).* **10.** *Jerusalem* **11.** *(b) Jordan River* **12.** *Egypt* **13.** *False (Canaan)* **14.** *(d) Laodicea* **15.** *Alexandria*

16. MATCHING

Match the ancient country with the modern nation in the same land.

1. Persia

2. Babylon

3. Phoenicia

4. Judah

5. Achaia

A. Iraq

B. Iran

C. Greece

D. Lebanon

E. Israel

17. True or False: Baby Moses' life was spared when Pharaoh's daughter found him floating in a papyrus basket on the Nile.

18. Judah married the daughter of a: (a) Hebrew; (b) Canaanite; (c) Philistine; (d) Egyptian.

19. Where was Jesus born?

20. Fill in the blank: Elijah told Ahab, "Have all Israel assemble for me at Mount _____, with the four hundred fifty prophets of Baal and the four hundred prophets of Asherah, who eat at Jezebel's table" (1 Ki 18:19).

21. In what city did Solomon build the Jewish temple?

22. True or False: Paul was on his way to Damascus to persecute Christians when he encountered Jesus.

23. Where did the daughter of Jephthah bewail her virginity for two months? (a) on the mountains; (b) on the Sea of Galilee; (c) in her home; (d) in the Sinai wilderness.

24. Fill in the blank: The Lord said to Jonah, "Go at once to _____, that great city, and cry out against it; for their wickedness has come up before me" (Jon 1:2).

25. Where did Pharoah command his people to throw all newborn Hebrew boys?

26. Where was Joseph taken when he was sold as a slave by his jealous brothers?

Answers for this page: **16.** *1B; 2A; 3D; 4E; 5C* **17.** *True* **18.** *(b) Canaanite* **19.** *Bethlehem* **20.** *Carmel* **21.** *Jerusalem* **22.** *True* **23.** *(a) on the mountains* **24.** *Nineveh* **25.** *the Nile* **26.** *Egypt*

27. True or False: John was on the island of Patmos when he received his vision of the end times.

28. Fill in the blank: "It was in _____ that the disciples were first called, 'Christians'" (Acts 11:26).

29. Noah's ark came to rest on this mountain after the flood: (a) Sinai; (b) Ararat; (c) Horeb; (d) Himilaya.

30. Fill in the blank: Paul began his defense before his people by declaring, "I am a Jew, born in _____ in Cilicia" (Acts 22:3).

31. True or False: At Endor, King Saul consulted with a witch to get information about how to kill David.

32. Where did Jacob dream of a stairway to heaven? (a) Sharon; (b) Shiloh; (c) Bethel; (d) Hebron.

33. Fill in the blank: Elisha sent a messenger to Naaman, saying, "Go, wash in the _____ seven times, and your flesh shall be restored and you shall be clean" (2 Ki 5:10).

34. True or False: Horeb was known as "the mountain of God."

---

35. UNSCRAMBLE AND SOLVE: SEA OF GALILEE (MATT 14:22–33)

Then rearrange the boxed letters to form the answer to the question. The answer is a play on words.

What did Peter experience at the Sea of Galilee when he tried to walk on water?

A "_ _ _ _ _ _ _   _ _ _ _ _ _ _"

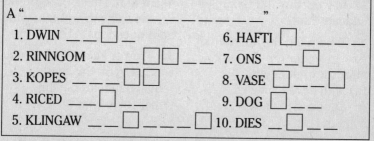

1. DWIN _ _ ☐ _

2. RINNGOM _ _ _ ☐☐ _ _

3. KOPES _ _ _ ☐☐

4. RICED _ _ ☐ _ _ _

5. KLINGAW _ _ ☐ _ _ _ _ ☐

6. HAFTI ☐ _ _ _ _ _

7. ONS _ _ ☐

8. VASE ☐ _ _ ☐

9. DOG ☐ _ _

10. DIES _ ☐ _ _

***Answers for this page: 27.** True **28.** Antioch **29.** (b) Ararat **30.** Tarsus **31.** False (he had her call up the ghost of Samuel) **32.** (c) Bethel **33.** Jordan **34.** True **35.** "sinking feeling" 1. wind; 2. morning; 3. spoke; 4. cried; 5. walking; 6. faith; 7. son; 8. save; 9. God; 10. side*

36. King Herod's threat to kill baby boys caused Joseph to take Mary and Jesus to what country?

37. Cain settled in this land after he murdered Abel: (a) Babel; (b) Canaan; (c) Eden; (d) Nod.

38. True or False: Esther became a queen in Babylon.

39. Moses parted what sea?

40. This river was not a branch of the river that flowed out of Eden: (a) Pishon; (b) Euphrates; (c) Nile; (d) Tigris.

41. Fill in the blank: God told Abraham, "Take your son, your only son Isaac, whom you love, and go to the land of _____, and offer him there as a burnt offering" (Gen 22:2).

42. In what city did Gamaliel educate Paul?

43. Where did the children of Israel wander for 40 years after they left Egypt? (a) Midian; (b) Sinai; (c) Edom; (d) Canaan.

44. True or False: Naboth's vineyard was located in Jezreel next to the palace of King Ahab of Samaria.

45. Fill in the blank: "A certain man named Simon had previously practiced magic in the city and amazed the people of _____" (Acts 8:9).

46. Cyrus ruled over what empire?

47. Mary and Martha's home was in this town: (a) Bethany; (b) Jerusalem; (c) Nazareth; (d) Capernaum.

48. True or False: Paul escaped from Damascus in a basket.

49. From what country was Hagar, Sarah's maid?

50. Fill in the blank: "When the queen of _____ heard of the fame of Solomon . . . she came to test him with hard questions" (1 Ki 10:1).

51. True or False: When Isaac was in Egypt, the king rebuked him for having Rebekah pose as his sister.

Answers for this page: **36.** *Egypt* **37.** *(d) Nod* **38.** *False (Persia)* **39.** *Red Sea* **40.** *(c) Nile* **41.** *Moriah* **42.** *Jerusalem* **43.** *(b) Sinai* **44.** *True* **45.** *Samaria* **46.** *Persian* **47.** *(a) Bethany* **48.** *True* **49.** *Egypt* **50.** *Sheba* **51.** *False (Gerar, not Egypt)*

52. MATCHING

Match the nation with the body of water.

1. Egypt   A. Euphrates

2. Israel   B. Ahava

3. Assyria   C. Nile

4. Moab   D. Jordan

5. Babylon   E. Arnon

53. The Promised Land was in this region: (a) Canaan; (b) Ammon; (c) Moab; (d) Edom.

54. Fill in the blank: After his resurrection, Jesus told Mary Magdalene, "Do not be afraid; go and tell my brothers to go to _____; there they will see me" (Matt 28:10).

55. True or False: The Philistines imprisoned a blinded Samson in Gaza, one of their chief cities.

56. In what nation did Joseph die?

57. Fill in the blank: "When we came into _____, Paul was allowed to live by himself, with the soldier who was guarding him" (Acts 28:16).

58. The place where Jacob saw God face to face: (a) Sharon; (b) Hebron; (c) Zoar; (d) Peniel.

59. True or False: Absalom drowned in the Jordan River.

60. Fill in the blank: "If in a safe land you fall down, how will you fare in the thickets of the _____?" (Jer 12:5).

61. The people made Saul their king at this place: (a) Salem; (b) Bethel; (c) Shiloh; (d) Gilgal.

62. Where was Nebuchadnezzar king?

63. Fill in the blank: "Solomon sought therefore to kill Jeroboam; but Jeroboam promptly fled to _____" (1 Ki 11:40).

Answers for this page: **52.** *1C; 2D; 3A; 4E; 5B* **53.** *(a) Canaan* **54.** *Galilee* **55.** *True* **56.** *Egypt* **57.** *Rome* **58.** *(d) Peniel* **59.** *False (did not drown)* **60.** *Jordan* **61.** *(d) Gilgal* **62.** *Babylon* **63.** *Egypt*

64. MATCHING

Match the location of these wells with the event.

1. Midian

A. God speaks to Hagar.

2. Samaria

B. Abraham's servant finds Rebekah.

3. Kadesh wilderness

C. Moses meets Zipporah.

4. Nahor

D. Jacob meets Rachel.

5. Haran

E. Jesus converses at Jacob's well.

65. Ruth was originally from what country? (a) Moab; (b) Midian; (c) Edom; (d) Ammon.

66. True or False: Jesus performed a miracle at a wedding in Cana of Galilee.

67. Fill in the blank: "In _____ there was a man named Cornelius, a centurion of the Italian Cohort, as it was called. He was a devout man who feared God with all his household" (Acts 10:1–2).

68. On which mountain did Moses receive the Ten Commandments from God?

69. True or False: Solomon was born in Hebron.

70. In what river did John the Baptist baptize people?

71. Abraham was 75 when he departed from this land: (a) Ur; (b) Haran; (c) Canaan; (d) Egypt.

72. After Esau settled in Seir, this country became known as what?

73. Fill in the blanks: "After this Paul left Athens and went to _____. There he found a Jew named Aquila, a native of _____, who had recently come from _____ with his wife Priscilla" (Acts 18:1–2).

74. True or False: Jonah rejoiced when the people in Babylon repented.

75. Job dwelled in this land: (a) Uz; (b) Ur; (c) Luz; (d) Oz.

Answers for this page: **64.** *1C; 2E; 3A; 4B; 5D* **65.** *(a) Moab* **66.** *True* **67.** *Caesarea* **68.** *Sinai* **69.** *False (Jerusalem)* **70.** *Jordan* **71.** *(b) Haran* **72.** *Edom* **73.** *Corinth, Pontus, Italy* **74.** *False (unhappy after Nineveh repented)* **75.** *(a) Uz*

76. True or False: The people in Lystra thought Paul and Barnabas were Roman gods.

77. Where did Moses flee and settle after he killed the Egyptian who had beaten one of the Hebrews?

78. Shalmaneser was king of this nation: (a) Sumer; (b) Assyria; (c) Babylon; (d) Persia.

79. Fill in the blank: "All King Solomon's drinking vessels were of gold, and all the vessels of the House of the Forest of _____ were of pure gold" (1 Ki 10:21).

80. In what region of Egypt did Jacob die?

81. True or False: At Mars Hill in Athens, Paul described the Christian faith to Greek philosophers.

82. Fill in the blank: Joshua declared before God and Israel, "Sun, stand still at _____" (Josh 10:12).

83. The tribes of Reuben and Gad decided to stay in this territory instead of going on into the Promised Land: (a) Sharon; (b) Hebron; (c) Edom; (d) Gilead.

84. What town was called the city of David?

85. True or False: After God put a mark on Cain, he dwelled west of Eden.

86. What city did Abraham try to persuade God not to devastate?

87. The Hebrews were defeated at this place as a result of Achan's sin: (a) Ai; (b) Zoar; (c) Arad; (d) Dibon.

---

88. CRYPTOGRAM: HOUSE OF PRAYER

Decode the letters in the words of this Bible verse. Each letter corresponds to a different letter in the alphabet.

NJ NS QYS LINSSWQ, "PV DYTJW JDGFF HW AGFFWB G DYTJW YX ZIGVWI XYI GFF QGSNYQJ"? HTS VYT DGKW PGBW NS G BWQ YX IYHHWIJ.

Answers for this page: **76.** *True* **77.** *Midian* **78.** *(b) Assyria* **79.** *Lebanon* **80.** *Goshen* **81.** *True* **82.** *Gibeon* **83.** *(d) Gilead* **84.** *Bethlehem* **85.** *False (east)* **86.** *Sodom* **87.** *(a) Ai* **88.** *"Is it not written, 'My house shall be called a house of prayer for all nations'? But you have made it a den of robbers" (Mark 11:17).*

89. WORD SEARCH: PLENTY OF PLACES *Answers on page 192.*

Find the 40 names of places in the puzzle below. You can find words diagonally, vertically, horizontally, backward, and forward. When you find a word in the puzzle, cross it off the list.

```
S  Q  M  O  U  N  T  O  F  O  L  I  V  E  S
I  E  N  A  B  E  T  H  E  L  Y  S  T  R  A
N  D  A  E  R  H  Q  A  P  P  O  J  O  G  P
A  E  U  O  B  S  M  E  L  A  S  U  R  E  J
I  N  I  S  F  O  T  R  E  S  E  D  R  L  O
D  S  Y  N  A  G  O  G  U  E  S  E  O  U  R
I  O  T  B  X  O  A  T  Q  L  A  A  H  A  D
M  A  E  A  I  Z  F  L  I  P  U  N  C  A  A
U  B  I  G  A  K  D  A  I  M  R  K  I  L  N
A  E  N  C  Y  N  A  H  T  E  B  E  R  E  R
N  T  U  A  O  P  T  N  V  T  E  S  E  M  I
R  H  A  N  V  E  T  I  H  G  T  I  J  R  V
E  E  C  A  R  A  R  A  T  R  H  A  D  A  E
P  S  T  A  B  E  R  N  A  C  L  E  U  C  R
A  D  Z  N  L  U  D  I  G  H  E  G  P  I  F
C  A  N  I  M  V  U  S  X  B  H  L  A  M  Q
N  O  N  G  A  D  A  R  E  N  E  S  K  T  D
B  O  T  S  A  M  A  R  I  A  M  A  R  O  H
R  A  H  C  Y  S  T  H  Y  A  T  I  R  A  X
```

Ararat (Mount)	Bethesda	Cana	Carmel
Bethany	Bethlehem	Canaan	Desert of Sin
Bethel	Calvary	Capernaum	Eden

89. WORD SEARCH: PLENTY OF PLACES *Continued*

Egypt	Joppa	Mount of Olives	Samaria
Gadarenes	Jordan River	Nain	Sinai (Mount)
Gath	Judea	Nazareth	Sychar
Gaza	Lystra	Nebo (Mount)	Synagogue
Goshen	Mars (Hill)	Nile River	Tabernacle
Jericho	Midian	Perea	Temple
Jerusalem	Moab	Red Sea	Thyatira

90. Fill in the blank: "Elijah ascended in a whirlwind into _____" (2 Ki 2:11).

91. True or False: Moses sent 12 spies into Egypt.

92. In what city did Nehemiah oversee the construction of a wall?

93. Nathaniel inferred that nothing "good" could come out of this town: (a) Bethlehem; (b) Capernaum; (c) Nazareth; (d) Bethany.

94. Fill in the blank: "Pharaoh's chariots and his army he cast into the sea; his picked officers were sunk in the _____ Sea" (Ex 15:4).

95. True or False: Laban lived in Haran.

96. Samaria was the capital of what nation?

97. Fill in the blank: "King Melchizedek of _____ brought out bread and wine; he was priest of God Most High" (Gen 14:18).

98. King Jeroboam placed the golden calves in this town as well as in Dan: (a) Shiloh; (b) Shechem; (c) Jerusalem; (d) Bethel.

99. True or False: Solomon built his palace in Hebron.

100. Fill in the blank: Paul wrote, "I commend to you our sister Phoebe, a deacon of the church at _____" (Rom 16:1).

Answers for this page: **90.** *heaven* **91.** *False (Canaan)* **92.** *Jerusalem* **93.** *(c) Nazareth* **94.** *Red* **95.** *True* **96.** *Israel* **97.** *Salem* **98.** *(d) Bethel* **99.** *False (Jerusalem)* **100.** *Cenchreae*

101. MATCHING

Match the city with its nation.

1. Rameses	A. Greece
2. Damascus	B. Assyria
3. Jerusalem	C. Syria
4. Corinth	D. Egpyt
5. Nineveh	E. Israel

102. Where did the Israelites set up the Tabernacle after they defeated the armies of Canaan?

103. True or False: God told Cain his brother's blood cried out to him from the ground.

104. At what port did Jonah find a ship going to Tarshish? (a) Dor; (b) Sidon; (c) Joppa; (d) Tyre.

105. Fill in the blanks: "But Moses said to God, 'Who am I that I should go to _____, and bring the Israelites out of _____?'" (Ex 3:11).

106. True or False: Og was the king of Bashan.

107. What town did Ruth go to with Naomi after the deaths of their husbands?

108. Where did Paul tell the church in Rome that he planned to go and would stop by to visit them on the way?

109. Hagar could not bear to watch Ishmael die in the desert so she put him: (a) in a cave; (b) by a stream; (c) under a bush; (d) by a large rock.

110. Fill in the blank: Two men in white robes told the disciples, "Men of _____, why do you stand looking up toward heaven? This Jesus, who has been taken up from you into heaven, will come in the same way as you saw him go into heaven" (Acts 1:11).

111. True or False: The devil tempted Jesus in the Judean wilderness.

Answers for this page: **101.** *1D; 2C; 3E; 4A; 5B* **102.** *Shiloh* **103.** *True* **104.** *(c) Joppa* **105.** *Pharaoh, Egypt* **106.** *True* **107.** *Bethlehem* **108.** *Spain* **109.** *(c) under a bush* **110.** *Galilee* **111.** *True*

112. The Israelites were engaged in battle in this valley when Joshua prayed for the sun and the moon to stand still: (a) Lachish; (b) Arabah; (c) Aijalon; (d) Death.

113. Fill in the blank: "I have heard," Jacob said to his sons, "that there is grain in _____; go down and buy grain for us there, that we may live and not die" (Gen 42:2).

114. Elijah fled from Jezebel to this mountain, where God told him to return to the wilderness of Damascus: (a) Carmel; (b) Nebo; (c) Ephraim; (d) Horeb.

115. True or False: Gideon built an altar, which he called, "The Lord is peace," at Ophrah.

116. Before David reigned over all Israel, he ruled over what kingdom?

117. Fill in the blanks: "During the night Paul had a vision: there stood a man of _____ pleading with him and saying, 'Come over to _____ and help us'" (Acts 16:9).

118. True or False: Ananias found a blinded Saul, who was later known as Paul, at a house on a street named "Straight."

---

119. QUOTATION PUZZLE: DEATH SITE

E	C	P	F	I	E	E	S	J	U	L	T	S	T	H	T	C	R	E	R
E	H	I	T	A	T	D	E	K	H	A	U	M	I	T	E	E	A	C	L
U	D	E	L	H	C	H		T	E	C	L		E	S	H	Y		L	H
W			N		E			Y		S	A					O		T	

Answers for this page: **112.** *(c) Aijalon* **113.** *Egypt* **114.** *(d) Horeb* **115.** *True* **116.** *Judah* **117.** *Macedonia, Macedonia* **118.** *True* **119.** *"When they came to the place that is called The Skull, they crucified Jesus there" (Luke 23:33).*

120. MATCHING

Match the town with the tribe.

1. Bethlehem
2. Bethel
3. Joppa
4. Shechem
5. Jerusalem

A. Ephraim
B. Dan
C. Manasseh
D. Benjamin
E. Judah

121. Fill in the blanks: After the Flood, God said to Noah, "I have set my bow in the _____, and it shall be a sign of the covenant between me and the _____" (Gen 9:13).

122. In what river did Jeremiah tell Seraiah to throw a scroll tied to a stone to indicate the fall of Babylon?

123. When Joseph was a young man, he searched for his brothers until a man told him that they had gone to this place: (a) Shechem; (b) Dothan; (c) Seir; (d) Egypt.

124. In what city did King Ahab construct his palace and citadel?

125. This was not one of the cities the Apostle John saw in his vision of the end times: (a) Ephesus; (b) Corinth; (c) Philadelphia; (d) Sardis.

126. True or False: Jacob was buried with his beloved wife, Rachel, in the cave in the field at Machpelah in the land of Canaan.

127. Fill in the blank: "Then Samuel took a stone and set it up between Mizpah and Jeshanah, and named it _____; for he said, 'Thus far the Lord has helped us'" (1 Sam 7:12).

128. To what hill did David bring the Ark of God (this hill later figuratively came to symbolize all of Jerusalem)?

Answers for this page: **120.** *1E; 2A; 3B; 4C; 5D* **121.** *clouds, earth* **122.** *Euphrates* **123.** *(b) Dothan* **124.** *Samaria* **125.** *(b) Corinth* **126.** *False (wife Leah)* **127.** *Ebenezer* **128.** *Zion*

129. Where was Rebekah when Abraham's servant chose her to be Isaac's wife? (a) at home; (b) on a camel; (c) in the market; (d) at a well.

130. True or False: The Mount of Olives was the place from which Jesus ascended into heaven.

131. What was the capital of Israel when David was king?

132. Moses went up from the plains of Moab to this mountain to the top of Pisgah, which is opposite Jericho, and God showed him the Promised Land: (a) Nebo; (b) Carmel; (c) Horeb; (d) Perazim.

---

133. HIDDEN WORDS: BIBLE PLACES

Find the names of these cities and towns hidden in the sentences below:

Bethany	Tarsus	Corinth	Rome	Galilee
Tyre	Emmaus	Cana	Nineveh	Babylon

1. Jean had her last baby long ago.

2. While visiting in Portugal, I leered at the strange man.

3. With our new program, we hope to eliminate pettiness and rancor in the group.

4. Singing and playing the guitar sustains me during my lonely times.

5. The road ran from east to west across the island.

6. Meeting again at the party revived their friendship.

7. We all laughed when Emma used her hairpin to repair her typewriter.

8. "That woman can act," admitted the drama critic.

9. Nine vehicles were in the convoy.

10. Don't give Elizabeth any more bananas; she's beginning to act like a monkey.

Answers for this page: **129.** *(d) at a well* **130.** *True* **131.** *Jerusalem* **132.** *(a) Nebo* **133.** *1. Babylon; 2. Galilee; 3. Corinth; 4. Tarsus; 5. Rome; 6. Tyre; 7. Emmaus; 8. Cana; 9. Nineveh; 10. Bethany*

134. Fill in the blank: Israel said to Joseph, "When I lie down with my ancestors, carry me out of _____ and bury me in their burial place" (Gen 47:30).

135. In what city was the Areopagus?

136. True or False: King Ahab ruled in Israel.

137. This man did not part the Jordan River: (a) Elijah; (b) Joshua; (c) Elisha; (d) Moses.

138. True or False: Pilate appointed Herod governor over Judea.

139. Fill in the blanks: "Abram settled in the land of _____, while Lot settled among the cities of the Plain and moved his tent as far as _____" (Gen 13:12).

140. This was not a city of refuge: (a) Bezer; (b) Bethlehem; (c) Hebron; (d) Shechem.

141. Where did Jacob use a stone to rest his head and then use it as a pillar for God's house?

142. The citizens of what city assaulted Gaius and Aristarchus, Paul's companions, because they were enraged with Paul whose teaching had swayed people from worshiping their Greek goddess?

143. True or False: Ezekiel never dwelled in the land of the Chaldeans.

144. Fill in the blank: Paul said to the Corinthians, "When I was with you and was in need, I did not burden anyone, for my needs were supplied by the friends who came from _____" (2 Cor 11:9).

145. In what valley did Samson meet Delilah? (a) Ashdod; (b) Ashkelon; (c) Sorek; (d) Etam.

146. True or False: The Prophet Amos was among the shepherds of Tekoa.

147. Fill in the blank: God told Moses, "Go back to _____; for all those who were seeking your life are dead" (Ex 4:19).

Answers for this page: **134.** *Egypt* **135.** *Athens* **136.** *True* **137.** *(d) Moses* **138.** *False* **139.** *Canaan, Sodom* **140.** *(b) Bethlehem* **141.** *Bethel* **142.** *Ephesus* **143.** *False* **144.** *Macedonia* **145.** *(c) Sorek* **146.** *True* **147.** *Egypt*

148. Where did Abraham make a treaty with King Abimelech and his commander for peace? (a) Shechem; (b) Moriah; (c) Beer-sheba; (d) Bethel.

149. True or False: In the village of Emmaus, Cleopas recognized the resurrected Jesus when the Lord blessed and broke bread.

150. What body of water has two gulfs that border the eastern and western borders of the Sinai peninsula?

151. Fill in the blank: "The next day we left and came to _____; and we went into the house of Philip the evangelist, one of the seven, and stayed with him" (Acts 21:8).

152. True or False: The cedars of Lebanon were floated down the Mediterranean so they could be used to build the temple in Jerusalem.

153. In what town was the house of the Lord, where Hannah left Samuel as a baby to fulfill her promise to God?

154. Where was Balaam headed when he encountered an angel who blocked his passage through a narrow path? (a) Edom; (b) Ammon; (c) Midian; (d) Moab.

155. Where did Jesus grow up?

156. Fill in the blank: "I am a rose of _____, a lily of the valleys" (Sol 2:1).

157. Where did Joshua gather the nation of Israel before his death to remind them of their covenant with God? (a) Bethel; (b) Shechem; (c) Jericho; (d) Shiloh.

158. True or False: Peter raised a disciple named Tabitha from the dead in Joppa.

159. Fill in the blanks: "There was a Levite, a native of _____, Joseph, to whom the apostles gave the name Barnabas (which means 'son of _____')" (Acts 4:36).

160. True or False: When the Hebrews came to Marah, they drank the water and praised God.

Answers for this page: **148.** *(c) Beer-sheba* **149.** *True* **150.** *Red Sea* **151.** *Caesarea* **152.** *True* **153.** *Shiloh* **154.** *(d) Moab* **155.** *Nazareth* **156.** *Sharon* **157.** *(b) Shechem* **158.** *True* **159.** *Cyprus, encouragement* **160.** *False (they complained)*

161. MATCHING

Match these places of war with the warriors who fought there.

1. Mount Tabor
2. Hill of Moreh
3. Valley of Elah
4. Lehi
5. Jericho

A. Joshua
B. Gideon
C. Barak
D. Samson
E. David

162. The natives of what island thought Paul was a god because a viper did not harm him?

163. Where did Isaac attempt to pass Rebekah off as his sister? (a) Edom; (b) Gerar; (c) Egypt; (d) Hebron.

164. Fill in the blank: God commanded Moses, "I will be standing there in front of you on the rock at _____. Strike the rock, and water will come out of it, so that the people may drink" (Ex 17:6).

165. Jethro was a priest in what land?

166. True or False: Jesus was arrested on the Mount of Olives.

167. Where was Samson going when he tore apart a lion by the power of the Lord? (a) Ashkelon; (b) Timnah; (c) Gaza; (d) Zorah.

168. Fill in the blanks: Paul wrote, "When Cephas came to _____, I opposed him to his face, because he stood self-condemned; for until certain people came from James, he used to eat with the _____" (Gal 2:11–12).

169. True or False: King Sennacherib returned to Nineveh from the outskirts of Jerusalem after the angel of the Lord struck down 185,000 of his soldiers, and later his sons murdered him in a pagan temple.

Answers for this page: **161.** *1C; 2B; 3E; 4D; 5A* **162.** *Malta* **163.** *(b) Gerar* **164.** *Horeb* **165.** *Midian* **166.** *True* **167.** *(b) Timnah* **168.** *Antioch, Gentiles* **169.** *True*

170. By what sea did Jesus feed over 5,000 people with five loaves and two fish?

171. At what spring did Gideon retain the soldiers who lapped like dogs? (a) Marah; (b) Siloam; (c) Harod; (d) Gerar.

172. True or False: God turned the waters of the Nile to blood because Pharoah would not release his Hebrew slaves.

173. On what island did Paul proclaim the gospel message to the proconsul Sergius Paulus and bring blindness to the magician Elymas?

174. Where did the Philistines capture the ark of the covenant of God from the Israelites after defeating their army? (a) Ashdod; (b) Ebenezer; (c) Aphek; (d) Shiloh.

175. Fill in the blank: "Then the prophet Isaiah came to King Hezekiah and said to him, 'What did these men say? From where did they come to you?' Hezekiah answered, 'They have come to me from a far country, from _____'" (Isa 39:3).

176. In what valley did King Amaziah and his soldiers strike down 10,000 men of Seir?

177. True or False: Joseph, who took Jesus' body and laid it in his own new tomb, was from Arimathea.

178. At this place God told Joshua that he had rolled away from his people the disgrace of Egypt: (a) Gilgal; (b) Bethel; (c) Shiloh; (d) Jericho.

179. In what town did Jesus heal Peter's mother-in-law?

---

180. Cryptogram: Depart From Haran

UQK EBW CQJA ZXVA EQ XGJXI, "HQ PJQI OQYJ
LQYUEJO XUA OQYJ SVUAJWA XUA OQYJ PXEBWJ'Z
BQYZW EQ EBW CXUA EBXE V KVCC ZBQK OQY."

Answers for this page: **170.** *Galilee* **171.** *(c) Harod* **172.** *True* **173.** *Cyprus* **174.** *(b) Ebenezer* **175.** *Babylon* **176.** *Valley of Salt* **177.** *True* **178.** *(a) Gilgal* **179.** *Capernaum* **180.** *"Now the Lord said to Abram, 'Go from your country and your kindred and your father's house to the land that I will show you'" (Gen 12:1).*

181. MATCHING

Match these places to the people who were imprisoned there.

1. Egypt	A. Samson
2. Gaza	B. John the Baptist
3. Rome	C. Joseph
4. Jerusalem	D. Paul
5. Galilee	E. Peter

182. Fill in the blank: "Then all the tribes of Israel came to David at _____.... and they anointed David king over Israel" (2 Sam 5:1, 3).

183. True or False: King Jehoshaphat constructed ships to go to Ophir for gold, but they were wrecked at Ezion-geber.

184. Where did the Israelites set up camp when Moses first went up the holy mountain to talk with God? (a) Canaan; (b) the Sinai wilderness; (c) Jericho; (d) Midian.

185. True or False: King Amaziah was murdered in Lachish, which was later destroyed by King Sennacherib's army.

186. Fill in the blank: "Now when Jesus came into the district of Caesarea _____, he asked his disciples, 'Who do people say that the Son of Man is?'" (Matt 16:13).

187. Aaron died on top of this mountain: (a) Ephraim; (b) Nebo; (c) Hor; (d) Sinai.

188. True or False: King Ahab was killed in the battle with the Arameans at Ramoth-gilead.

189. Fill in the blank: "The Lord rained hail on the land of Egypt; ... Only in the land of _____, where the Israelites were, there was no hail" (Ex 9:23, 26).

190. What great Assyrian city did Nahum prophesy against?

Answers for this page: **181.** *1C; 2A; 3D; 4E; 5B* **182.** *Hebron* **183.** *True* **184.** *(b) the Sinai wilderness* **185.** *True* **186.** *Philippi* **187.** *(c) Hor* **188.** *True* **189.** *Goshen* **190.** *Nineveh*

191. In what town did Jesus meet with Zacchaeus, the tax collector, and change his dishonest ways?

192. From what town did the Benjaminite men take wives so their tribe could continue to exist? (a) Shiloh; (b) Bethel; (c) Shechem; (d) Lachish.

193. True or False: Ur of the Chaldeans was located in Assyria.

194. Fill in the blank: Paul wrote to the Romans, "Greet my beloved Epaenetus, who was the first convert in _____ for Christ" (Rom 16:5).

195. The Sea of Chinnereth (or Chinneroth or Kinnereth) we know today was what in the days of Moses and Joshua?

196. True or False: Hazael ruled over Syria.

---

197. UNSCRAMBLE AND MATCH: HOMETOWN

Unscramble the names of the people on the left and match them with their hometown.

1. SEUSJ	_ _ _ _ _	A. Ur
2. THEZALIBE	_ _ _ _ _ _ _ _ _	B. Arimathea.
3. HAMBARA	_ _ _ _ _ _ _	C. Nazareth
4. HESOPJ	_ _ _ _ _ _	D. Jerusalem
5. HABEERK	_ _ _ _ _ _ _	E. Jericho
6. HAISIA	_ _ _ _ _ _	F. Ain Karim (hill country of Judea)
7. CHAZSUCEA	_ _ _ _ _ _ _ _ _	G. Tarsus
8. SCRIPIALL	_ _ _ _ _ _ _ _ _	H. Uz
9. LUAS	_ _ _ _	I. Haran
10. BOJ	_ _ _	J. Rome

Answers for this page: **191.** *Jericho* **192.** *(a) Shiloh* **193.** *False (Babylonia)* **194.** *Asia* **195.** *Sea of Galilee* **196.** *True* **197.** *1. Jesus/C; 2. Elizabeth/F; 3. Abraham/A; 4. Joseph/B; 5. Rebekah/I; 6. Isaiah/D; 7. Zacchaeus/E; 8. Priscilla/J; 9. Saul/G; 10. Job/H*

198. MATCHING

Match the pagan god to the place it was worshiped.

1. Marduk
2. Dagon
3. Baal
4. Jupiter
5. Artemis

A. Rome
B. Canaan
C. Philistia
D. Ephesus
E. Babylon

199. This was not true of the city of Laish: (a) former inhabitants were quiet and unsuspecting; (b) Danites burned it to the ground; (c) it was rebuilt and renamed Dan; (d) Micah's idol was never set up there.

200. What broad, fertile region east of the Sea of Galilee, extending roughly from Gilead in the south to Mount Hermon in the north was celebrated in the Old Testament for its cattle, sheep, and oak trees?

201. Why did Barnabas go to Tarsus? (a) to preach the gospel; (b) to escape persecution; (c) to look for Saul; (d) to bring Peter back to Jerusalem.

202. Fill in the blanks: On the day of Pentecost, Peter stood with the eleven and addressed the crowd, "Men of _____ and all who live in _____, let this be known to you, and listen to what I say" (Acts 2:14).

203. True or False: Whenever Elisha passed through the town of Shunem, a wealthy woman always urged him to stop and have a meal, and he rewarded her by promising her that the Lord would bless her with a daughter.

204. Fill in the blanks: Gabriel said to Daniel, "As for the ram that you saw with the two horns, these are the kings of _____ and _____" (Dan 8:20).

Answers for this page: **198.** *1E; 2C; 3B; 4A; 5D* **199.** *(d) Micah's idol was never set up there* **200.** *Bashan* **201.** *(c) to look for Saul* **202.** *Judea, Jerusalem* **203.** *False (son)* **204.** *Media, Persia*

205. QUOTATION PUZZLE: WISDOM'S CALL

S	T	A	C	R	T	S	E	R	W	A	D	T	A	S	H	T
H	I	D	K	H	O	H	S	E	O	G	Y	T	A	T	D	E
O	E		T	E	E		H	E	I	A	S	S	S	N	B	E
	N		E	S	S		H		R	H	H					

206. In what city are located the Abana and Pharpar rivers, which Naaman, commander of the army of the king of Aram, praised?

207. God appeared to Solomon in a dream at this place and asked Solomon what he could give him: (a) Shiloh; (b) Gibeon; (c) Hebron; (d) Jerusalem.

208. Fill in the blank: Jesus "left Judea and started back to Galilee. But he had to go through _____" (John 4:3–4).

209. True or False: Jacob saw a vision of a staircase at the top of which stood Abraham.

210. Near what village did Rachel die?

211. Ezekiel was held a prisoner by this river and saw visions: (a) Chebar; (b) Nile; (c) Euphrates; (d) Tigris.

212. Fill in the blank: God said to Elijah, "Go now to _____, which belongs to Sidon, and live there; for I have commanded a widow there to feed you" (1 Ki 17:9).

213. In what town did Jesus raise Lazarus from the dead?

214. True or False: Ravens brought bread and meat to the Prophet Elijah by the Wadi Cherith.

Answers for this page: **205.** *"On the heights, beside the way, at the crossroads she takes her stand" (Prov 8:2).* **206.** *Damascus* **207.** *(b) Gibeon* **208.** *Samaria* **209.** *False (did not see Abraham)* **210.** *Bethlehem* **211.** *(a) Chebar* **212.** *Zarephath* **213.** *Bethany* **214.** *True*

215. Queen Esther resided in this city in the Persian Empire: (a) Pura; (b) Persepolis; (c) Bactra; (d) Susa.

216. Fill in the blank: "As they went out, they came upon a man from _____ named Simon; they compelled this man to carry his cross" (Matt 27:32).

217. True or False: Elisha retrieved an ax head from the Euphrates.

218. From what city did the author of Ecclesiastes say he ruled as king?

219. Lydia, a Christian convert, was from this city: (a) Ephesus; (b) Corinth; (c) Thyatira; (d) Philippi.

220. Fill in the blank: "They buried the bones of Saul and of his son Jonathan in the land of _____ in Zela, in the tomb of his father Kish" (2 Sam 21:14).

221. Asa was king of this kingdom: (a) Judah; (b) Israel; (c) Syria; (d) Tyre.

222. The Acts of the Apostles concludes in what city?

223. True or False: Jesus told the man born blind to go and wash in the pool of Siloam.

224. What land did Joshua and Caleb spy?

225. The tower of Babel was built in this land: (a) Uz; (b) Shinar; (c) Ur; (d) Havilah.

226. True or False: Evil-merodach ruled in Assyria.

227. Fill in the blank: Paul wrote to Titus, "I left you behind in _____ for this reason, so that you should put in order what remained to be done, and should appoint elders in every town, as I directed you" (Titus 1:5).

228. Daniel had a vision of a ram and a goat by this river: (a) Tigris; (b) Euphrates; (c) Ulai; (d) Gihon.

229. True or False: Cain built a city and named it Enoch after his son.

230. Where was the church to which Paul wrote about the fruit of the Spirit?

Answers for this page: **215.** *(d) Susa* **216.** *Cyrene* **217.** *False (Jordan)* **218.** *Jerusalem* **219.** *(c) Thyatira* **220.** *Benjamin* **221.** *(a) Judah* **222.** *Rome* **223.** *True* **224.** *Canaan* **225.** *(b) Shinar* **226.** *False (Babylon)* **227.** *Crete* **228.** *(c) Ulai* **229.** *True* **230.** *Galatia*

231. MATCHING

Match these women to the places where they are found in the Acts of the Apostles.

1. Dorcas   A. Philippi

2. Sapphira   B. Lystra

3. Lydia   C. Corinth

4. Priscilla   D. Joppa

5. Eunice   E. Jerusalem

232. Fill in the blank: "So you shall know that I, the Lord your God, dwell in _____, my holy mountain" (Joel 3:17).

233. True or False: In order to disgrace Israel, the Ammonites threatened to gouge out the right eye of every person in Jabesh-gilead, but they were defeated by Saul.

234. During the Exodus, the Hebrews discovered 12 wells and 70 palm trees at this location: (a) Kibroth; (b) Rephidim; (c) Marah; (d) Elim.

235. Mentioned in the Acts of the Apostles, Candace was queen of what nation?

236. True or False: A spirit lifted Jeremiah between earth and heaven by the lock of his head.

237. Fill in the blanks: Jesus said, "Woe to you, Chorazin! Woe to you, Bethsaida! For if the deeds of power done in you had been done in _____ and _____, they would have repented long ago in sackcloth and ashes" (Matt 11:21).

238. This king did not rule over all of Israel: (a) David; (b) Solomon; (c) Josiah; (d) Saul.

239. Who outran Ahab's chariot from Mount Carmel to Jezreel?

Answers for this page: **231.** *1D; 2E; 3A; 4C; 5B* **232.** *Zion* **233.** *True* **234.** *(d) Elim* **235.** *Ethiopia* **236.** *False (Ezekiel)* **237.** *Tyre, Sidon* **238.** *(c) Josiah* **239.** *Elijah*

240. Crisscross Puzzle: Events *Answers on page 193.*

Fit each of the following 70 words into the puzzle below. Words are arranged alphabetically according to the number of letters.

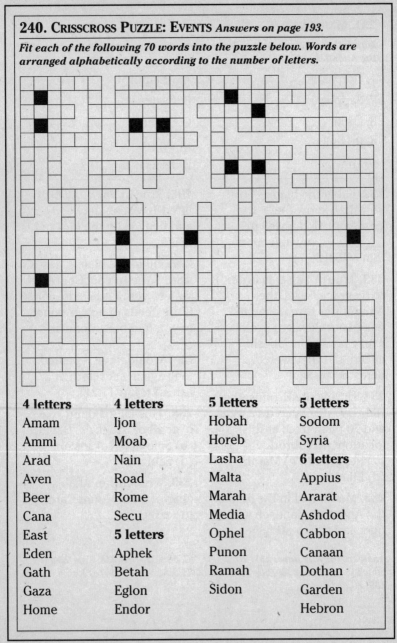

4 letters	4 letters	5 letters	5 letters
Amam	Ijon	Hobah	Sodom
Ammi	Moab	Horeb	Syria
Arad	Nain	Lasha	**6 letters**
Aven	Road	Malta	Appius
Beer	Rome	Marah	Ararat
Cana	Secu	Media	Ashdod
East	**5 letters**	Ophel	Cabbon
Eden	Aphek	Punon	Canaan
Gath	Betah	Ramah	Dothan
Gaza	Eglon	Sidon	Garden
Home	Endor		Hebron

240. CRISSCROSS PUZZLE: EVENTS *continued*

6 letters	7 letters	8 letters	10 letters
Ithnan	Antioch	Berothai	Alexandria
Jordan	Assyria	Damascus	Appollonia
Kartan	Corinth	Neapolis	**11 letters**
Lystra	Ephesus	Thyatira	Trachonitis
Rabbah	Galilee	**9 letters**	**12 letters**
Sardis	Lachish	Areopagus	Thessalonica
Shinar	Samaria	Beer-sheba	
Thebes	**8 letters**	Jerusalem	
	Arubboth	Synagogue	
	Ashkelon		

241. Fill in the blank: "Once every three years the fleet of ships of _____ used to come bringing gold, silver, ivory, apes, and peacocks. Thus King Solomon excelled all the kings of the earth in riches and in wisdom" (1 Ki 10:22–23).

242. Jephthah's hometown was: (a) Mizpah; (b) Miletus; (c) Hebron; (d) Gilgal.

243. Where did the Christians have a confrontation with Demetrius, a silversmith, and his fellow artisans on Paul's third missionary journey?

244. The church in this city in Revelation is warned about tolerating the fornication and idolatry of Jezebel: (a) Smyrna; (b) Thyatira; (c) Sardis; (d) Laodicea.

245. What ancient city was situated where Tel Aviv is now located?

246. True or False: The Israelites buried the bones of Joseph at Shechem.

247. Where did Peter heal a paralytic named Aeneas? (a) Caesarea; (b) Lydda; (c) Antioch; (d) Jerusalem.

Answers for this page: **241.** *Tarshish* **242.** *(a) Mizpah* **243.** *Ephesus* **244.** *(b) Thyatira* **245.** *Joppa* **246.** *True* **247.** *(b) Lydda*

248. Fill in the blank: "But you, O _____ of Ephrathah, who are one of the little clans of Judah, from you shall come forth for me one who is to rule in Israel" (Mic 5:2).

249. True or False: Eliezer, Abraham's servant, was from Haran.

250. Fill in the blank: "At that time prophets came down from Jerusalem to _____. One of them named Agabus stood up and predicted by the Spirit that there would be a severe famine over all the world" (Acts 11:27–28).

89. Word Search: Plenty of Places *Puzzle on page 174.*

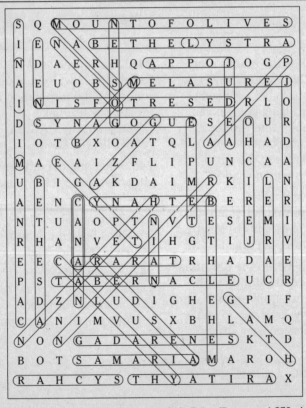

Answers for this page: **248.** *Bethlehem* **249.** *False (Damascus)* **250.** *Antioch*

240. CRISSCROSS PUZZLE: EVENTS *Puzzle on page 190.*

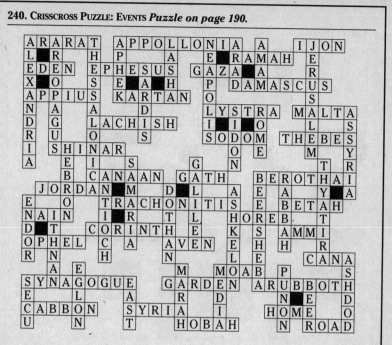

Crossword Puzzle #6: Animals *Answers on page 280.*

Across

1. "_____ the eyes of the blind..." (Isa 35:5).
5. Dog-like animal (Jer 12:9)
7. Domesticated
11. Function
12. Levites' land (1 Chron 6:70)
13. Asian river
14. Fed Elijah (1 Ki 17:6)
15. Wild pig (Psa 80:13)
16. "Desert owl" (Lev 11:18; footnote)
18. John ate them (Matt 3:4)
20. Beast of burden (Deut 25:4)

Across *continued*

22. "Tell _____ one..." (Mark 9:9).
23. Hooters (Zeph 2:14)
25. "Agnus _____."
27. Ravenous creature (Gen 49:27)
30. James _____ his nets (Matt 4:21)
33. High flier (Prov 30:19)
34. Makeup (Jer 4:30)
36. Owed (Rom 13:7)
37. Light of the _____ (Matt 5:14)
38. West Africa (abbr)
40. Gallium (chem sym)

Across *continued*

41. Bird imported by Solomon (1 Ki 10:22)

43. Grazing land (Gen 47:4)

46. "_____ homo!" (Latin for John 19:5)

49. Adam's son

52. Time-teller (Isa 38:8)

53. "The _____ of his pasture" (Psa 100:3).

54. Rabbit

Down

1. Snare (Josh 23:13)

2. Residence (John 12:1)

3. Jewish month

4. Ancestor of Jesus (Luke 3:27)

5. Coney (Psa 104:18)

6. David's son (2 Sam 13:1)

7. Forbidden (alt. sp.)

8. A bone or a mouth (two words)

9. Animal flesh

10. Sins

17. Greek Island

19. Female herd animal

21. Infectious disease

24. "The heart of a _____" (2 Sam 17:10).

Down *continued*

25. Condition of Samson's lion

26. Unemployed (Prov 19:15)

28. Roman emperor

29. Venomous snake (Isa 11:8)

30. "As for _____ and my household..." (Josh 24:15).

31. Southeast (abbr)

32. Kept out of sight (Ex 2:2)

35. Pair (Gen 6:19)

37. Past of "to be"

39. Jesus died on ___ _____. (2 wds)

40. Horse's gait (Judg 5:22)

41. Scraped the ground (Job 39:21)

42. Desert taxi (Gen 24:64)

44. Hebrew Scriptures

45. Babylonian captivity (1 Chron 9:1)

47. Color index (abbr)

48. Calcium (symbol)

50. Barium (symbol)

51. Son of Judah (Gen 38:3)

How Did You Do?

You must be eager to take a trip to the holy lands now that you have learned so many interesting facts about the various sites in Israel, Egypt, and other places mentioned in the Bible. Meanwhile, determine how you fared on this topic by counting what you answered correctly and seeing where your score lies in the following chart.

The total number of points for this chart includes the questions in chapter 6 and Crossword Puzzle #6:

411 to 457: You are truly a Bible scholar!
343 to 410: You have an excellent grasp of Bible facts.
274 to 342: You have some knowledge of the Bible.
228 to 273: You could brush up on the Bible.
0 to 227: You may want to start studying the Bible.

Animals are quite prominent in the Bible, as you probably noticed in Crossword Puzzle #6. In fact, you'll be amazed at the wide variety of animals there are. So be ready to utilize your vast knowledge of the animal kingdom in the next chapter.

CHAPTER SEVEN
Know Your Bible Animals and Plants

1. In the Creation account, who named the animals?

2. Which kind of plants grew in Palestine in Jesus' day? (a) trees; (b) vines; (c) herbs; (d) all three.

3. True or False: After Joseph's brothers cast him into a pit, took his coat, and then sold him into slavery, they dipped his coat in camel's blood to deceive their father.

4. Fill in the blanks: The lover in the Song of Solomon declared, "I am a _____ of Sharon, a _____ of the valleys" (Sol 2:1).

5. On Mount Horeb, Moses encountered what amazing plant?

6. True or False: The tree of life will be in the New Jerusalem.

---

7. MATCHING

Match the son with the description Jacob gave each on his deathbed.

1. Dan
2. Judah
3. Benjamin
4. Issachar
5. Naphtali

A. Doe
B. Snake
C. Donkey
D. Wolf
E. Lion

Answers for this page: **1.** *Adam* **2.** *(d) all three* **3.** *False (goat's blood)* **4.** *rose, lily* **5.** *burning bush* **6.** *True* **7.** *1B; 2E; 3D; 4C; 5A*

8. QUOTATION PUZZLE: HOPE FOR THE FUTURE

To find the verse, put the letters that appear in the bottom half of the puzzle into the column of boxes above them. The letters may not be listed in the exact order in which they appear in the quote. Mark off used letters at the bottom. A letter may be used only once. The black boxes represent the space between words.

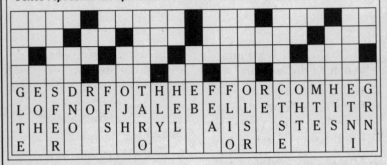

9. Because the Israelites complained about eating manna in the wilderness, God sent them: (a) olives; (b) fish; (c) turkeys; (d) quail.

10. Fill in the blank: Paul said, "You shall not muzzle an _____ while it is treading out the grain" (1 Tim 5:18).

11. Who was the first person to plant a vineyard?

12. Which animals would faithful Israelites not raise? (a) sheep; (b) goats; (c) pigs; (d) donkeys.

13. True or False: Joshua said that if the people didn't chase their enemies out of the Promised Land, they would become thorns in their eyes.

14. Fill in the blank: God said, "Let the earth bring forth living _____ of every kind" (Gen 1:24).

15. Jesus said we will know people by their (a) fruits; (b) crops; (c) number of sheep they own; (d) land.

16. What kind of animal did King Solomon keep in 40,000 stalls?

Answers for this page: **8.** *"Then shall all the trees of the forest sing for joy before the Lord; for he is coming" (Psa 96:12–13).* **9.** *(d) quail* **10.** *ox* **11.** *Noah* **12.** *(c) pigs* **13.** *True* **14.** *creatures* **15.** *(a) fruits* **16.** *horses*

17. True or False: Isaiah spoke of a time when a child would play with snakes and not be hurt.

18. Fill in the blank: "What was sown among _____, this is the one who hears the word, but the cares of the world and the lure of wealth choke the word" (Matt 13:22).

19. To what insect did Moses compare the Amorites?
(a) locusts; (b) bees; (c) flies; (d) beetles.

20. True or False: Jesus permitted his disciples to pluck and eat grain on the sabbath, which the Pharisees called work.

21. Samson's riddle had to do with honey inside the carcass of what animal?

22. Fill in the blank: Isaiah declared, "He will not cry or lift up his voice . . . a bruised _____ he will not break" (Isa 42:2–3).

23. True or False: When David guarded his flocks, he killed lions and bears.

24. Which of the following trees is not mentioned in the Bible? (a) terebinth; (b) olive; (c) myrtle; (d) maple.

25. When Aaron threw down his staff before Pharaoh, it turned into what animal?

---

26. MATCHING

Match the animals with their use.

1. Mules	A. War
2. Deer	B. Carried royalty
3. Horses	C. Travel
4. Camels	D. Herd sheep
5. Dogs	E. Food

Answers for this page: **17.** *True* **18.** *thorns* **19.** *(b) bees* **20.** *True* **21.** *lion* **22.** *reed* **23.** *True* **24.** *(d) maple* **25.** *snake* **26.** *1B; 2E; 3A; 4C; 5D*

27. CRYPTOGRAM: LIKE EAGLES

Decode the letters in the words of this Bible verse. Each letter corresponds to a different letter in the alphabet.

ITXEJ STX SNOI LXZ ITJ RXZM ETNRR ZJGJS ITJOZ EIZJGWIT, ITJU ETNRR PXFGI FK SOIT SOGWE ROHJ JNWRJE, ITJU ETNRR ZFG NGM GXI VJ SJNZU, ITJU ETNRR SNRH NGM GXI LNOGI.

28. Fill in the blank: "Can a fig tree, my brothers and sisters, yield _____, or a grapevine figs? No more can salt water yield fresh" (Jas 3:12).

29. True or False: Joseph dreamed that his brothers were binding sheaves and all of their sheaves bowed to his.

30. Compared to the size of the people of Canaan, the spies saw themselves as this small creature: (a) ants; (b) grasshoppers; (c) bees; (d) moths.

31. The first of all crops belonged to whom?

32. Fill in the blank: The psalmist said, "As a _____ longs for flowing streams, so my soul longs for you, O God" (Psa 42:1).

33. True or False: The mustard tree grows so high that birds nest in its branches.

34. Moses placed this bronze creature on a pole to stop a plague among the Hebrews: (a) lion; (b) bear; (c) eagle; (d) serpent.

35. Fill in the blank: Jesus taught, "Consider the _____ of the field, how they grow; they neither toil nor spin" (Matt 6:28).

36. What animal's hair did John the Baptist wear?

37. The 12 spies did not bring these fruits out of Canaan: (a) figs; (b) pomegranates; (c) grapes; (d) apples.

38. True or False: King Ahab coveted the vineyard of Naboth.

Answers for this page: **27.** *"Those who wait for the Lord shall renew their strength, they shall mount up with wings like eagles, they shall run and not be weary, they shall walk and not faint" (Isa 40:31).* **28.** olives **29.** True **30.** *(b) grasshoppers* **31.** God **32.** deer **33.** True **34.** *(d) serpent* **35.** lilies **36.** camel's **37.** *(d) apples* **38.** True

39. Fill in the blank: The psalmist prayed, "O that I had wings like a _____!" (Psa 55:6).

40. Jude said ungodly sinners are like autumn trees that lack what?

41. True or False: The Bible never mentions the leopard.

42. What kind of branches were in people's hands before the Lamb in John's vision of the end times? (a) olive; (b) willow; (c) poplar; (d) palm.

43. What did Pharaoh refuse to provide the Israelites with for them to make bricks?

44. Fill in the blanks: Jesus said, "Do not throw your pearls before _____" (Matt 7:6).

45. This animal could not be brought to the priest as a sacrifice: (a) a bird; (b) a goat; (c) a rabbit; (d) a sheep.

46. True or False: The Bible does not identify the kind of fruit Adam and Eve ate from the tree of the knowledge of good and evil.

47. Fill in the blank: The psalmist declared, "How sweet are your words to my taste, sweeter than _____ to my mouth!" (Psa 119:103).

---

48. UNSCRAMBLE AND SOLVE: ELIJAH AND THE BIRDS *(1Ki 17:1-7)*

Then rearrange the boxed letters to form the answer to the question. The answer is a play on words.

How Elijah felt in the wilderness before God sent some birds to feed him:

He was "___ ___ ___ ___ ___-___ ___ ___."

1. DEFE ___ ☐ ___ ___

2. KRIND ___ ___ ___ ☐ ___

3. BADER ___ ☐ ___ ___ ___

4. TEAM ___ ___ ☐ ___

5. DEVIL ___ ___ ___ ☐ ___ ___

6. ORWD ___ ☐ ___ ___

7. SATE ___ ___ ___ ☐

8. RUNT ___ ☐ ___ ___

Answers for this page: **39.** *dove* **40.** *fruit* **41.** *False* **42.** *(d) palm* **43.** *straw* **44.** *swine* **45.** *(c) a rabbit* **46.** *True* **47.** *honey* **48.** *..."raven-ous"* **1.** *feed;* **2.** *drink;* **3.** *bread;* **4.** *meat;* **5.** *lived;* **6.** *word;* **7.** *eats;* **8.** *turn*

49. MATCHING

Match the men with their occupations.

1. Cain	A. Kept sheep
2. Peter	B. Beat wheat
3. Abel	C. Raised fruit
4. Gideon	D. Caught fish

50. What hung on Paul's hand on the island of Malta but did not kill him?

51. God asked David why he had not built him a house made out of what? (a) cedar; (b) cypress; (c) sycamore; (d) birch.

52. Fill in the blank: Jesus said, "You blind guides! You strain out a gnat, but swallow a _____!" (Matt 23:24).

53. What tall plant is mentioned in the Bible, has purple blossoms, and can be used as a writing instrument?

54. True or False: On his deathbed Jacob referred to Reuben, his eldest son, as a weasel.

55. John the Baptist's diet consisted of what two foods?

56. Fill in the blanks: Isaiah proclaimed, "The _____ withers, the _____ fades; but the word of our God will stand forever" (Isa 40:8).

57. When the people proclaimed King Herod god, what ate and killed him? (a) dogs; (b) a lion; (c) worms; (d) ants.

58. True or False: The Hebrews use tree limbs to celebrate the Feast of Tabernacles.

59. This flower is not mentioned in the Bible: (a) tulip; (b) rose; (c) lily; (d) mandrake.

60. Fill in the blank: Jesus said to Simon and Andrew, "Follow me and I will make you _____ for people" (Mark 1:17).

Answers for this page: **49.** *1C; 2D; 3A; 4B* **50.** *viper* **51.** *(a) cedar* **52.** *camel* **53.** *reed* **54.** *False* **55.** *locusts, wild honey* **56.** *grass, flower* **57.** *(c) worms* **58.** *True* **59.** *(a) tulip* **60.** *fish*

61. With what thing in the field did James compare the rich?

62. True or False: God told Noah to bring animals that Hebrews later considered "unclean" into the ark.

63. What kind of tree did Jesus wither because it had no fruit?

64. During his affliction Job cried out that his flesh was clothed with these creatures: (a) worms; (b) beetles; (c) lice; (d) ants.

65. Fill in the blank: "These are they who have come out of the great ordeal; they have washed their robes and made them white in the blood of the _____" (Rev 7:14).

66. True or False: At the siege of Samaria, food became so scarce that traders charged five shekels of silver for a small amount of dove dung.

67. What did the dove have in its beak when it returned to Noah's ark?

68. Fill in the blank: The spies told Moses, "We came to the land to which you sent us; it flows with milk and _____" (Num 13:27).

69. True or False: When people presented offerings to God, a portion of it went to the priests.

70. These animals ruin the vineyards in the Song of Solomon: (a) gazelles; (b) doves; (c) does; (d) foxes.

71. MATCHING

Match the product and the country associated with it in the Bible.

1. Oak trees
2. Cedar trees
3. Papyrus or reed
4. Dill

A. Egypt
B. Bashan
C. Israel
D. Lebanon

Answers for this page: **61.** *flower* **62.** *True* **63.** *fig* **64.** *(a) worms* **65.** *Lamb* **66.** *True* **67.** *olive leaf* **68.** *honey* **69.** *True* **70.** *(d) foxes* **71.** *1B; 2D; 3A; 4C*

---

72. MATCHING

Match the clean and unclean.

1. Clean animal   A. Shellfish

2. Unclean animal   B. Goat

3. Clean fish   C. Perch

4. Unclean fish   D. Land crocodile

---

73. What kind of branches did the people bring to Jesus when he came to Jerusalem?

74. Fill in the blank: After John baptized Jesus, he "saw the Spirit of God descending like a _____ and alighting on him" (Matt 3:16).

75. True or False: Seth offered fruit of the ground, which the Lord accepted.

76. What kind of animal did Jesus say false prophets are inwardly?

77. Noah used this kind of wood to build the ark:
(a) cypress; (b) oak;
(c) redwood; (d) cedar.

78. True or False: The Israelites used acacia wood in building the tabernacle.

79. Fill in the blank: The psalmist said that God's "delight is not in the strength of the _____, nor his pleasure in the speed of a runner" (Psa 147:10).

80. Gideon chose his 300 men because they lapped water at the river like this type of animal: (a) dog; (b) horse; (c) sheep; (d) goat.

81. After his resurrection, Jesus ate a piece of broiled what in the presence of his disciples?

82. The writer of Hebrews said that ground that produces these things is worthless: (a) thorns; (b) thistles; (c) both a and b; (d) neither a nor b.

Answers for this page: **72.** *1B; 2D; 3C; 4A* **73.** *palm* **74.** *dove* **75.** *False (God had no regard for Cain's fruit offering)* **76.** *wolves* **77.** *(a) cypress* **78.** *True* **79.** *horse* **80.** *(a) dog* **81.** *fish* **82.** *(c) both a and b*

83. Fill in the blank: The psalmist declared, "Know that the Lord is God. It is he that made us, and we are his; we are his people, and the _____ of his pasture" (Psa 100:3).

84. True or False: Zacchaeus saw Jesus from a sycamore tree.

85. What kind of animal spoke to Balaam?

86. The Prophet Amos was a dresser of what kind of trees? (a) walnut; (b) sycamore; (c) almond; (d) apple.

87. True or False: When an angel told Manoah and his wife that they would have a son (Samson), they sacrificed a goat.

88. Fill in the blanks: Jesus said, "If you had faith the size of a _____ seed, you could say to this mulberry _____, 'Be uprooted and planted in the sea,' and it would obey you" (Luke 17:6).

89. What was the only creature (other than a human) to lie?

90. True or False: The Bible mentions animals before it mentions plants.

91. Under what kind of stalks did Rahab hide the Hebrew spies? (a) corn; (b) bean; (c) wheat; (d) flax.

92. Fill in the blank: Jeremiah asked, "Can Ethiopians change their skin or _____ their spots?" (Jer 13:23).

---

93. QUOTATION PUZZLE: A HEALTHY SIGN

F	H	E	U	P	A	G	M	T	L	I	E	S
T	H	O		R	R	L	H		E	O	K	E
T	L	E		R	I	S	H	T	R	U	E	

Answers for this page: **83.** *sheep* **84.** *True* **85.** *donkey* **86.** *(b) sycamore*
87. *True* **88.** *mustard, tree* **89.** *the serpent* **90.** *False* **91.** *(d) flax*
92. *leopards* **93.** *"The righteous flourish like the palm tree" (Psa 92:12).*

94. Word Search: Bible Plants, Fruit, and Herbs

Answers on page 224.
Find the 35 members of the plant kingdom in the puzzle below. You can find words diagonally, vertically, horizontally, backward, and forward. When you find a word in the puzzle, cross it off the list on the next page.

```
B  F  E  A  Q  C  A  L  A  M  U  S  O
G  A  L  L  S  G  I  F  A  N  P  O  L
R  J  L  A  B  H  U  N  L  O  I  U  I
S  O  O  M  X  M  D  X  K  P  C  S  V
R  P  S  O  D  R  A  T  S  U  M  X  E
E  O  I  E  A  N  X  R  M  X  W  M  T
D  S  Q  K  O  L  M  M  B  O  X  O  R
N  S  E  Q  E  F  I  W  L  Z  V  D  E
A  Y  L  L  I  N  S  L  O  M  P  O  E
I  H  U  T  T  X  A  H  Y  Y  P  S  X
R  W  C  U  M  M  O  R  A  R  V  F  D
O  H  A  N  N  M  T  V  D  R  U  O  G
C  W  S  X  P  L  X  I  S  H  O  E  O
I  N  S  H  E  N  N  A  K  W  U  N  P
N  Q  I  B  X  B  U  S  M  Z  M  I  H
U  B  A  N  R  E  I  R  B  X  N  V  E
S  E  P  A  R  G  O  A  K  U  S  S  R
W  O  L  L  I  W  C  E  D  A  R  W  P
```

94. WORD SEARCH: BIBLE PLANTS, FRUIT, AND HERBS

Anise	Coriander	Henna	Oak
Ash	Cummin	Hyssop	Olive tree
Balm	Figs	Lily	Rose of Sharon
Box	Fitch	Mallow	
Bramble	Flax	Mandrake	Rue
Brier	Gall	Mint	Spikenard
Calamus	Gopher	Mustard	Vine of Sodom
Cassia	Gourd	Myrrh	Willow
Cedar	Grapes	Myrtle	Wormwood

95. King Darius of Persia had Daniel thrown into a den occupied by what animals?

96. Fill in the blanks: God said to Adam, "_____ and _____ it shall bring forth for you; and you shall eat the plants of the field" (Gen 3:18).

97. During the sabbath year, the only food crops the Israelites could eat were those that (a) grew by themselves; (b) strangers brought to them; (c) they could buy; (d) they planted by hand.

98. True or False: Peter had a dream in which God told him to kill and eat unclean animals.

99. What plant tasted bitter and symbolized sorrow and tragedy?

100. Fill in the blank: "Consider the _____: they neither sow nor reap, they have neither storehouse nor barn, and yet God feeds them" (Luke 12:24).

101. True or False: During Bible times it was a compliment to refer to someone as a dog.

102. Nathan rebuked David for stealing a man's wife by comparing David to a rich man who stole what kind of animal?

Answers for this page: **95.** *lions* **96.** *thorns, thistles* **97.** *(a) grew by themselves* **98.** *True* **99.** *wormwood* **100.** *ravens* **101.** *False* **102.** *lamb*

103. MATCHING

Match the creature with the plague on Egypt.

1. Flies   A. Second

2. Locusts   B. Third

3. Frogs   C. Fourth

4. Gnats   D. Eighth

104. Which food did the Israelites not mention in their complaint about no longer being in Egypt? (a) cucumbers; (b) melons; (c) onions; (d) grapes.

105. Fill in the blanks: "Then, opening their treasure chests, [the wise men] offered [the baby Jesus] gifts of gold, _____, and _____" (Matt 2:11).

106. This animal is the most frequently mentioned animal in the Bible: (a) sheep; (b) horse; (c) lion; (d) dog.

107. True or False: Isaiah promised that the desert would blossom like a rose.

108. What kind of crown did the Roman soldiers put on Jesus' head?

109. After the Philistines stole the Ark of the Covenant, they tried to stop a plague among them by making five golden what?

110. Fill in the blank: "She considers a field and buys it; with the fruit of her hands she plants a _____" (Prov 31:16).

111. True or False: The Mosaic laws listed bats as being unclean and forbid God's people from eating them.

112. The writer of Proverbs did not include this animal as being among the four things on earth that are small and exceedingly wise: (a) lizards; (b) snails; (c) locusts; (d) badgers.

Answers for this page: **103.** *1C; 2D; 3A; 4B* **104.** *(d) grapes* **105.** *frankincense, myrrh* **106.** *(a) sheep* **107.** *True* **108.** *thorns* **109.** *mice* **110.** *vineyard* **111.** *True* **112.** *(b) snails*

113. HIDDEN WORDS: BIBLE ANIMALS

These animals appear in the Bible. Find their names hidden in the sentences below:

goat	camel	wolf	donkey	lion
boar	eagle	sheep	oxen	horse

1. The Tower of London Key Ceremony is an event you don't want to miss.

2. I abhor seeing what the beetles are doing to our elm trees.

3. Private Smith has been AWOL for three days.

4. She epitomizes our image of the liberated woman.

5. The groom was on time for the wedding, but the bride came late.

6. The zoo keeps the fox enclosed in a simulated natural environment.

7. Those who ordered seafood gumbo are being served first.

8. "When you come to the area, glean in the fields behind the reapers," Naomi told Ruth.

9. Elena danced the tango at her wedding.

10. My new purifier will ionize the air in this room in less than 30 minutes.

114. Fill in the blanks: Peter said, "All flesh is like _____. . . . The _____ withers, and the flower falls" (1 Pet 1:24).

115. True or False: Hagar placed Ishmael under a bush so she wouldn't have to watch him die.

Answers for this page: **113.** *1. donkey; 2. horse; 3. wolf; 4. sheep; 5. camel; 6. oxen; 7. boar; 8. eagle; 9. goat; 10. lion* **114.** *grass, grass* **115.** *True*

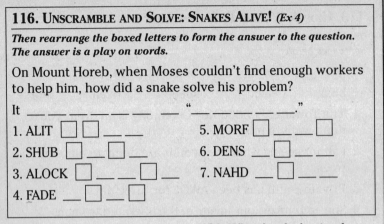

116. Unscramble and Solve: Snakes Alive! *(Ex 4)*

Then rearrange the boxed letters to form the answer to the question. The answer is a play on words.

On Mount Horeb, when Moses couldn't find enough workers to help him, how did a snake solve his problem?

It __ __ __ __ __ __ __ __ "__ __ __ __ __ __."

1. ALIT ☐ ☐ __ __

2. SHUB ☐ __ ☐ __

3. ALOCK ☐ __ __ ☐ __

4. FADE __ ☐ __ ☐

5. MORF ☐ __ __ ☐

6. DENS __ ☐ __ __

7. NAHD __ ☐ __ __

---

117. True or False: Eve ate the fruit from the tree of life in the Garden of Eden.

118. Before Jael killed Sisera, she gave him: (a) fish; (b) wine; (c) milk; (d) deer meat.

119. Fill in the blank: "The glory of _____ shall come to you, the cypress, the plane, and the pine, to beautify the place of my sanctuary" (Isa 60:13).

120. What is the animal that the King James Version of the Bible calls a "unicorn"? (a) gazelle; (b) oryx; (c) elk; (d) jackalope.

121. What kind of animals mauled the boys who taunted Elisha?

122. Fill in the blank: Paul said, "To keep me from being too elated, a _____ was given me in the flesh, a messenger of Satan to torment me, to keep me from being too elated" (2 Cor 12:7).

123. True or False: God created fish and birds on the same day.

124. When the Jews were exiled in Babylon, they hung their harps on what kind of tree?

Answers for this page: **116.**...*became a "staff."* *1. tail; 2. bush; 3. cloak; 4. deaf; 5. form; 6. send; 7. hand* **117.** *False (the tree of the knowledge of good and evil)* **118.** *(c) milk* **119.** *Lebanon* **120.** *(b) oryx* **121.** *bears* **122.** *thorn* **123.** *True* **124.** *willow*

125. Fill in the blank: "The wicked flee when no one pursues, but the righteous are as bold as a _____" (Prov 28:1).

126. What plant did Jotham use to describe the Lords of Shechem: (a) trees; (b) vines; (c) brambles; (d) weeds.

127. What kind of leaves did Adam and Eve use to make aprons for themselves?

128. Fill in the blanks: Jesus said, "See, I am sending you out like sheep in the midst of wolves; so be wise as _____ and innocent as _____" (Matt 10:16).

129. True or False: People did not eat meat until after the Flood.

130. The story of Ruth and Boaz takes place during the harvest of this grain: (a) barley; (b) corn; (c) wheat; (d) rice.

131. Fill in the blank: "Anyone who tends a _____ tree will eat its fruit" (Prov 27:18).

132. What is one of the most destructive weeds in Palestine, which Jesus used in his parable to describe nonbelievers in the church?

133. God provided Abraham with this animal caught in a thicket to replace Isaac as an offering: (a) lamb; (b) deer; (c) dove; (d) ram.

134. In reference to the Messiah, what did Isaiah say would grow out of the roots of Jesse?

---

135. MATCHING

Match the creature with its human characteristics.

1. Dove	A. Courage
2. Lion	B. Swiftness
3. Eagle	C. Gentleness
4. Deer	D. Fleetness of foot

Answers for this page: **125.** *lion* **126.** *(a) trees* **127.** *fig* **128.** *serpents, doves* **129.** *True* **130.** *(a) barley* **131.** *fig* **132.** *tare* **133.** *(d) ram* **134.** *branch* **135.** *1C; 2A; 3B; 4D*

136. True or False: To explain the coming of the Babylonians, Jeremiah told the Israelites that God was letting loose snakes and adders to bite them.

137. Fill in the blank: Jesus said to Peter, "Truly I tell you, this very night, before the _____ crows, you will deny me three times" (Matt 26:34).

138. True or False: The Bible says Abel's offering of his crops was pleasing to God.

139. Fill in the blank: Isaiah told the Israelites, "All we like _____ have gone astray; we have all turned to our own way" (Isa 53:6).

140. Jacob did not use the rods of this tree to breed his flocks: (a) plane; (b) almond; (c) cherry; (d) poplar.

141. The writer of Proverbs advises the lazy to consider which insect?

142. True or False: Jesus said the smallest seed is the mustard seed.

143. What kind of stew did Jacob give Esau for his birthright? (a) potato; (b) lentil; (c) bean; (d) corn.

144. What kind of animal did Jesus call Herod?

145. True or False: Leah gave Rachel mandrake so she could lie with Jacob.

---

146. MATCHING

Match the tree or plant with its product.

1. Grape   A. Ornament on a high priest's vestment

2. Frankincense   B. Fig-like fruit

3. Myrtle   C. Perfume as a medicine

4. Sycamore   D. Booths for the Feast of Tabernacles

5. Pomegranate   E. Wine

Answers for this page: **136.** *True* **137.** *cock* **138.** *False (Abel offered the firstlings of his flock)* **139.** *sheep* **140.** *(c) cherry* **141.** *the ant* **142.** *True* **143.** *(b) lentil* **144.** *fox* **145.** *True* **146.** *1E; 2C; 3D; 4B; 5A*

147. CRYPTOGRAM: FOXES AND BIRDS

YAS IQLHL LYZS JX KZC, "OXBQL KYFQ KXEQL, YAS WZNSL XO JKQ YZN KYFQ AQLJL; WHJ JKQ LXA XO CYA KYL AXDKQNQ JX EYP KZL KQYS."

148. What animals ate the corpse of queen Jezebel? (a) dogs; (b) wolves; (c) worms; (d) vultures.

149. Fill in the blanks: "I am the true _____, and my Father is the _____" (John 15:1).

150. How many days was Jonah inside the great fish?

151. True or False: The Bible says Adam was the first to eat the forbidden fruit.

152. Fill in the blanks: "Do not be afraid of them, and do not be afraid of their words, though briers and _____ surround you and you live among _____" (Ezek 2:6).

153. Joel's prophecy did not mention the withering of this tree, symbolizing the doom of God's people: (a) pomegranate; (b) palm; (c) apple; (d) peach.

154. True or False: To describe the coming evil, the Prophet Amos said it was as though someone fled from a lion and met a bear.

155. What kind of herbs are the Hebrews supposed to eat with the Passover meal?

156. The Bible refers to this animal 40 times: (a) cat; (b) dog; (c) zebra; (d) dove.

157. Fill in the blanks: "You will know them by their fruits. Are grapes gathered from _____, or figs from _____?" (Matt 7:16).

158. True or False: After the flood, God told Noah that animals would fear humankind.

159. What food did Jacob's sons not take with them when they brought Benjamin to Egypt? (a) gum; (b) cashews; (c) pistachio nuts; (d) almonds.

Answers for this page: **147.** *"And Jesus said to him, 'Foxes have holes, and birds of the air have nests; but the Son of Man has nowhere to lay his head'"* *(Matt 8:20).* **148.** *(a) dogs* **149.** *vine, vinegrower* **150.** *three* **151.** *False (Eve)* **152.** *thorns, scorpions* **153.** *(d) peach* **154.** *True* **155.** *bitter* **156.** *(b) dog* **157.** *thorns, thistles* **158.** *True* **159.** *(b) cashews*

160. MATCHING

Match the plant with one of its functions.

1. Reed	A. Perfume
2. Leeks	B. Measuring device
3. Spikenard	C. Purifying dead bodies
4. Aloe	D. Medicine

161. Jesus said it was easier for what animal to go through the eye of a needle than for a rich man to enter heaven?

162. Fill in the blank: Absalom's "head caught fast in the _____, and he was left hanging between heaven and earth" (2 Sam 18:9).

163. True or False: Cats are frequently mentioned in the Old Testament.

164. The serpent said the fruit from what tree will make a person wise?

165. What did David compare himself to when King Saul pursued him? (a) dead dog; (b) single flea; (c) both a and b; (d) neither a nor b.

166. True or False: Jesus was arrested at the Mount of Olives.

167. What kind of animal did Samson tie tail to tail and then put a torch between each set of tails?

168. The psalmist said this creature dissolves into slime: (a) worm; (b) snail; (c) slug; (d) caterpillar.

169. Fill in the blanks: "From the _____ tree learn its lesson: as soon as its _____ becomes tender and puts forth its leaves, you know that summer is near" (Matt 24:32).

170. True or False: King Solomon imported peacocks to decorate his palace.

171. What did Jesus note that the Pharisees tithed? (a) mint; (b) cummin; (c) dill; (d) all three.

Answers for this page: **160.** *1B; 2D; 3A; 4C* **161.** *camel* **162.** *oak* **163.** *False* **164.** *the tree of the knowledge of good and evil* **165.** *(c) both* **166.** *True* **167.** *foxes* **168.** *(b) snail* **169.** *fig, branch* **170.** *True* **171.** *(d) all three*

172. Fill in the blanks: Moses sang to the Lord, "I will sing to the Lord, for he has triumphed gloriously; _____ and _____ he has thrown into the sea" (Ex 15:1).

173. True or False: Joseph refused to give any grain to his brothers because they had sold him into slavery.

174. The writer of Hebrews 11 said that because of their faith, some people shut the mouths of what kind of animal?

175. Solomon imported this kind of tree from Lebanon: (a) mahogany; (b) oak; (c) cedar; (d) cypress.

176. Fill in the blanks: Jesus said, "Look at the _____ of the _____; they neither sow nor reap nor gather into barns, and yet your heavenly Father feeds them" (Matt 6:26).

177. True or False: Spices were not used in anointing the tabernacle.

178. What looked like coriander seeds to the Israelites in the wilderness?

179. Women weaved 11 curtains for the tabernacle from the skin of this animal: (a) ram; (b) deer; (c) lion; (d) goat.

180. Jesus said not to give what is holy to which animal?

---

181. QUOTATION PUZZLE: MESSENGER SERVICE

E	W	T	T	E	M	S	A	I	E	D	O	O	O	B	E	I	D	G	F	O	F	H	O
M	H	F	H	O	R	E	H	C	M	N	T	F	U	S	S	E	T	H	D		T	R	D
T		A	N	E	H	F		H	E		T	S		T	T	E		I	R		D	N	V
		E	R					S	A					U	H			E	E		U	O	E

Answers for this page: **172.** *horse, rider* **173.** *False* **174.** *lion* **175.** *(c) cedar* **176.** *birds, air* **177.** *False* **178.** *manna* **179.** *(d) goat* **180.** *dogs* **181.** *"Then he sent out the dove from him, to see if the waters had subsided from the face of the ground" (Gen 8:8).*

182. UNSCRAMBLE AND MATCH: PLANTS AND ANIMALS

Unscramble the names of the plants and animals on the left and match them with the person associated with each one.

1. CASYROEM REET (Luke 19:4) _____ BALAAM

2. NILO (Dan 6:16–24) _____ SAMSON

3. LAQUI (Num 11:31) _____ DANIEL

4. LIVEO ELFA (Gen 8:11) _____ ZACCHAEUS

5. KOCC (Mark 13:35) _____ MOSES

6. EBSE (Judg 14:8) _____ JEWISH EXILES

7. PHEES (1 Sam 17:15) _____ PETER

8. KENDOY (Num 22:28–30) _____ DAVID

9. LOWWIL REET (Psa 137:2) _____ SOLOMON

10. DARCE REETS (1 Ki 5:6) _____ NOAH

---

183. True or False: Paul advised Timothy to drink a little wine for his stomach ailments.

184. Fill in the blank: "They have venom like the venom of a _____" (Psa 58:4).

185. James compared the human tongue to a small fire that can set this ablaze: (a) house; (b) garden; (c) crops; (d) forest.

186. True or False: God told Samuel that the kings of Israel would seize the best olive orchards from the people.

187. What kind of animal did Rebekah water to indicate to Abraham's servant that she would become the wife of Isaac? (a) donkey; (b) camel; (c) horse; (d) sheep.

188. What is the healing ointment associated with Gilead?

Answers for this page: **182.** *1. sycamore tree/Zacchaeus; 2. lion/Daniel; 3. quail/Moses; 4. olive leaf/Noah; 5. cock/Peter; 6. bees/Samson; 7. sheep/David; 8. donkey/Balaam; 9. willow tree/Jewish exiles; 10. cedar trees/Solomon* **183.** *True* **184.** *serpent* **185.** *(d) forest* **186.** *True* **187.** *(b) camel* **188.** *balm of Gilead*

189. Fill in the blank: "Do not store up for yourselves treasures on earth, where _____ and rust consume and where thieves break in and steal" (Matt 6:19).

190. True or False: The Law allowed people to eat grasshoppers and locusts.

191. Jesus used what kind of seed to explain faith?

192. Mosaic law forbid yoking an ox with what animal in order to plow? (a) donkey; (b) camel; (c) horse; (d) another ox.

193. True or False: King Saul committed suicide when he consumed hemlock.

194. Fill in the blanks: The writer of Proverbs 23:32 warned against drinking too much wine because: "At the last it bites like a _____, and stings like an _____."

195. In the Song of Solomon, what flower among brambles is compared to the love among maidens? (a) rose; (b) lily; (c) poppy; (d) crocus.

196. According to Jesus, what kind of clothing do false prophets wear?

197. True or False: The almond tree blooms in winter and its fruit ripens in late summer in Israel.

---

198. MATCHING

Match the colored horse in Revelation with what its rider holds or is named.

1. Bright red   A. Bow

2. White   B. "Death"

3. Pale green   C. Sword

4. Black   D. Pair of scales

Answers for this page: **189.** *moth* **190.** *True* **191.** *mustard* **192.** *(a) donkey* **193.** *False* **194.** *serpent, adder* **195.** *(b) lily* **196.** *sheep's* **197.** *True* **198.** *1C; 2A; 3B; 4D*

199. Crisscross Puzzle: Plants and Animals

Answers on page 225.

Fit each of the following 54 words into the puzzle on this page. Words are arranged below and on the next page alphabetically according to the number of letters.

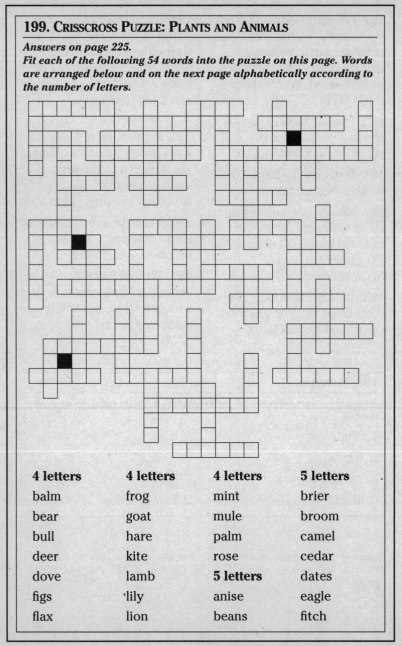

4 letters	**4 letters**	**4 letters**	**5 letters**
balm	frog	mint	brier
bear	goat	mule	broom
bull	hare	palm	camel
deer	kite	rose	cedar
dove	lamb	**5 letters**	dates
figs	lily	anise	eagle
flax	lion	beans	fitch

---

199. CRISSCROSS PUZZLE: PLANTS AND ANIMALS *continued*

5 letters	6 letters	6 letters	8 letters
gourd	almond	myrtle	mulberry
horse	barley	**7 letters**	wormwood
olive	cassia	bramble	**9 letters**
plant	gopher	leopard	spikenard
quail	grapes	mustard	**11 letters**
sheep	hyssop	**8 letters**	grasshopper
vines	locust	cucumber	pomegranate
wheat	mallow	mandrake	

---

200. Fill in the blank: "Worthy is the _____ that was slaughtered to receive power and wealth and wisdom and might and honor and glory and blessing" (Rev 5:12).

201. What reedlike plant grows in Egypt and is used to make the earliest known paper?

202. The Prophet Habakkuk said God made his feet like what animal treading upon high places? (a) horse; (b) goat; (c) deer; (d) sheep.

203. True or False: The Levitical priests were not allowed to use spices for burning incense within the tabernacle.

204. In Bible times, what were oxen not used for? (a) agricultural work; (b) food; (c) religious ceremonies; (d) royal parades.

205. Fill in the blank: The Prophet Amos declared, "You have turned justice into poison and the fruit of righteousness into _____" (Amos 6:12).

206. True or False: On the third day God created vegetation.

207. Fill in the blank: John the Baptist proclaimed, "Here is the _____ of God who takes away the sin of the world!" (John 1:29).

Answers for this page: **200.** *Lamb* **201.** *papyrus (or bulrush)* **202.** *(c) deer* **203.** *False* **204.** *(d) royal parades* **205.** *wormwood* **206.** *True* **207.** *Lamb*

208. Abraham pitched his tent and built an altar by what kind of trees in Mamre?

209. What kind of animal was in Pharaoh's dream, which he told to Joseph? (a) lion; (b) tiger; (c) cow; (d) donkey.

210. True or False: Jesus' first recorded miracle in the Gospel of John is turning stones into grapes at the wedding in Cana.

211. The Ethiopian eunuch was reading a passage from Isaiah about an animal led to the slaughter. What is this animal?

212. Fill in the blanks: The writer of Ecclesiastes declared, "For everything there is a season . . . a time to _____, and a time to pluck up what is _____" (Eccl 3:1–2).

213. True or False: An asp killed James, the brother of Jesus, on the island of Cyprus.

214. What was the first bird Noah sent from the ark?

215. In Psalm 19, David declared that the law and the fear of the Lord are sweeter than what? (a) honey; (b) sugar; (c) wine; (d) none of the three.

216. Fill in the blank: Jesus said, "Are not two _____ sold for a penny? Yet not one of them will fall to the ground apart from your Father" (Matt 10:29).

217. True or False: The Jews use the fruit from the citron tree in their Feast of Tabernacles.

218. What is the first plant to be specifically named in the Bible?

219. Fill in the blanks: "Purge me with _____, and I shall be clean; wash me, and I shall be whiter than _____" (Psa 51:7).

220. Samson used the jawbone of what animal to slay a thousand Philistines? (a) bear; (b) donkey; (c) lion; (d) horse.

Answers for this page: **208.** *oak* **209.** *(c) cow* **210.** *False (turning water into wine at the wedding in Cana)* **211.** *sheep* **212.** *plant, planted* **213.** *False (James was martyred)* **214.** *raven* **215.** *(a) honey* **216.** *sparrows* **217.** *True* **218.** *fig* **219.** *hyssop, snow* **220.** *(b) donkey*

221. MATCHING

Match the bird to its type as described in the Bible.

1. Eagle   A. Migratory

2. Quail   B. Decorative

3. Swallow   C. Predatory

4. Peacock   D. Food

222. The law of Moses forbid the Hebrews from planting what as a sacred pole beside the altar?

223. True or False: Frogs symbolized only good.

224. Where was King Manasseh of Judah buried? (a) in the field of Shiloh; (b) in the Jordan River; (c) in the garden of his house; (d) he wasn't buried.

225. Fill in the blank: A Gentile woman said to Jesus, "Sir, even the _____ under the table eat the children's crumbs" (Mark 7:28).

226. True or False: On Mount Sinai, God wrote the Ten Commandments on a bay tree for Moses.

227. What did King Mesha of Moab breed and give as a tribute to King Ahab? (a) donkeys; (b) horses; (c) sheep; (d) none of the three.

228. Fill in the blank: "The wilderness and the dry land shall be glad, the desert shall rejoice and _____; like the crocus" (Isa 35:1).

229. What killed the bush that protected Jonah from the sun outside of Nineveh?

230. True or False: The Benjaminites hid in the vineyards in order to abduct the women of Shiloh so they could rebuild their tribe.

231. What did Absalom's servants set on fire that belonged to Joab?

Answers for this page: **221.** *1C; 2D; 3A; 4B* **222.** *tree* **223.** *False* **224.** *(c) in the garden of his house* **225.** *dogs* **226.** *False (tablets of stone)* **227.** *(c) sheep* **228.** *blossom* **229.** *worm* **230.** *True* **231.** *barley*

232. Fill in the blank: Jesus said about Jerusalem: "How often have I desired to gather your children together as a _____ gathers her brood under her wings" (Luke 13:34).

233. What kind of wood was the Ark of the Covenant made out of? (a) oak; (b) cedar; (c) chestnut; (d) acacia.

234. When Samuel went to Bethlehem to choose a new king to displace Saul, what kind of animal was David tending to?

235. Fill in the blank: "Look at Behemoth, which I made just as I made you; it eats _____ like an ox" (Job 40:15).

236. In John's vision three foul spirits like frogs did not come out of whose mouth? (a) dragon; (b) Babylonian whore; (c) beast; (d) false prophet.

237. True or False: Adam blamed both God and Eve for his eating the forbidden fruit.

238. Fill in the blanks: Jesus said about the final judgment: "All the nations will be gathered before him, and he will separate people one from another as a shepherd separates the _____ from the _____" (Matt 25:32).

239. True or False: In Jesus' day people mixed myrrh with wine to work as a painkiller.

240. Daniel had a vision of four beasts coming up out of the sea. Which of the following beasts did not look like the ones he saw? (a) serpent; (b) lion; (c) bear; (d) leopard.

241. Fill in the blank: God told his people, "If you besiege a town for a long time, making war against it in order to take it, you must not destroy its _____ by wielding an ax against them" (Deut 20:19).

242. What animal was Rachel sitting on in order to hide and steal the household gods that belonged to Laban, her father?

Answers for this page: **232.** *hen* **233.** *(d) acacia* **234.** *sheep* **235.** *grass* **236.** *(b) Babylonian whore* **237.** *True* **238.** *sheep, goats* **239.** *True* **240.** *(a) serpent* **241.** *trees* **242.** *camel*

243. True or False: The Bible says the Nephilim were famous for producing new kinds of crops.

244. What animal was not in Peter's dream before he went to Cornelius's home? (a) four-footed creatures; (b) birds; (c) reptiles; (d) fish.

245. What kind of fruit did the chief cupbearer dream about and ask Joseph about?

246. Fill in the blank: "Do not weep. See, the _____ of the tribe of Judah, the Root of David, has conquered, so that he can open the scroll and its seven seals" (Rev 5:5).

247. True or False: The Prophet Isaiah described the Jewish nation as the "vineyard of God."

248. King Hezekiah did not indicate that he made a sound like this bird during his illness: (a) dove; (b) swallow; (c) crow; (d) crane.

249. Whose staff blossomed and bore ripe almonds after a devastating plague came upon the rebellious Israelites in the wilderness?

250. True or False: A "shofar" is made out of the horn of a ram.

Answers for this page: **243.** *False* **244.** *(d) fish* **245.** *grapes* **246.** *Lion*
247. *True* **248.** *(c) crow* **249.** *Aaron* **250.** *True*

94. WORD SEARCH: BIBLE PLANTS, FRUIT, AND HERBS *Puzzle on page 206.*

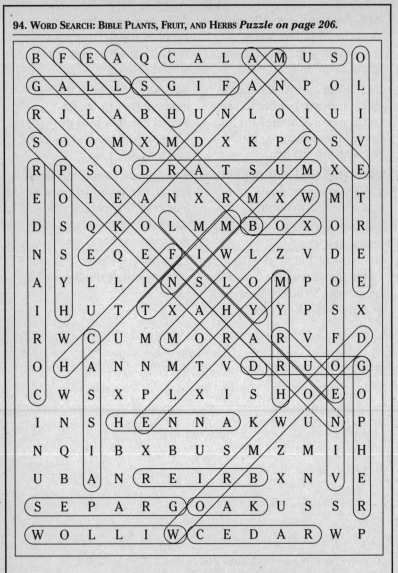

```
B  F  E  A  Q  C  A  L  A  M  U  S  O
G  A  L  L  S  G  I  F  A  N  P  O  L
R  J  L  A  B  H  U  N  L  O  I  U  I
S  O  O  M  X  M  D  X  K  P  C  S  V
R  P  S  O  D  R  A  T  S  U  M  X  E
E  O  I  E  A  N  X  R  M  X  W  M  T
D  S  Q  K  O  L  M  M  B  O  X  O  R
N  S  E  Q  E  F  I  W  L  Z  V  D  E
A  Y  L  L  I  N  S  L  O  M  P  O  E
I  H  U  T  T  X  A  H  Y  Y  P  S  X
R  W  C  U  M  M  O  R  A  R  V  F  D
O  H  A  N  N  M  T  V  D  R  U  O  G
C  W  S  X  P  L  X  I  S  H  O  E  O
I  N  S  H  E  N  N  A  K  W  U  N  P
N  Q  I  B  X  B  U  S  M  Z  M  I  H
U  B  A  N  R  E  I  R  B  X  N  V  E
S  E  P  A  R  G  O  A  K  U  S  S  R
W  O  L  L  I  W  C  E  D  A  R  W  P
```

199. CRISSCROSS PUZZLE: PLANTS AND ANIMALS *Puzzle on page 218.*

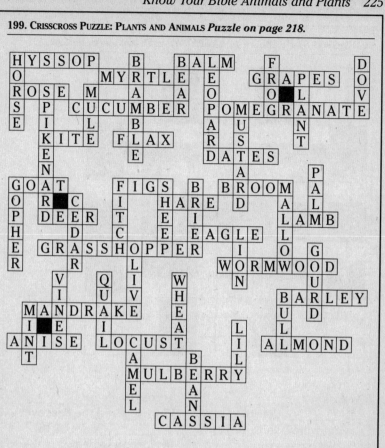

CROSSWORD PUZZLE #7: EVERYDAY LIFE *Answers on page 281.*

Across

1. "I _____ that they may have life" (John 10:10).
5. "We have seen _____ glory" (John 1:14).
8. Body of water (Luke 5:1)
12. Descendant of Ishmael (Neh 2:19)
13. Altar (Latin)
14. Fragrant African plant (Psa 45:8)
15. Second letter of Greek alphabet
16. Dashed (Luke 15:20)

Across *continued*

17. "Prepared the Passover _____" (Mark 14:16).
18. Joseph wore a _____ _____. (Gen 37:3) (2 wds)
20. "They kept heaping many other _____ on [Jesus]" (Luke 22:65).
23. Ornate priestly vestment (Ex 25:7)
24. Objects of worship (Acts 17:16)
27. Cause of a flood (Gen 7:12)

CROSSWORD PUZZLE #7: EVERYDAY LIFE *continued*

Across *continued*

28. Peter's protective garment (Acts 12:8)
29. Oven for pottery or bricks (Ex 9:8)
30. Armor (1 Ki 22:34)
34. Hebrew month
36. Latin prefix for "three"
37. Toward (Matt 2:8)
39. Jesus turned water to _____. (John 2:9)
41. Poetic evening
42. The kingdom of God has come _____. (Mark 1:15)
44. Father of Gaal (Judg 9:26)
45. A rule (abbr) (Lev 5:10)
46. "The Lord is the _____ God" (Jer 10:10).

Down

1. Ancient Hebrew measure
2. "Why _____ you angry?" (Gen 4:6).
3. Used for sleeping (Mark 6:55)
4. Mountain in the Promised Land (Josh 8:30)
5. Gather crops (Ruth 2:21)
6. "Dies _____" (medieval Latin hymn)

Down *continued*

7. Footwear (John 1:27)
8. Sacrificial animal (Gen 22:7)
9. Leeward side
10. Enemy of the Hebrews (Ezek 23:23)
11. Snakelike fish
19. Built the tabernacle (Ex 31:6)
20. Father of Zechariah (Ezra 5:1)
21. "_____ to the Lord a new song" (Psa 98:1).
22. Nationality of Ruth (Ruth 1:4)
25. Wall covering (Dan 5:5)
26. Living in temporary shelter (Num 24:2)
31. Plant that hid Moses (Ex 2:3)
32. Olive or fig (Judg 9:9, 11)
33. Portable shelter (Gen 9:21)
34. Wonder (Mark 4:41)
35. Baby's napkin
37. 19th Greek letter
38. Metal-bearing rock (Job 28:2)
40. Northeast (abbr)
43. Son of Judah (Gen 38:3)

How Did You Do?

You probably feel as though you have just taken a long stroll through a large zoo. The Bible is filled with a wide variety of animal and plant life, and now you are acquainted with many of them.

The total number of points possible for this chart includes the questions in chapter 7 and Crossword Puzzle #7:

410 to 456: You are truly a Bible scholar!
342 to 409: You have an excellent grasp of Bible facts.
273 to 341: You have some knowledge of the Bible.
228 to 272: You could brush up on the Bible.
0 to 227: You may want to start studying the Bible.

Perhaps even of more interest to you are the cultures of the ancient peoples mentioned in the Bible. The next chapter focuses on many of their customs—some that will astonish you.

CHAPTER EIGHT
Life During Bible Times

1. What ten special laws did God give Moses on Mount Sinai?

2. True or False: Paul said that a woman disgraces her head if she prophesies with her head veiled.

3. Which type of food was considered "unclean" for the Israelites? (a) oxen; (b) pork; (c) beef; (d) lamb.

4. Fill in the blank: The Mosaic laws command "you shall love your _____ as yourself" (Lev 19:18).

5. True or False: The Israelites did not have to continue celebrating Passover after Jesus' death.

6. How many miles could a Roman soldier demand that a civilian carry his pack? (a) 1; (b) 2; (c) 3; (d) any number.

7. What is the day set aside for rest called?

8. True or False: Before the tower of Babel, there were two common languages among all humankind.

---

9. MATCHING

Match the person with the sign of mourning for which he is noted.

1. Jacob	A. Wept
2. Job	B. Put sackcloth on
3. Jesus	C. Shaved head; tore robe
4. David	D. Fasted; lay on the ground

Answers for this page: **1.** *Ten Commandments* **2.** *False (she should be veiled)* **3.** *(b) pork* **4.** *neighbor* **5.** *False* **6.** *(a) 1* **7.** *sabbath* **8.** *False (one)* **9.** *1B; 2C; 3A; 4D*

10. QUOTATION PUZZLE: A DAILY DEMAND

To find the verse, put the letters that appear in the bottom half of the puzzle into the column of boxes above them. The letters may not be listed in the exact order in which they appear in the quote. Mark off used letters at the bottom. A letter may be used only once. The black boxes represent the space between words.

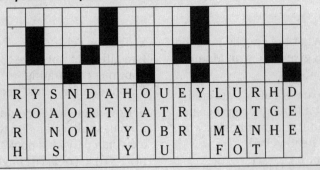

11. Fill in the blank: Paul taught that husbands and wives were to "be _____ to one another out of reverence for Christ" (Eph 5:21).

12. The sacred lots Jewish high priests used to determine God's will were called: (a) oracles; (b) phylacteries; (c) urim and thummim; (d) star charts.

13. What percentage of the crops of the land had to be tithed to the Lord?

14. Fill in the blank: God told his people not to worship idols, "for I the Lord your God am a _____ God" (Ex 20:5).

15. True or False: A woman's testimony had weight in ancient courts of law.

16. A kinsman-redeemer in Hebrew society was expected to be this: (a) nearest male relative; (b) a close friend; (c) a distant relative; (d) nearest female relative.

Answers for this page: **10.** *"Honor your father and your mother, so that your days may be long" (Ex 20:12).* **11.** *subject* **12.** *(c) urim and thummim* **13.** *one tenth* **14.** *jealous* **15.** *False* **16.** *(a) nearest male relative*

17. Any person who was executed and then was hung on a tree was under whose curse?

18. Fill in the blanks: In reference to the government, the Bible commands, "_____ your leaders and _____ to them" (Heb 13:17).

19. True or False: Although other nations had temple prostitutes, Israel was forbidden to do so.

20. Which year was the prescribed "fallow" year for land according to the law of Moses? (a) first; (b) fifth; (c) sixth; (d) seventh.

21. According to Paul, what is the minimum number of witnesses necessary to bring a charge against someone in the church?

22. Fill in the blanks: "If your _____ are hungry, give them bread to eat; and if they are thirsty, give them water to drink; . . . and the _____ will reward you" (Prov 25:21–22).

23. True or False: When Jacob confronted Laban about his deceit, Laban claimed that a family custom was to marry off the oldest daughter first.

24. What was an ephod? (a) king's robe; (b) priest's linen garment; (c) priest's hat; (d) Roman garment.

25. When a Jewish king was anointed with oil, on what part of his body was the oil placed?

26. True or False: Women usually drew water during the evening because it was the coolest time of the day.

27. Fill in the blank: "The Lord commanded that those who proclaim the _____ should get their living by the gospel" (1 Cor 9:14).

28. According to the law of Moses, what penalty did David and Bathsheba merit for their adultery?

29. The Jews looked down on this group of people: (a) Pharisees; (b) Sadducees; (c) Samaritans; (d) scribes.

Answers for this page: **17.** *God's* **18.** *obey, submit* **19.** *True* **20.** *(d) seventh* **21.** *two* **22.** *enemies, Lord* **23.** *True* **24.** *(b) priest's linen garment* **25.** *head* **26.** *True* **27.** *gospel* **28.** *death* **29.** *(c) Samaritans*

30. MATCHING

Match the commandment with the person who broke it.

1. "You shall not commit adultery" (Ex 20:14)   A. Aaron

2. "You shall not steal" (Ex 20:15)   B. Cain

3. "You shall not murder" (Ex 20:13)   C. Ananias

4. "You shall not make . . . an idol" (Ex 20:4)   D. Rachel

5. "You shall not lie" (Lev 19:11)   E. Bathsheba

31. Fill in the blank: The Lord said to Moses, "You shall hallow the _____ year and you shall proclaim liberty throughout the land to all its inhabitants" (Lev 25:10).

32. True or False: The oldest son was entitled to a double portion of the inheritance.

33. A man in the Israelite military was released from his duties for how long once he became a newlywed? (a) 6 months; (b) 1 year; (c) 2 years; (d) 3 years.

34. Fill in the blank: After Paul learned that he had insulted the high priest, he quoted Scripture, saying, "You shall not speak evil of a _____ of your people" (Acts 23:5).

35. What is the feast of unleavened bread known as?

36. True or False: The stigma of barrenness was not as important to a woman as that associated with being unmarried.

37. Fill in the blank: "This was the custom in former times in Israel concerning redeeming and exchanging: to confirm a transaction, the one took off a _____ and gave it to the other" (Ruth 4:7).

38. The Israelites had a number of laws concerning the fair treatment of these people: (a) widows; (b) aliens; (c) orphans; (d) all of the above.

Answers for this page: **30.** *1E; 2D; 3B; 4A; 5C* **31.** *fiftieth* **32.** *True* **33.** *(b) 1 year* **34.** *leader* **35.** *Passover* **36.** *False* **37.** *sandal* **38.** *(d) all of the above*

39. True or False: In the ancient Israelite culture, an engagement was considered just as binding as being married.

40. What type of dwelling did nomadic patriarchs like Abraham prefer?

41. What was a cupbearer's main responsibility? (a) to pour the king's wine; (b) to clean the king's cup; (c) to taste the king's wine; (d) to buy the king's cup.

42. Fill in the blanks: Jesus said to Simon, "Do you see this woman? I entered your house; you gave me no water for my _____, but she has bathed my _____ with her tears and dried them with her hair" (Luke 7:44).

43. True or False: A Hebrew woman who just delivered a baby would be considered ceremonially unclean for seven days.

44. The person who fled to the city of refuge had to remain there until the death of this person: (a) king; (b) avenger of blood; (c) father of victim; (d) high priest.

45. What was the sacred box Israel carried into battle?

46. Fill in the blank: "Do not boast about _____, for you do not know what a day may bring" (Prov 27:1).

47. This grain was the universal symbol of poverty in the Near East: (a) rice; (b) corn; (c) wheat; (d) barley.

48. CRYPTOGRAM: A TIME FOR EVERYTHING

Decode the letters in the words of this Bible verse. Each letter corresponds to a different letter in the alphabet.

PCS AYASEDWNXT DWASA NL M LAMLCX, MXF M DNRA
PCS AYASE RMDDAS OXFAS WAMYAX: M DNRA DC VA
VCSX, MXF M DNRA DC FNA; M DNRA DC QKMXD, MXF
M DNRA DC QKOJG OQ IWMD NL QKMXDAF.

Answers for this page: **39.** True **40.** tents **41.** (c) to taste the king's wine **42.** feet, feet **43.** True **44.** (d) high priest **45.** the Ark of the Covenant **46.** tomorrow **47.** (d) barley **48.** "For everything there is a season, and a time for every matter under heaven: a time to be born, and a time to die; a time to plant, and a time to pluck up what is planted" (Eccl 3:1–2).

49. MATCHING

The birthright went to the first son. Match the father with his eldest son.

1. Abraham   A. Esau

2. Isaac   B. Amnon

3. Jacob   C. Ishmael

4. Joseph   D. Reuben

5. David   E. Manasseh

50. True or False: Paul said that a man disgraces his head if he prays with something on his head.

51. During the Israelites' wandering in the wilderness, what was the penalty for breaking the sabbath?

52. This misdeed merited crucifixion: (a) political insurrection; (b) slander; (c) adultery; (d) rape.

53. Fill in the blank: Paul stood in front of the Areopagus and said, "Athenians, I see how extremely _____ you are in every way" (Acts 17:22).

54. Which day of the week are burials forbidden in Jewish society?

55. True or False: God forbid the Israelites from eating eagles.

56. Fill in the blank: Moses said, "When a man makes a vow to the _____ . . . he shall not break his word" (Num 30:2).

57. What Jewish sect in Jesus' day did not believe in the resurrection or angels?

58. For Abraham and Jacob, asking someone to put his hand under the asker's thigh meant this: (a) I trust you; (b) peace to you; (c) we are friends; (d) swear an oath.

59. According to Proverbs, a good wife is worthy of wearing clothing dyed in what color?

Answers for this page: **49.** *1C; 2A; 3D; 4E; 5B* **50.** *True* **51.** *death* **52.** *(a) political insurrection* **53.** *religious* **54.** *sabbath* **55.** *True* **56.** *Lord* **57.** *Sadducees* **58.** *(d) swear an oath* **59.** *purple*

60. True or False: A harem was a symbol of a king's status and power in the ancient Near East.

61. Fill in the blanks: Jesus said, "Woe to you, scribes and Pharisees, hypocrites! For you tithe mint, dill, and cummin, and have neglected the weightier matters of the law: _____ and _____ and _____" (Matt 23:23).

62. What does the word *manna* mean? (a) bread; (b) What is it?; (c) precious food; (d) from God.

63. Besides pomegranates, what was placed on the hem of the priest's garment?

64. Fill in the blanks: God indicated how long is the sabbath: "From _____ to _____ you shall keep your sabbath" (Lev 23:32).

65. How did Solomon make an alliance with Pharaoh? (a) gave him gold; (b) gave Pharaoh his daughter; (c) married Pharaoh's daughter; (d) gave him slaves.

66. What shall become one flesh with a man?

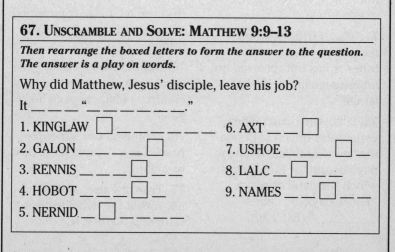

67. UNSCRAMBLE AND SOLVE: MATTHEW 9:9–13

Then rearrange the boxed letters to form the answer to the question. The answer is a play on words.

Why did Matthew, Jesus' disciple, leave his job?

It __ __ __ "__ __ __ __ __ __ __."

1. KINGLAW ☐ __ __ __ __ __ __

2. GALON __ __ __ __ ☐

3. RENNIS __ __ __ ☐ __ __

4. HOBOT __ __ __ ☐ __

5. NERNID __ ☐ __ __ __ __

6. AXT __ __ ☐

7. USHOE __ __ __ ☐ __

8. LALC __ ☐ __ __

9. NAMES __ __ ☐ __ __

Answers for this page: **60.** *True* **61.** *justice, mercy, faith* **62.** *(b) What is it?* **63.** *bells* **64.** *evening, evening* **65.** *(c) married Pharaoh's daughter* **66.** *his wife* **67.** . . . *was "taxing." 1. walking; 2. along; 3. sinner; 4. booth; 5. dinner; 6. tax; 7. house; 8. call; 9. means*

68. MATCHING

Forty is a significant number in the Bible. Match the person with the 40 something.

1. Noah   A. Wandered in the wilderness for 40 years

2. Moses   B. Was tempted in the wilderness for 40 days

3. Joshua   C. Became a spy at 40

4. David   D. Watched it rain for 40 days

5. Jesus   E. Reigned over Judah for 40 years

---

69. Fill in the blank: Jesus said, "Truly I tell you, no prophet is accepted in the prophet's _____" (Luke 4:24).

70. True or False: The Romans never took a census of non-Romans.

71. Which tribe of Israel received a tithe from the other tribes but received no inheritance in the land of Israel?

72. Fill in the blank: When Esther was queen of Persia, the Jews established a two-day custom for themselves, which they still observe. "These days are called _____" (Est 9:26).

73. True or False: After the Assyrians conquered a nation, they would scatter its people throughout foreign lands.

74. The way Paul became a Roman citizen: (a) bought it; (b) born a citizen; (c) married a Roman; (d) saved a Roman prince.

75. Besides silver, out of what precious metal were the children of Israel not to make gods?

76. In biblical times, people prayed at any time of the day or night.

77. True or False: Moses did not forbid the Israelites from tattooing themselves.

Answers for this page: **68.** *1D; 2A; 3C; 4E; 5B* **69.** *hometown* **70.** *False* **71.** *Levi* **72.** *Purim* **73.** *True* **74.** *(b) born a citizen* **75.** *gold* **76.** *True* **77.** *False*

78. Fill in the blank: "They took the body of Jesus and wrapped it with the spices in linen cloths, according to the _____ custom of the Jews" (John 19:40).

79. The Sanhedrin consisted of the high priest and how many members? (a) 20; (b) 40; (c) 50; (d) 70.

80. What Greek goddess did the Ephesians worship and build a famous temple for?

81. Which civilization devised the crucifixion? (a) the Romans; (b) the Israelites; (c) the Greeks; (d) the Phoenicians.

82. Fill in the blank: "Whoever curses father or _____ shall be put to death" (Ex 21:17).

83. What did Esau give to Jacob for bread and lentil stew?

84. How many days does each month of the Jewish calendar have? (a) 24; (b) 28; (c) 30; (d) 32.

85. The Israelites strapped a pouch or small box to their foreheads and wrists. They were called frontlets in the Old Testament and phylacteries in the New Testament. What did they contain?

---

86. QUOTATION PUZZLE: A DAILY PRAYER

L	E	L	H	R	O	G	O	S	O	N	I
H		O	O	R			A	D	D	A	E
E		T	U	R			O	L	R	T	E
S		A	R				I	R			H

Answers for this page: **78.** *burial* **79.** *(d) 70* **80.** *Artemis* **81.** *(d) Phoenicians* **82.** *mother* **83.** *his birthright* **84.** *(b) 28* **85.** *Scriptures* **86.** *"Hear, O Israel: The Lord is our God, the Lord alone" (Deut 6:4).*

87. WORD SEARCH: A DAILY WORD *Answers on page 250.*

The passage below comes from the Shema, *a daily confession of faith for the Israelites. In the puzzle below, find the 31 words or phrases in bold. You can find words diagonally, vertically, horizontally, backward, and forward. When you find a word in the puzzle, cross it out.*

```
K  O  D  E  G  O  D  C  A  S  E  S  S
P  A  T  W  L  O  V  H  Y  L  N  E  T
X  O  Q  M  R  T  U  A  N  O  E  W  A
O  W  H  E  N  I  W  R  O  R  U  O  Y
Y  O  U  L  B  L  T  G  C  D  Y  R  M
D  U  E  B  A  R  T  E  B  I  N  D  O
C  O  M  M  A  N  D  M  E  N  T  S  N
L  D  O  E  S  U  O  H  E  A  H  U  O
I  A  H  R  P  U  T  O  L  N  E  A  R
E  E  B  H  P  E  E  K  L  C  R  U  E
D  H  O  L  A  O  I  G  L  E  E  N  T
O  E  X  C  O  N  S  A  A  S  F  O  U
W  R  H  U  G  V  D  T  H  M  O  R  E
N  O  F  I  X  H  E  E  S  N  R  U  D
W  F  S  G  O  O  D  S  A  M  E  P  L
```

You shall **LOVE** the **LORD** your **GOD**, **THEREFORE**, and **KEEP** his **CHARGE**, his **DECREES**, his **ORDINANCES**, and his **COMMANDMENTS ALWAYS**. . . . You **SHALL PUT** these **WORDS** of mine in your **HEART** and **SOUL**, and you shall **BIND** them as a **SIGN** on your **HAND**, and **FIX** them as an

87. WORD SEARCH: A DAILY WORD *Continued*

EMBLEM on your **FOREHEAD**. **TEACH** them to your children, **TALKING** about them **WHEN** you are at **HOME** and when you are away, and when you **LIE DOWN** [one answer] and when you rise. **WRITE** them on the **DOORPOSTS** of your **HOUSE** and on your **GATES**. —DEUTERONOMY 11:1, 18–20

88. True or False: According to the Mosaic dietary laws, rabbit stew could be served in a Jewish household.

89. Fill in the blank: Paul once said to a centurion, "Is it legal for you to flog a _____ citizen who is uncondemned?" (Acts 22:25).

90. True or False: The laws of Moses allowed God's people to eat the blood of some animals.

91. Fill in the blank: God told the Israelites, "When you reap the harvest of your land, you shall not reap to the very edges of your fields. . . . you shall leave them for the _____ and the alien" (Lev 19:9–10).

92. What kind of men usually guarded a king's harem?

93. What is a sepulchre? (a) a cup for royalty; (b) a couch in the temple; (c) a cave for burial; (d) none of these.

94. True or False: People in Jesus' day were not required to make sacrifices. They did them voluntarily.

95. What was used as a sweetener because there was no sugar?

96. While at Mount Sinai, Moses told the Hebrews that this act would render them ritually unclean: (a) sleep; (b) sex; (c) fighting; (d) eating.

97. Fill in the blank: "In the _____ of the year, the time when kings go out to battle" (2 Sam 11:1).

98. True or False: Like the Hebrews, the Philistine men were circumcised.

Answers for this page: **88.** *False* **89.** *Roman* **90.** *False (no blood)* **91.** *poor* **92.** *eunuchs* **93.** *(c) a cave for burial* **94.** *False* **95.** *honey* **96.** *(b) sex* **97.** *spring* **98.** *False*

99. MATCHING

Match the empire during Bible times with the letter in chronological order.

1. Persia	A. First
2. Rome	B. Second
3. Babylon	C. Third
4. Assyria	D. Fourth
5. Greece	E. Fifth

100. Fill in the blank: Paul asked Christians, "When any of you has a grievance against another, do you dare to take it to _____ before the unrighteous, instead of taking it before the saints?" (1 Cor 6:1).

101. True or False: Brotherless women could inherit land under the law of Moses.

102. The Bible says the trip from Babylon to Jerusalem was dangerous for returning exiles for this reason: (a) robbers; (b) terrain; (c) climate; (d) vipers.

103. Instead of graves, in what were people in the ancient Middle East buried after their death?

104. It was an Israelite custom for the daughters of Israel to lament the daughter of Jephthah how many days a year? (a) 1 day; (b) 3 days; (c) 4 days; (d) 7 days.

105. Fill in the blanks: Jesus taught his followers, "Whenever you _____, do not look dismal, like the hypocrites, for they disfigure their faces so as to show others that they are _____" (Matt 6:16).

106. True or False: The Zealots supported the Roman occupation of Judea.

107. Number of soldiers under a Roman centurion: (a) 25; (b) 50; (c) 100; (d) 150.

Answers for this page: **99.** *1C; 2E; 3B; 4A; 5D* **100.** *court* **101.** *True* **102.** *(a) robbers* **103.** *caves* **104.** *(c) 4 days* **105.** *fast, fasting* **106.** *False* **107.** *(c) 100*

108. HIDDEN WORDS: EVERYDAY LIFE

Find these words from everyday life in Bible times, hidden in the sentences below:

robe   veil   sandals   turban   barley

grapes   bread   olives   fishing   temple

1. Small children frequently have illnesses throughout the winter season.

2. Her voice has a timbre a drama coach would love.

3. All through school, I've studied hard.

4. After you choose an item, please stand in this line to make your payment.

5. Whether you are an automobile driver or a biker, obey the traffic signals!

6. On the menu tonight are breads, meats, and also plenty of vegetables.

7. Kevin has always acted standoffish in gatherings of more than three people.

8. Never disturb an elephant, especially when it is guarding its young.

9. As we sailed around the sandbar, Leyte, an island in the Philippines, came into view.

10. Willie enjoys performing rap, especially when the audience is appreciative.

109. True or False: Paul encouraged Gentiles to enter the inner court of the temple in Jerusalem to worship God.

110. Fill in the blank: "Observe the sabbath day and keep it _____" (Deut 5:12).

Answers for this page: **108.** *1. veil; 2. bread; 3. olives; 4. temple; 5. robe; 6. sandals; 7. fishing; 8. turban; 9. barley; 10. grapes* **109.** *False* **110.** *holy*

111. On what day of the month were the Israelites to give their monthly offerings?

112. True or False: The Bible teaches that God's people should not be wealthy.

113. What is the Jewish feast with a musical theme?

114. Male Israelites were not required to attend this festival: (a) Passover; (b) Lights; (c) Harvest or Weeks; (d) Tabernacles or Booths.

115. Fill in the blank: "Keep your lives free from the love of _____, and be content with what you have" (Heb 13:5).

116. If you took a Nazirite vow, what was not permitted? (a) drinking wine; (b) touching a dead body; (c) cutting one's hair; (d) all of the above.

117. Fill in the blank: The Book of Judges concludes, "In those days there was no _____ in Israel; all the people did what was right in their own eyes" (Judg 21:25).

118. True or False: The Ishmaelites were merchants who traveled in large caravans.

119. What is the term Jesus used to indicate how the Pharisees used their tradition to nullify God's Word, which commands the honoring of parents? (a) Bekah; (b) Omer; (c) Corban; (d) Menorah.

120. When people in the ancient Near East wanted to express their contrition publicly, they wore ashes and what?

121. Fill in the blank: Paul's teaching on marriage: "Do not be mismatched with _____" (2 Cor 6:14).

122. True or False: In days of the patriarchs, there were no silos or barns.

123. What is the term for beating grain with sticks or grinding it under big rocks to separate the seed?

124. What was the "staff of life" in the ancient Near East? (a) bread; (b) corn; (c) potatoes; (d) french fries.

Answers for this page: **111.** *first* **112.** *False* **113.** *Feast of Trumpets* **114.** *(b) Lights* **115.** *money* **116.** *(d) all of the above* **117.** *king* **118.** *True* **119.** *(c) Corban* **120.** *sackcloth* **121.** *unbelievers* **122.** *False* **123.** *threshing* **124.** *(a) bread*

125. MATCHING

Match the crime with the penalty.

1. Kidnapping someone	A. Five head of cattle
2. Beating a slave (no injury)	B. Payment for loss of time
3. Stealing an ox	C. "Eye for eye"
4. Physically injuring someone (not seriously)	D. No punishment
5. Serious injury to someone	E. Death

126. Fill in the blank: "Where there is no prophecy, the people cast off restraint, but happy are those who keep the _____" (Prov 29:18).

127. True or False: Old Testament laws do not forbid lending or even taking interest.

128. What were the Israelite women called who functioned as visiting nurses when a woman needed help delivering a baby?

129. Fill in the blank: Paul said this about church leaders: "If someone does not know how to manage his own household, how can he take care of God's _____" (1 Tim 3:5).

130. Which of the following did the Hebrews use as a liquid measure? (a) hin; (b) cubit; (c) seah; (d) mina.

131. True or False: None of the musical instruments mentioned in the Bible were made out of wood.

132. In Jesus' day what coin was considered fair pay for a day's work?

133. Fill in the blank: "A good _____ is better than precious ointment" (Eccl 7:1).

134. True or False: In Bible times, scales were used to measure money.

135. When a Hebrew boy was eight days old, his father or a rabbi did what to him?

Answers for this page: **125.** *1E; 2D; 3A; 4B; 5C* **126.** *law* **127.** *True* **128.** *midwives* **129.** *church* **130.** *(a) hin* **131.** *False (e.g., harp)* **132.** *a Roman denarius* **133.** *name* **134.** *True* **135.** *circumcised him*

136. QUOTATION PUZZLE: BABY NEEDS ONE?

W	E	A	C	A	I	A	C	E	T	T	H	I	N	L	I	R	C	T
I	H	E	Y	E	W	F	O	S	R	A	D	E	A	G	O	N	O	R
T	H	I	L		O	S	F	F	O	R	T	A	D		S	A	D	
H	F		T					C		E	D					T		

137. How long did a Hebrew wedding feast usually last? (a) 1 day; (b) 3 days; (c) 7 days; (d) 2 weeks.

138. What Greek city was like the "Las Vegas" of Paul's day?

139. True or False: Jubilee was a time when land was returned to the original Hebrew owner.

140. Fill in the blank: Jesus said, "But to what will I compare this generation? It is like children sitting in the _____ and calling to one another" (Matt 11:16).

141. True or False: The Mosaic laws forbid the eating of goat's meat.

142. In ancient Palestine, people did not commonly drink this liquid: (a) goat's milk; (b) well water; (c) orange juice; (d) wine.

143. Fill in the blanks: "A _____ shall not wear a man's apparel, nor shall a _____ put on a woman's garment" (Deut 22:5).

144. How many cities did the Israelites set aside for cities of refuge: (a) 3; (b) 5; (c) 6; (d) 7.

145. True or False: Unleavened bread is made without yeast.

146. In Bible times, when did a day begin?

Answers for this page: **136.** *"They offered a sacrifice according to what is stated in the law of the Lord" (Luke 2:24).* **137.** *(c) 7 days* **138.** *Corinth* **139.** *True* **140.** *marketplaces* **141.** *False* **142.** *(c) orange juice* **143.** *woman, man* **144.** *(c) 6* **145.** *True* **146.** *at sunrise*

147. Hebrew priests sounded these musical instruments prior to a battle: (a) trumpets; (b) drums; (c) lyres; (d) bagpipes.

148. Fill in the blank: "The farmer waits for the precious crop from the earth, being patient with it until it receives the early and the late _____" (Jas 5:7).

149. What kind of Roman coin did Jesus' enemies use to try to entrap him?

150. True or False: Hebrew priests were expected to fulfill medical duties.

151. What did the Israelites call the altars on hills? (a) temples; (b) high places; (c) tabernacles; (d) high booths.

152. According to the Mosaic law, if a bull gored someone to death, what would become of it?

153. Fill in the blank: "Happy are those whose way is blameless, who walk in the _____ of the Lord" (Psa 119:1).

154. True or False: Slaves were forbidden to take part in any of the special feast days of Israel.

155. When does the sabbath begin?

156. The word *jeremiad* was derived from Jeremiah's name because of what habitual occurrence? (a) anger over Israel's sin; (b) prophecies against Israel; (c) prolonged sorrow over Israel's sin; (d) preaching.

157. True or False: The more valuable the animal to be sacrificed, the higher the standing of the person within the ancient Hebrew community.

---

158. CRYPTOGRAM: LEFTOVERS

EUTA HMJ RODUTC DUT RCOBTK MS HMJC IWATHOCP, PM AMD RZTOA EUOD WK ZTSD; WD KUOZZ NT SMC DUT OZWTA, DUT MCBUOA, OAP DUT EWPME.

Answers for this page: **147.** *(a) trumpets* **148.** *rains* **149.** *denarius* **150.** *True* **151.** *(b) high places* **152.** *stoned to death* **153.** *law* **154.** *False* **155.** *sundown* **156.** *(c) prolonged sorrow over Israel's sin* **157.** *True* **158.** *"When you gather the grapes of your vineyard, do not glean what is left; it shall be for the alien, the orphan, and the widow" (Deut 24:21).*

159. MATCHING

Match the Jewish feast with the month it's observed.

1. Pentecost	A. October
2. Passover	B. March
3. Purim	C. June
4. Tabernacles	D. December
5. Hanukkah	E. April

160. Fill in the blanks: "Do not neglect to show hospitality to _____, for by doing that some have entertained _____ without knowing it" (Heb 13:2).

161. Jewish women could go no farther than this area in the temple in Jerusalem:
(a) Court of Women;
(b) Court of the Gentiles;
(c) Court of the Priests;
(d) Court of Israel.

162. True or False: As Esther and Daniel well knew, Persian laws could not be repealed even by the king.

163. King Josiah reinstituted the celebration of what feast, once the Book of the Law was found?

164. In Bible times poor yet respectable women were not expected to do this: (a) collect water; (b) bake bread; (c) work in the fields; (d) go to the threshing floor during harvests.

165. True or False: Levitical law did not allow Israelite priests to participate in the mourning at funeral services.

166. Fill in the blanks: "For _____ years you shall sow your land and gather in its yield; but the _____ year you shall let it rest and lie fallow, so that the poor of your people may eat" (Ex 23:10–11).

Answers for this page: **159.** *1C; 2E; 3B; 4A; 5D* **160.** *strangers, angels* **161.** *(a) Court of Women* **162.** *True* **163.** *Passover* **164.** *(d) go to the threshing floor during harvests* **165.** *True* **166.** *six, seventh*

167. UNSCRAMBLE AND MATCH: COMMON ITEMS

Unscramble the words for common items of everyday life in Bible times, then match them with the definitions.

1. DRAN _____
A. Coin representing a day's wages (Mark 12:15).

2. TOLCUS _____
B. Leather case containing Scriptures (Matt 23:5).

3. SUIREDAN _____
C. Very thin cake (Ex 16:31).

4. CHLPAYRETY_____
D. Oil used as perfume (John 12:3).

5. LOTSHACCK _____
E. A medicinal spice (Psa 45:8).

6. AWREF _____
F. Swarming insect, used as food by the poor (Deut 28:38).

7. MAR'S ROHN _____
G. Large, sleeveless outer garment (1 Ki 19:13).

8. RHYRM _____
H. Chest containing the tablets of law (Deut 10:5).

9. TANMEL _____
I. Rough material used for mourning garments (Psa 30:11).

10. KAR _____
J. Musical instrument used in temple ceremonies (Josh 6:4).

168. What is the Aramaic word for "riches," which Jesus taught not to serve?

169. Whose head was inscribed on a Roman denarius in Jesus' day?

Answers for this page: **167.** *1. nard/D; 2. locust/F; 3. denarius/A; 4. phylactery/B; 5. sackcloth/I; 6. wafer/C; 7. ram's horn/J; 8. myrrh/E; 9. mantle/G; 10. ark/H* **168.** *Mammon* **169.** *the Roman emperor*

170. CRISSCROSS PUZZLE: EVERYDAY LIFE *Answers on page 251.*

Fit each of the following 55 words into the puzzle below. Words are arranged below alphabetically according to the number of letters.

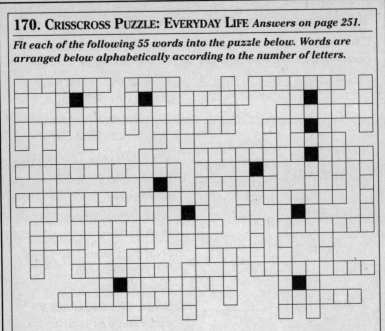

4 Letters	4 Letters	5 letters	6 letters	8 letters
Abib	omer	Torah	shekel	banquets
Adar	seed	tunic	temple	blessing
Amen	soil	visit	trades	kindness
beka	tomb	**6 letters**	**7 letters**	neighbor
calf	**5 letters**	depend	command	offering
care	deeds	equate	denarii	**9 letters**
cord	doers	girdle	nomadic	direction
land	grain	gleans	sabbath	encourage
meat	manna	hallow	waiting	**12 letters**
mill	Purim	learns	wedding	thankfulness
mina	quail	lepton	weights	
need	Shema	praise		
oath	tests	Shebat		

171. Fill in the blank: "Keep away from believers who are living in idleness.... Anyone unwilling to _____ should not eat" (2 Thes 3:6, 10).

172. This Jewish group is not mentioned in the New Testament: (a) Herodians; (b) Pharisees; (c) Sadducees; (d) Essenes.

173. True or False: The Hebrew prophets pled the cause of widows and orphans because the Israelites refused to obey the Law.

174. Fill in the blank: "You shall not bear false witness against your _____" (Ex 20:16).

175. This grain is not mentioned in the Bible: (a) rice; (b) corn; (c) wheat; (d) barley.

176. True or False: Lamps were left burning all night in many Jewish homes in Jesus' day.

177. Where do the Jewish people go to pray and read Scriptures on the sabbath?

178. Fill in the blanks: Jesus said, "So if I, your Lord and Teacher, have washed your _____, you also ought to wash one another's _____" (John 13:14).

179. In Hebrew society a man had to pay a fee to the woman's father so they could marry. What was this fee called? (a) zeresh; (b) mohar; (c) haman; (d) gomer.

180. Fill in the blank: The Mosaic laws state that a leper "shall remain _____ as long as he has the disease" (Lev 13:46).

181. What was the large tent that housed the Ark of the Covenant called?

182. True or False: Famine and drought were extremely rare in Palestine.

183. Fill in the blanks: Jesus said, "If the same person sins against you _____ times a day, and turns back to you _____ times and says, 'I repent,' you must _____" (Luke 17:4).

Answers for this page: **171.** *work* **172.** *(d) Essenes* **173.** *True* **174.** *neighbor* **175.** *(a) rice* **176.** *True* **177.** *synagogue* **178.** *feet, feet* **179.** *(b) mohar* **180.** *unclean* **181.** *tabernacle* **182.** *False* **183.** *seven, seven, forgive*

87. WORD SEARCH: A DAILY WORD *Puzzle on page 238.*

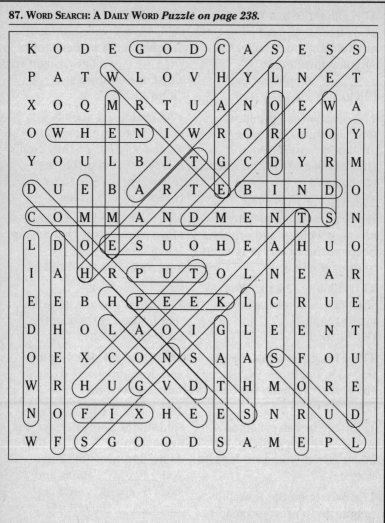

```
K  O  D  E  G  O  D  C  A  S  E  S  S
P  A  T  W  L  O  V  H  Y  L  N  E  T
X  O  Q  M  R  T  U  A  N  O  E  W  A
O  W  H  E  N  I  W  R  O  R  U  O  Y
Y  O  U  L  B  L  T  G  C  D  Y  R  M
D  U  E  B  A  R  T  E  B  I  N  D  O
C  O  M  M  A  N  D  M  E  N  T  S  N
L  D  O  E  S  U  O  H  E  A  H  U  O
I  A  H  R  P  U  T  O  L  N  E  A  R
E  E  B  H  P  E  E  K  L  C  R  U  E
D  H  O  L  A  O  I  G  L  E  E  N  T
O  E  X  C  O  N  S  A  A  S  F  O  U
W  R  H  U  G  V  D  T  H  M  O  R  E
N  O  F  I  X  H  E  E  S  N  R  U  D
W  F  S  G  O  O  D  S  A  M  E  P  L
```

170. Crisscross Puzzle: Everyday Life *Puzzle on page 248.*

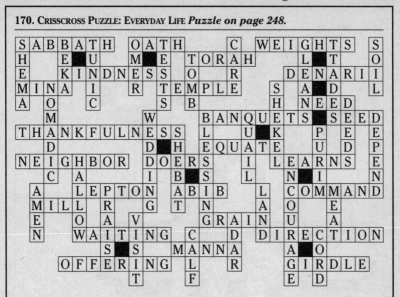

How Did You Do?

This was a tough chapter, but the next one is even more challenging!

The total number of points possible for this chart includes the questions in chapter 8 and Crossword Puzzle #8:

347 to 386: You are truly a Bible scholar!
289 to 346: You have an excellent grasp of Bible facts.
231 to 288: You have some knowledge of the Bible.
193 to 230: You could brush up on the Bible.
0 to 192: You may want to start studying the Bible.

CROSSWORD 8: BIBLE DETAILS *Answers on page 281.*

(*Denotes name of Bible book)

Across

*1. A priest after the exile

*7. Fourth Gospel

11. Gather crops (Lev 19:9)

13. Geber was _____'_ son (1 Ki 4:19)

14. 17th letter of Greek alphabet

15. Cave or lair (Nah 2:11)

17. A record of events in the Bible

21. Babylonian god of wisdom

*23. Prophet concerned with social evils

24. Copper coin of ancient Rome

Across *continued*

25. Speak to God (Job 33:26)

27. Rave (Prov 29:9)

29. Aid (Ex 18:4)

*33. Devoted daughter-in-law

34. God's Word

37. Philistine seaport (Gen 10:19)

38. A city of Judah (Josh 15:15)

39. One who colors a garment (Job 38:14)

42. Associate with (Psa 26:4)

48. Asian city visited by Paul (Acts 18:19)

Across *continued*

53. Sacred writings
    (Acts 18:24)
56. He rebuked Job's friends
    (Job 32:2)
60. Pair (Gen 6:19)
61. Lord (Hebrew)
*65. Prophet with unfaithful
    wife
*66. Prophet who called
    Nineveh to repent

Down

1. Judah's son (Gen 38:3)
2. Fortified town (Josh 19:35)
3. Cheer
4. "Hidden" books of the
   Bible
5. Violent weather
   (Acts 27:18)
6. Lit stick (Gen 15:17)
*7. Bible letter writer; sinned
   (2 wds)
8. Metal-bearing rock
   (Job 28:2)
9. Hebrew measure
   (Ex 30:24)
10. Opposite directions
    (abbr)
12. Metallic element
16. A son of David
    (2 Sam 5:15)
18. Liquid from olives
    (Ex 27:20)
19. God's name (Ex 3:14)
*20. Jewish queen of Persia
22. Plural of is
24. A model worker
    (Prov 6:6)
26. Aluminum (symbol)

Down *continued*

28. Gold (symbol)
30. Noah was 500 years
    _____. (Gen 5:32)
31. Aramaic for "father"
    (Mark 14:36)
32. Shortened (abbr)
35. Ancient form of "you"
36. Roman two
*40. He led invasion of
    Canaan
41. "Though only ____ ____
    being. . ." (John 10:33).
    (2 wds)
43. Old Testament (abbr)
44. New Hampshire (abbr)
45. Southeast (abbr)
46. Roman Catholic (abbr)
47. "Speaking the _____ in
    love" (Eph 4:15).
48. Priestly garment
    (Ex 28:4)
49. Platinum (symbol)
50. Hesitation in speech
51. Selenium (abbr)
52. Self and another
*54. He rebuilt Jerusalem's
    walls (abbr)
*55. Friend to Paul
    (abbr)(Acts 16:1)
57. Behold (Isa 17:14)
58. "It ____ written"
    (Mark 1:2).
59. "____ is the Son of God"
    (Acts 9:20).
62. Day (abbr)
63. Expression of surprise
64. 13th letter of Greek
    alphabet

Chapter Nine
Facts About the Bible

1. What is the name of the first book in the Bible?

2. Which New Testament book recounts the history of the early Christian church? (a) Acts; (b) John; (c) Revelation; (d) Hebrews.

3. True or False: The Old Testament was originally written in Hebrew and Aramaic.

4. How many books are in the New Testament?

5. Fill in the blanks: Jesus said to the devil, "One does not live by _____ alone, but by every _____ that comes from the mouth of God" (Matt 4:4).

6. True or False: Jonah was a minor prophet.

7. Fill in the blank: "Every _____ of God proves true" (Prov 30:5).

8. This is not a Gospel book: (a) Luke; (b) Peter; (c) John; (d) Matthew.

---

9. Matching

Match the theme with the book.

1. Flight from Egypt   A. Genesis
2. Clans of Israel   B. Exodus
3. God's Law   C. Leviticus
4. Creation   D. Numbers
5. Ceremonial laws   E. Deuteronomy

Answers for this page: **1.** *Genesis* **2.** *(a) Acts* **3.** *True* **4.** *27* **5.** *bread, word*
6. *True* **7.** *word* **8.** *(b) Peter* **9.** *1B; 2D; 3E; 4A; 5C*

10. QUOTATION PUZZLE: GOD'S WORD

To find the verse, put the letters that appear in the bottom half of the puzzle into the column of boxes above them. The letters may not be listed in the exact order in which they appear in the quote. Mark off used letters at the bottom. A letter may be used only once. The black boxes represent the space between words.

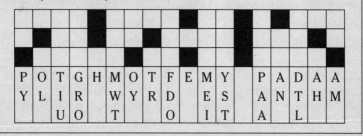

11. True or False: Abraham wrote the first five books of the Bible.

12. Who wrote the most books of the Bible?

13. This type of book is not in the Old Testament: (a) poetry; (b) history; (c) epistle; (d) prophecy.

14. Fill in the blanks: "For I am not ashamed of the _____; it is the power of God for salvation to _____" (Rom 1:16).

15. True or False: The Old Testament is shorter than the New Testament.

16. This person was not an author of a New Testament letter: (a) Peter; (b) John; (c) James; (d) Mark.

17. What Old Testament book precedes Psalms?

18. True or False: The Book of Titus is a New Testament book.

19. Fill in the blanks: "The _____ withers, the _____ fades; but the word of our God will stand forever" (Isa 40:8).

20. How many Gospels are in the New Testament?

Answers for this page: **10.** *"Your word is a lamp to my feet and a light to my path" (Psa 119:105).* **11.** *False (Moses)* **12.** *Paul (13)* **13.** *(c) epistle* **14.** *gospel, everyone* **15.** *False* **16.** *(d) Mark* **17.** *Job* **18.** *True* **19.** *grass, flower* **20.** *4*

21. MATCHING

Match the Bible book with its author.

1. Exodus	A. John
2. Proverbs	B. Paul
3. Psalms	C. Solomon and others
4. Galatians	D. Moses
5. Revelation	E. David and others

22. The first five books of the Bible are known as: (a) Prophecy; (b) Pentateuch; (c) Apocalypse; (d) Wisdom Books.

23. Fill in the blank: Jesus said, "All this has taken place, so that the _____ of the prophets may be fulfilled" (Matt 26:56).

24. True or False: The name of the first book of the Bible means "beginnings."

25. Which book in the Bible is a collection of wise sayings?

26. Fill in the blanks: "Indeed, the word of God is living and active, sharper than any two-edged _____, piercing until it divides _____ from spirit" (Heb 4:12).

27. The subject of this letter by Paul is Onesimus, a slave: (a) Philemon; (b) Romans; (c) 1 Timothy; (d) 2 Timothy.

28. Fill in the blank: "By the _____ of the Lord the heavens were made" (Psa 33:6).

29. Besides the Song of Solomon, what book of the Bible does not mention God?

30. What is the technical term for the first three Gospels? (a) Pentateuch; (b) Codex; (c) Syntax; (d) Synoptic.

31. True or False: Obadiah is the shortest book in the Old Testament.

32. Which Old Testament book is about a prophet swallowed by a large fish?

Answers for this page: **21.** *1D; 2C; 3E; 4B; 5A* **22.** *(b) Pentateuch* **23.** *scriptures* **24.** *True* **25.** *Proverbs* **26.** *sword, soul* **27.** *(a) Philemon* **28.** *word* **29.** *Esther* **30.** *(d) Synoptic* **31.** *True* **32.** *Jonah*

33. True or False: All the writers of the New Testament were Jewish.

34. Fill in the blank: The word of God "is able to judge the thoughts and intentions of the _____" (Heb 4:12).

35. The Hebrew name for the first five books is: (a) Torah; (b) Masorah; (c) Talmud; (d) Midrash.

36. True or False: The Book of Ecclesiastes tells the history of the Israelites before David became their king.

37. What is the first book of the New Testament?

38. Fill in the blank: Daniel declared, "I am to tell you what is inscribed in the book of _____" (Dan 10:21).

39. This is not an Old Testament book of "poetry": (a) Psalms; (b) Lamentations; (c) Ezra; (d) Song of Solomon.

40. True or False: The Song of Solomon is about the love between a woman and a man.

41. What New Testament book is between Ephesians and Colossians?

42. This book expresses the sorrow of Jeremiah: (a) 1 Kings; (b) 2 Kings; (c) Ecclesiastes; (d) Lamentations.

43. Fill in the blank: "The _____ has imprisoned all things under the power of sin" (Gal 3:22).

44. Which Bible book has the chapter with the most verses?

---

45. CRYPTOGRAM: ALL SCRIPTURE

Decode the letters in the words of this Bible verse. Each letter corresponds to a different letter in the alphabet.

JAA GHYLSCNYK LG LZGSLYKP OT QMP JZP LG NGKUNA
UMY CKJHVLZQ, UMY YKSYMMU, UMY HMYYKHCLMZ,
JZP UMY CYJLZLZQ LZ YLQVCKMNGZKGG.

Answers for this page: **33.** *False (Luke was not)* **34.** *heart* **35.** *(a) Torah* **36.** *False (this book belongs to the Wisdom Literature)* **37.** *Matthew* **38.** *truth* **39.** *(c) Ezra* **40.** *True* **41.** *Philippians* **42.** *(d) Lamentations* **43.** *scripture* **44.** *Psalms* **45.** *"All scripture is inspired by God and is useful for teaching, for reproof, for correction, and for training in righteousness" (2 Tim 3:16).*

46. MATCHING

Match the Bible book with its classification.

1. Psalm	A. Prophecy
2. 1 Samuel	B. Epistle
3. Hebrews	C. Poetry
4. Nahum	D. Gospel
5. Luke	E. History

47. True or False: John the Baptist wrote the Book of Revelation.

48. Fill in the blanks: "So shall my word be that goes out from my _____; it shall not return to me _____, but it shall accomplish that which I purpose" (Isa 55:11).

49. This book was the earliest Gospel about the life of Jesus: (a) Matthew; (b) Luke; (c) Peter; (d) Mark.

50. True or False: Moses wrote at least one psalm in the Book of Psalms.

51. Fill in the blanks: "How sweet are your _____ to my taste, sweeter than _____ to my mouth!" (Psa 119:103).

52. Who was the author of the Acts of the Apostles?

53. This book is not about a minor prophet: (a) Daniel; (b) Micah; (c) Habakkuk; (d) Haggai.

54. True or False: Jesus was the author of two of the New Testament Books.

55. Which New Testament letter teaches that faith without deeds is dead?

56. Fill in the blank: "For whatever was written in former days was written for our instruction, so that by steadfastness and by the encouragement of the _____ we might have hope" (Rom 15:4).

Answers for this page: **46.** *1C; 2E; 3B; 4A; 5D* **47.** *False (John the Apostle)* **48.** *mouth, empty* **49.** *(d) Mark* **50.** *True* **51.** *words, honey* **52.** *Luke* **53.** *(a) Daniel* **54.** *False (none)* **55.** *James* **56.** *scriptures*

57. True or False: Early biblical manuscripts had no vowel markings and no verse and chapter divisions.

58. In this New Testament letter, Paul mentioned a "thorn" in his flesh: (a) 1 Corinthians; (b) 2 Corinthians; (c) 1 Thessalonians; (d) 2 Thessalonians.

59. What is the last book that chronicles Old Testament history?

60. Fill in the blank: "After he was raised from the dead, his disciples remembered that he had said this; and they believed the _____ " (John 2:22).

61. The word *selah* in Psalms means: (a) Amen; (b) Halleluia; (c) the meaning is uncertain; (d) be quiet.

62. What does the word *Gospel* mean?

63. True or False: Deuteronomy is the longest book in the Old Testament.

64. Which New Testament book says nothing can "separate us from the love of God"? (a) John; (b) Romans; (c) Philippians; (d) James.

65. Fill in the blank: "Incline your ear and hear my words, and apply your _____ to my teaching" (Prov 22:17).

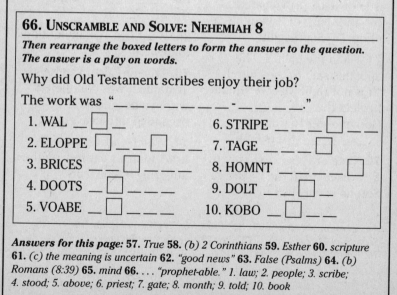

66. UNSCRAMBLE AND SOLVE: NEHEMIAH 8

Then rearrange the boxed letters to form the answer to the question. The answer is a play on words.

Why did Old Testament scribes enjoy their job?

The work was "__ __ __ __ __ __ __ - __ __ __ __ ."

1. WAL __ ☐ __
2. ELOPPE ☐ __ __ ☐ __ __ __
3. BRICES __ __ ☐ __ __ __
4. DOOTS __ ☐ __ __ __
5. VOABE __ ☐ __ __ __

6. STRIPE __ __ __ ☐ __ __
7. TAGE __ __ __ ☐
8. HOMNT __ __ __ __ ☐
9. DOLT __ __ ☐ __
10. KOBO __ ☐ __ __

Answers for this page: **57.** *True* **58.** *(b) 2 Corinthians* **59.** *Esther* **60.** *scripture* **61.** *(c) the meaning is uncertain* **62.** *"good news"* **63.** *False (Psalms)* **64.** *(b) Romans (8:39)* **65.** *mind* **66.** *. . . "prophet-able."* *1. law; 2. people; 3. scribe; 4. stood; 5. above; 6. priest; 7. gate; 8. month; 9. told; 10. book*

67. MATCHING

Match the famous phrase with the Bible verse.

1. "Fight the good fight."	A. Exodus 5:1
2. "All is vanity."	B. John 20:19
3. "Let my people go."	C. 1 Timothy 6:12
4. "Peace be with you."	D. Psalm 23:1
5. "The Lord is my shepherd."	E. Ecclesiastes 12:8

68. What was the literary device Jesus used to teach a lesson through stories?

69. True or False: The Old Testament has three major divisions: the Law, the Prophets, and the Writings.

70. The ancient Greek translation of the Old Testament is known as: (a) Vulgate; (b) Midrash; (c) Pseudepigraphon; (d) Septuagint.

71. Fill in the blanks: The apostles said to the church, "It is not right that we should neglect the _____ of God in order to wait on _____" (Acts 6:2).

72. True or False: A shepherd boy discovered the Dead Sea Scrolls in clay jars in a cave.

73. The Sermon on the Mount is found in Luke and: (a) Peter; (b) Matthew; (c) John; (d) Mark.

74. Fill in the blank: "When God finished speaking with Moses on Mount Sinai, he gave him the two tablets of the covenant . . . written with the _____ of God" (Ex 31:18).

75. What Old Testament book follows Judges?

76. True or False: The New Testament was completed within a decade after Jesus ascended into heaven.

77. Which Old Testament book focuses entirely on the suffering of one man?

Answers for this page: **67.** *1C; 2E; 3A; 4B; 5D* **68.** *parable* **69.** *True* **70.** *(d) Septuagint* **71.** *word, tables* **72.** *True* **73.** *(b) Matthew* **74.** *finger* **75.** *Ruth* **76.** *False* **77.** *Job*

78. Fill in the blanks: Jesus stated, "Until _____ and _____ pass away, not one letter, not one stroke of a letter, will pass from the law until all is accomplished" (Matt 5:18).

79. What is the first letter in the Hebrew alphabet? (a) alpha; (b) taw; (c) aleph; (d) omega.

80. True or False: Revelation is the last book in the Bible.

81. This New Testament letter mentions Paul's plan to visit Spain: (a) Romans; (b) Galatians; (c) Ephesians; (d) Colossians.

82. Fill in the blank: "The unfolding of your words gives _____" (Psa 119:130).

83. What Old Testament book does the New Testament refer to the most?

84. True or False: Besides Jesus, David is mentioned the most in the Bible.

85. What Old Testament book includes the stories of Deborah, Gideon, and Samson?

86. Fill in the blank: "You shall read the words of the _____ from the scroll that you have written at my dictation" (Jer 36:6).

---

87. QUOTATION PUZZLE: THE REASON FOR THE WORD

M	S	S	O	T	I	H	A	L	I	Y	V	U	E	S	H	Y	A	C	J
N	E	U	T	O	H	B	E	E	H	E	R	E		M	R	I	T	T	O
B					T	S	S	T		A	O	M		T	A	I		H	E
						E				E				W					

---

88. WORD SEARCH: BOOKS OF THE BIBLE *Answers on page 275.*

The Bible has 66 books, but you'll need to find only 46 of them in the puzzle on this page. You can find words diagonally, vertically, horizontally, backward, and forward. When you find a word in the puzzle, cross it off the list. On the lines below, write the puzzle's leftover letters in the order in which they appear in the puzzle. The leftover letters spell out a promise from the Bible that you can bank on.

```
Z  E  P  H  A  N  I  A  H  E  B  R  E  W  S  Z
H  M  I  J  S  N  A  I  P  P  I  L  I  H  P  E
E  S  U  T  I  T  H  S  M  E  R  S  C  I  S  C
Z  D  O  H  H  C  S  N  E  V  A  E  R  U  M  H
E  C  S  N  A  I  H  T  N  I  R  O  C  I  A  A
K  D  O  L  G  N  M  E  A  T  U  I  C  I  T  R
I  I  A  O  G  O  O  H  A  N  T  A  M  E  T  I
E  M  N  N  A  N  F  J  D  I  H  E  T  H  H  A
L  E  Y  G  I  P  R  O  V  E  R  B  S  A  E  H
R  E  H  T  S  E  R  E  F  E  E  L  N  E  W  P
W  E  Z  A  E  T  L  L  J  S  U  D  O  X  E  H
V  E  L  R  M  E  M  A  R  K  O  R  Y  M  O  I
R  M  N  I  A  R  N  E  E  G  G  L  R  E  A  L
S  T  I  J  J  O  B  A  D  I  A  H  O  S  Y  E
O  U  R  O  F  M  A  I  M  T  C  H  O  M  F  M
J  O  S  H  U  A  T  I  M  O  T  H  Y  S  O  O
U  L  N  N  E  N  G  E  N  E  S  I  S  S  E  N
J  U  D  G  E  S  N  A  I  S  S  O  L  O  C  A
K  U  K  K  A  B  A  H  A  I  M  E  H  E  N  S
```

_____

_____

_____

88. WORD SEARCH: BOOKS OF THE BIBLE *Continued*

Old Testament	Old Testament	New Testament
Genesis	Isaiah	Matthew
Exodus	Jeremiah	Mark
Leviticus	Ezekiel	Luke
Numbers	Daniel	John (the Gospel; 1, 2, & 3)
Joshua	Hosea	
Judges	Joel	Acts
Ruth	Amos	Romans
Kings (1 & 2)	Obadiah	Corinthians (1 & 2)
Ezra	Jonah	Philippians
Nehemiah	Micah	Colossians
Esther	Habakkuk	Timothy (1 & 2)
Job	Zephaniah	Titus
Psalms	Haggai	Philemon
Proverbs	Zechariah	Hebrews
Song of Solomon	Malachi	James
		Peter (1 & 2)
		Jude

89. MATCHING

Match version/translation with its author.

1. Latin to English
2. Greek New Testament
3. Greek to German
4. Greek to English
5. Living Bible paraphrase

A. Martin Luther
B. Kenneth Taylor
C. John Wycliffe
D. Erasmus
E. William Tyndale

Answers for this page: **89.** *1C; 2D; 3A; 4E; 5B*

90. True or False: Hezekiah is an Old Testament book.

91. Which Bible book has the shortest chapter?

92. This Bible book is not a New Testament letter: (a) Timothy; (b) James; (c) Joel; (d) Jude.

93. True or False: In 1250, the Bible was first divided into chapters.

94. Which Bible book has the famous phrase: "For God so loved the world..."?

95. Fill in the blank: Joshua declared, "See, this _____ shall be a witness against us; for it has heard all the words of the Lord that he spoke to us" (Josh 24:27).

96. True or False: Andrew wrote 1 Peter.

97. This is not an Apocryphal book: (a) Judith; (b) Tobit; (c) Zephaniah; (d) 1 Maccabees.

98. Fill in the blank: Paul told Timothy, "I solemnly urge you: _____ the message" (2 Tim 4:1–2).

99. Which Bible book says "for everything there is a season"?

100. Another name for Revelation is: (a) Annunication; (b) Apocryphal; (c) Apocalypse; (d) Pericope.

101. Fill in the blank: Jesus declared, "Do not think that I have come to abolish the law or the prophets; I have come not to abolish but to _____" (Matt 5:17).

102. True or False: The Bible is the world's best-selling book.

103. This event is in all the Gospels: (a) feeding 5,000; (b) Jesus' birth; (c) transfiguration; (d) Jesus' baptism.

104. What is the last book in the Old Testament?

105. Fill in the blanks: "_____ died for our _____ in accordance with the scriptures" (1 Cor 15:3).

106. True or False: The Book of Job recounts the early history of Israel.

Answers for this page: **90.** *False (not a book)* **91.** *Psalms (117)* **92.** *(c) Joel* **93.** *True* **94.** *John (3:16)* **95.** *stone* **96.** *False (Peter)* **97.** *(c) Zephaniah* **98.** *proclaim* **99.** *Ecclesiastes* **100.** *(c) Apocalypse* **101.** *fulfill* **102.** *True* **103.** *(a) feeding 5,000* **104.** *Malachi* **105.** *Christ, sins* **106.** *False*

107. To avoid misinterpretation of Hebrew Scriptures, scribes adopted a system of vowels and accent markings called: (a) Masorah; (b) Torah; (c) Talmud; (d) Midrash.

108. Which Gospel includes Mary's song of praise known as the "Magnificat"?

109. True or False: The New Testament was originally written in Greek.

110. Fill in the blanks: "Moses came and told the people all the _____ of the Lord.... And Moses wrote down all the _____ of the Lord" (Ex 24:3–4).

111. The shorter prophetic books in the Old Testament are called "minor" for this reason: (a) nothing about the Messiah; (b) less important prophets; (c) less important prophecy; (d) shorter length.

112. True or False: Some Bible books existed in spoken form long before they were written down.

113. Which letter by Paul describes the "fruit of the Spirit"?

114. Fill in the blank: Jesus said, "You abandon the commandment of God and hold to human _____ " (Mark 7:8).

115. True or False: In Talmudic times, Genesis was known as the "Book of the Creation of the World."

116. The word "Bible" is taken from Greek *biblia,* which means: (a) books; (b) good tidings; (c) sacred text; (d) chronicles.

117. Which Bible book has the longest verse?

118. True or False: The Gospel of Thomas is a New Testament book.

119. Fill in the blanks: "I treasure your word in my _____, so that I may not _____ against you" (Psa 119:11).

120. What New Testament book precedes Jude?

Answers for this page: **107.** *(a) Masorah* **108.** *Luke* **109.** *True* **110.** *words, words* **111.** *(d) shorter length* **112.** *True* **113.** *Galatians* **114.** *tradition* **115.** *True* **116.** *(a) books* **117.** *Esther (8:9)* **118.** *False* **119.** *heart, sin* **120.** *3 John*

121. HIDDEN WORDS: BIBLE TYPES

Among the contents of the Bible are the following types of writing. Find these words hidden in the sentences below.

law	history	prophecy	prayer	poetry
hymn	gospel	letters	sermon	parable

1. "Be sure to bring your #2 pencils and an eraser Monday for the test," announced the teacher.

2. Don't try to enlist in the Marines if your health is below par. Able-bodied recruits are the only ones being accepted.

3. My cousin Lila works in a doctor's office.

4. The Whigs opposed the British king and his Tory sympathizers.

5. A good author for mystery lovers is Edgar Allan Poe. Try reading some of his macabre short stories.

6. "Cheer up, Ray; Eric has volunteered to work your shift tonight."

7. "Let terse, angry words be put aside in the interest of peace," the ambassador pleaded.

8. The Galapagos, Pelau, and Canary Islands are among the places I hope to visit.

9. Unless you approach them with complete apathy, mnemonic techniques really can assist your memory.

10. When asked to design a stage prop, he cycled back to the office and got right to work.

Answers for this page: **121.** *1. sermon; 2. parable; 3. law; 4. history; 5. poetry; 6. prayer; 7. letters; 8. gospel; 9. hymn; 10. prophecy*

122. This Old Testament book was detached from the end of 2 Chronicles: (a) 1 Chronicles; (b) Nehemiah; (c) 1 Kings; (d) Ezra.

123. Fill in the blank: "Those who are taught the _____ must share in all good things" (Gal 6:6).

124. True or False: The Book of Ezekiel is written entirely in the first person, apart from the note in 1:2–3.

125. Which New Testament letter contains Paul's description of "the whole armor of God"?

126. Which Bible book has the famous phrase: "Love is patient; love is kind"?

127. What Old Testament book states, "The word of the Lord was rare in those days; visions were not widespread"? (a) Joshua; (b) Judges; (c) 1 Samuel; (d) 2 Samuel.

128. This is not an Old Testament "wisdom" book: (a) Job; (b) Proverbs; (c) Ecclesiastes; (d) Song of Solomon.

129. Fill in the blank: After Saul fought the Philistines, Samuel said to Saul, "Now therefore listen to the words of the _____" (1 Sam 15:1).

130. True or False: Luke wrote the longest book in the New Testament.

---

131. MATCHING

Match the Bible book with its actual Hebrew title.

1. Genesis
2. Exodus
3. Leviticus
4. Numbers
5. Deuteronomy

A. Vayikra
B. Devarim
C. Bereshit
D. Shemot
E. Bamidbar

Answers for this page: **122.** *(d) Ezra* **123.** *word* **124.** *True* **125.** *Ephesians* **126.** *1 Corinthians* **127.** *(c) 1 Samuel* **128.** *(d) Song of Solomon* **129.** *Lord* **130.** *True* **131.** *1C; 2D; 3A; 4E; 5B*

132. CRYPTOGRAM: SPOKE FROM GOD

GY MTYMLWFS YU EFTXMHZTW XE V QVHHWT YU
YGW'E YCG XGHWTMTWHVHXYG, JWFVZEW GY
MTYMLWFS WNWT FVQW JS LZQVG CXAA, JZH QWG
VGK CYQWG QYNWK JS HLW LYAS EMXTXH EMYOW
UTYQ PYK.

133. The Hebrew word for "meditation" (*hagah*) is not used to describe: (a) the coo of a dove; (b) the growl of a lion; (c) the pecking of a woodpecker; (d) the reading of the Bible.

134. Fill in the blank: Jesus said in the synagogue, "Today this _____ has been fulfilled in your hearing" (Luke 4:21).

135. True or False: Ancient Scripture was written in a script from left to right.

136. The maxim "God helps those who help themselves" is found in what Bible book? (a) Proverbs; (b) Matthew; (c) Romans; (d) none.

137. True or False: The Gospel of John was written after the other Gospels.

138. Fill in the blanks: "In _____, whose word I praise, in _____ I trust" (Psa 56:4).

139. What is the name of the collection of ancient scriptural texts found in caves near Qumran?

140. Fill in the blank: Jesus said, "The _____ cannot be annulled" (John 10:35).

141. True or False: The first books of the Bible were written about 3,500 years ago.

142. Which Gospel relates the conversation between Jesus and Nicodemus?

143. The Torah, or the Law, is derived from the Hebrew word whose meaning is: (a) to write; (b) to hear; (c) to teach; (d) to speak.

Answers for this page: **132.** *"No prophecy of scripture is a matter of one's own interpretation, because no prophecy ever came by human will, but men and women moved by the Holy Spirit spoke from God" (2 Pet 1:20–21).* **133.** *(c) the pecking of a woodpecker* **134.** *scripture* **135.** *False (right to left)* **136.** *(d) none (it is not in the Bible)* **137.** *True* **138.** *God, God* **139.** *The Dead Sea Scrolls* **140.** *scripture* **141.** *True* **142.** *John* **143.** *(c) to teach*

144. True or False: The Book of Revelation presents John's vision of the end times.

145. Fill in the blank: "For the _____ of the Lord is upright" (Psa 33:4).

146. In this letter an apostle noted that some things Paul said are sometimes difficult to understand: (a) 1 Peter; (b) 2 Peter; (c) 1 John; (d) 3 John.

147. What Old Testament book is between Haggai and Malachi?

148. True or False: Jesus' words are found only in the Gospels.

149. Fill in the blanks: "Has not the _____ said that the Messiah is descended from David and comes from _____, the village where David lived?" (John 7:42).

150. Which Bible book is rigidly structured with chapters of 22 verses or a multiple of 22 verses?

151. This Old Testament book is about a prophet whom God told to marry a whore: (a) Joel; (b) Micah; (c) Hosea; (d) Obadiah.

152. What book in the Bible has the fewest verses?

---

153. Quotation Puzzle: School's In

B	W	E	I	T	N	O	G	N	S	T	H	A	C	T	A	C	E	U	A
F	L	E	M	K	C	N	I	L	D	H	O	U	D	S	A	R	O	E	H
A	R	R		T	O	H	W	N		T	H	E	T		Y	Y	U		D
	V	O			I		I	S		T	R	O				O	R		

---

154. Fill in the blank: "I shall have an answer for those who taunt me, for I trust in your _____" (Psa 119:42).

155. True or False: Both the Old and the New Testaments include poetry.

156. This is not a modern translation of the Bible:
(a) King James Version;
(b) New International Version;
(c) New Revised Standard Version; (d) Jerusalem Bible.

157. Fill in the blank: "Take the helmet of salvation, and the _____ of the Spirit, which is the word of God" (Eph 6:17).

158. What is the first Old Testament book of the prophets?

159. True or False: The Acts of the Apostles includes an account of Jesus' last days on earth.

160. Fill in the blanks: "My soul languishes for your _____; I hope in your _____" (Psa 119:81).

161. This is not an ancient source that aids our understanding of languages in Bible times: (a) the Rosetta Stone; (b) the Behistun Rock; (c) Ugarit clay tablets; (d) Ark of the Covenant.

162. What New Testament book follows 2 Peter?

163. True or False: In 1560 the Geneva Bible was the first entire English Bible to have verse divisions.

---

164. MATCHING

Match the theme with Paul's letter.

1. Christ's second coming	A. Romans
2. Legalism of the Judaizers	B. 1 Corinthians
3. The Lord's Supper	C. Ephesians
4. Governing authorities	D. Galatians
5. Family roles	E. 1 Thessalonians

Answers for this page: **154.** *word* **155.** *True* **156.** *(a) King James Version* **157.** *sword* **158.** *Isaiah* **159.** *True* **160.** *salvation, word* **161.** *(d) Ark of the Covenant* **162.** *1 John* **163.** *True* **164.** *1E; 2D; 3B; 4A; 5C*

165. Which Old Testament book contains many examples of acrostic poems?
(a) Proverbs; (b) Psalms; (c) Song of Solomon; (d) Ecclesiastes.

166. Fill in the blank: Luke decided "to write an orderly account . . . so that you may know the _____" (Luke 1:3–4).

167. The story of Israel's captivity in Egypt is found in which book?

168. Who wrote Hebrews? (a) Paul; (b) Apollos; (c) Barnabas; (d) unknown.

169. True or False: The Book of Revelation makes it clear what year Jesus will return.

170. Fill in the blank: "The sum of your word is _____" (Psa 119:160).

171. What is the first epistle in the New Testament?

172. What kind of "Criticism" is the study of ancient Bible documents? (a) Form; (b) Textual; (c) Redaction; (d) Source.

173. Fill in the blanks: Peter declared, "'The _____ of the Lord endures forever.' That _____ is the good news that was announced to you" (1 Pet 1:25).

174. What Old Testament book describes the beginning of the Jewish people?

175. This Old Testament book contains the Lord's command "to love your neighbor as yourself": (a) Proverbs; (b) Leviticus; (c) Amos; (d) Isaiah.

176. True or False: Jewish tradition maintains that the scribe Ezra probably arranged the canon of the Hebrew Bible.

177. What New Testament letter mentions the dispute between the archangel Michael and the devil over Moses' body?

178. Fill in the blank: "Then beginning with Moses and all the prophets, he interpreted to them the things about himself in all the _____" (Luke 24:27).

Answers for this page: **165.** *(b) Psalms* **166.** *truth* **167.** *Exodus* **168.** *(d) unknown* **169.** *False* **170.** *truth* **171.** *Romans* **172.** *(b) Textual* **173.** *word, word* **174.** *Genesis* **175.** *(b) Leviticus* **176.** *True* **177.** *Jude* **178.** *scriptures*

179. UNSCRAMBLE AND MATCH: BIBLE BOOKS AND STYLE

Unscramble the names of the Bible books and match them with their style by writing the name next to the style:

1. Poetry _____ AHISAI

2. Law _____ WETHTAM

3. History _____ MONTERYEUOD

4. Prayers & Songs _____ GONS FO MONSOLO

5. Prophecy _____ MELAUS 1 & 2

6. Biography _____ AVELERINTO

7. Letter _____ SPORBREV

8. Vision of End Times _____ SLAMPS

9. Wise Sayings _____ MANSOR

180. Fill in the blanks: Jeremiah said to God, "Your words were found, and I ate them, and your words became to me a _____ and the delight of my _____" (Jer 15:16).

181. True or False: The Gospel of Luke and the Acts of the Apostles compose almost one-fourth of the New Testament.

182. What Old Testament book provides the most information about the end times?

183. This Old Testament book tells how a Moabite woman was an ancestor of King David and Jesus Christ: (a) Joshua; (b) Judges; (c) Ruth; (d) Esther.

184. This Gospel concludes with a painful discussion between Jesus and Peter: (a) Luke; (b) Peter; (c) John; (d) Matthew.

185. Fill in the blank: "Teach me your way, O Lord, that I may walk in your _____" (Psa 86:11).

Answers for this page: **179.** *1. Song of Solomon; 2. Deuteronomy; 3. 1 & 2 Samuel; 4. Psalms; 5. Isaiah; 6. Matthew; 7. Romans; 8. Revelation; 9. Proverbs* **180.** *joy, heart* **181.** *True* **182.** *Daniel* **183.** *(c) Ruth* **184.** *(c) John* **185.** *truth*

186. CRISSCROSS PUZZLE: BIBLE BOOKS *Answers on page 276.*

Fit each of the following 31 words into the puzzle below. Words are arranged below alphabetically according to the number of letters.

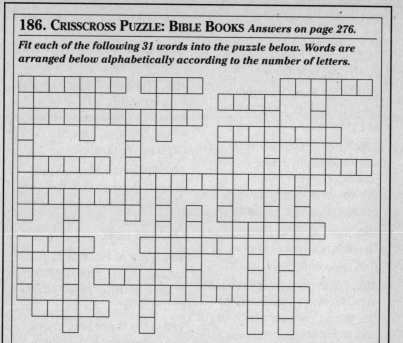

4 letters
Acts
Amos
Ezra
Joel
John
Mark
Ruth
Song
[of Solomon]

5 letters
James
Jonah
Kings
Nahum

6 letters
Daniel
Exodus
Haggai
Isaiah
Joshua

6 letters
Judges
Psalms

7 letters
Genesis
Numbers
Obadiah
Timothy

8 letters
Nehemiah
Proverbs

9 letters
Ephesians
Galatians
Leviticus

11 letters
Corinthians

12 letters
Lamentations

13 letters
Thessalonians

187. What Gospel is not a Synoptic Gospel?

188. True or False: Amos is an Old Testament book.

189. What New Testament book describes the ministries of Peter and Paul?

190. The Dead Sea Scrolls were hidden in caves to protect them from: (a) Romans; (b) Egyptians; (c) Assyrians; (d) Pharisees.

191. True or False: Both Habakkuk and Job are books that question God's justice.

192. Fill in the blank: "I thank my God every time I remember you . . . because of your sharing in the _____ from the first day until now" (Phlp 1:3, 5).

193. The Aramaic translations of the Hebrew Bible were called: (a) Talmud; (b) Torah; (c) Targums; (d) Midrash.

194. What New Testament book mentions Melchizedek?

195. True or False: The Jewish Masoretic scholars invented vowel signs for the Hebrew Bible.

196. The New Testament was written within a span of about: (a) 20 years; (b) 50 years; (c) two centuries; (d) three centuries.

197. Fill in the blank: King Jehoshaphat said to the king of Israel, "Inquire first for the _____ of the Lord" (2 Chron 18:4).

198. True or False: Archaeological discoveries have not helped verify accounts given in the Bible.

199. This is not true about the Gutenberg Bible: (a) in the Latin Vulgate; (b) first printing of Bible; (c) printed in fourteenth century; (d) printed in Germany.

200. What New Testament book concludes with Jesus' promise that he will come back soon?

Answers for this page: **187.** *John* **188.** *True* **189.** *Acts* **190.** *(a) Romans* **191.** *True* **192.** *gospel* **193.** *(c) Targums* **194.** *Hebrews* **195.** *True* **196.** *(b) 50 years* **197.** *word* **198.** *False* **199.** *(c) printed in fourteenth century* **200.** *Revelation*

88. WORD SEARCH: BOOKS OF THE BIBLE *Puzzle on page 268.*

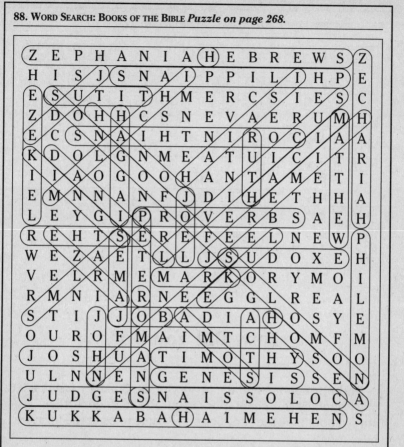

Leftover letters [there should be 71 of them]: "His mercies never come to an end; they are new every morning; great is your faithfulness" (Lam 3:22–23).

186. CRISSCROSS PUZZLE: BIBLE BOOKS *Puzzle on page 273.*

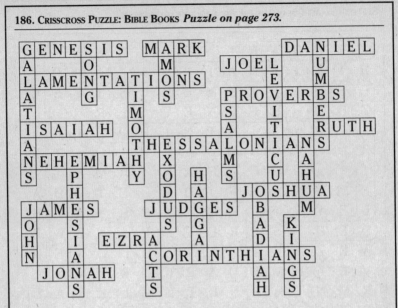

How Did You Do?

Both the content and the history of the Bible are fascinating. Hopefully this chapter has inspired you to do further study about how the Holy Scripture came to us in the form we have today.

The total number of points possible for this chart includes the questions in chapter 9:

291 to 324: You are truly a Bible scholar!
243 to 290: You have an excellent grasp of Bible facts.
194 to 242: You have some knowledge of the Bible.
162 to 193: You could brush up on the Bible.
0 to 161: You may want to start studying the Bible.

How Did You Do—Overall?

Now that you have completed this book, you are probably curious how you have done overall. List your scores for each chart on the following lines and total:

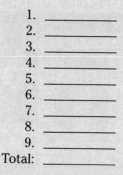

    1. _____
    2. _____
    3. _____
    4. _____
    5. _____
    6. _____
    7. _____
    8. _____
    9. _____
Total: _____

Determine within what range your total score falls in this last chart:

3627 to 4030: You are truly a Bible scholar!
3022 to 3626: You have an excellent grasp of Bible facts.
2418 to 3021: You have some knowledge of the Bible.
2015 to 2417: You could brush up on the Bible.
0 to 2014: You may want to start studying the Bible.

You probably did much better than you thought you would when you first started. You might also want to consider going through this book again in a few months and see how much you have learned. In any case, congratulations on finishing this book. No doubt, you learned a lot . . . and had fun in the process.

CROSSWORD PUZZLE #1: PRODIGAL SON *Puzzle on page 38.*

CROSSWORD PUZZLE #2: BIBLE COUPLES *Puzzle on page 72.*

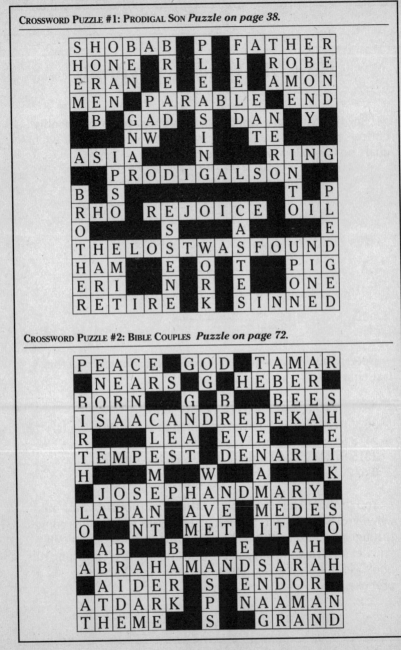

CROSSWORD PUZZLE #3: WHERE ARE THE CHILDREN? *Puzzle on page 102.*

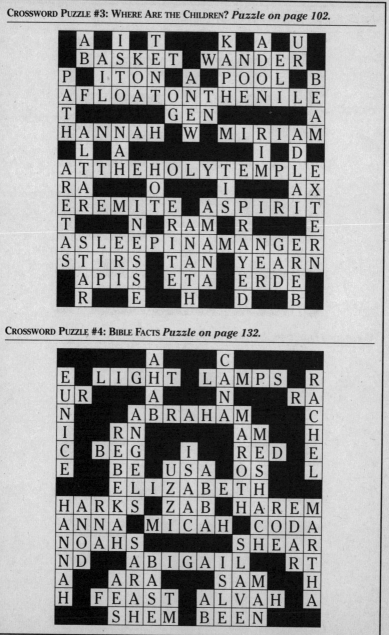

CROSSWORD PUZZLE #4: BIBLE FACTS *Puzzle on page 132.*

CROSSWORD #5: BIBLE PLACES *Puzzle on page 164.*

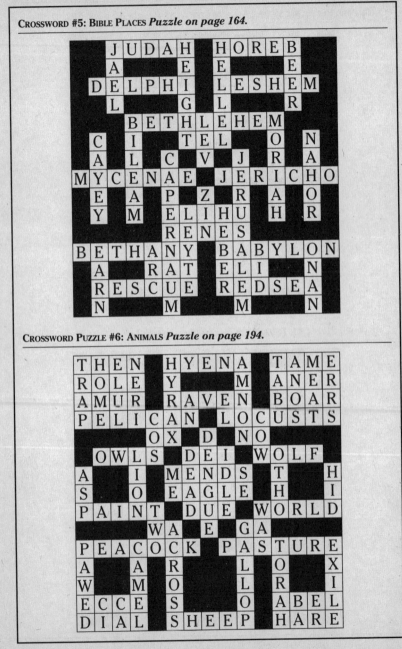

CROSSWORD PUZZLE #6: ANIMALS *Puzzle on page 194.*

CROSSWORD PUZZLE #7: EVERYDAY LIFE *Puzzle on page 226.*

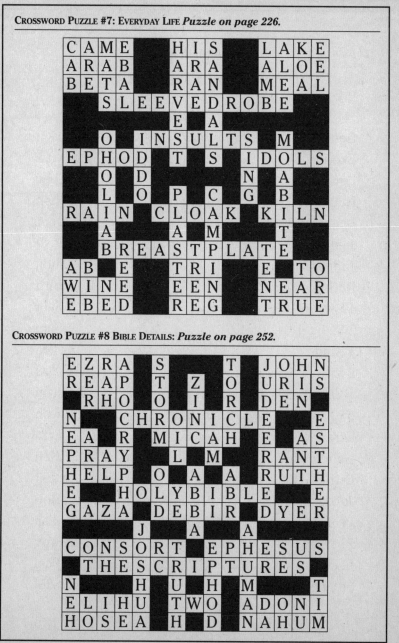

CROSSWORD PUZZLE #8 BIBLE DETAILS: *Puzzle on page 252.*

Abbreviations

Old Testament

Genesis . . . . .Gen

Exodus . . . . .Ex

Leviticus . . . . .Lev

Numbers . . . . .Num

Deuteronomy . . . . .Deut

Joshua . . . . .Josh

Judges . . . . .Judg

Ruth . . . . .Ruth

1 Samuel . . . . .1 Sam

2 Samuel . . . . .2 Sam

1 Kings . . . . .1 Ki

2 Kings . . . . .2 Ki

1 Chronicles . . . . .1 Chron

2 Chronicles . . . . .2 Chron

Ezra . . . . .Ezra

Nehemiah . . . . .Neh

Esther . . . . .Est

Job . . . . .Job

Psalms . . . . .Psa

Proverbs . . . . .Prov

Ecclesiastes . . . . .Eccl

Song of Solomon . . . . .Sol

Old Testament

Isaiah .... Isa
Jeremiah .... Jer
Lamentations .... Lam
Ezekiel .... Ezek
Daniel .... Dan
Hosea .... Hos
Joel .... Joel
Amos .... Amos
Obadiah .... Oba
Jonah .... Jon
Micah .... Mic
Nahum .... Nah
Habakkuk .... Hab
Zephaniah .... Zeph
Haggai .... Hag
Zechariah .... Zec
Malachi .... Mal

New Testament

Matthew . . . . .Matt

Mark . . . . .Mark

Luke . . . . .Luke

John . . . . .John

Acts of the Apostles . . . . .Acts

Romans . . . . .Rom

1 Corinthians . . . . .1 Cor

2 Corinthians . . . . .2 Cor

Galatians . . . . .Gal

Ephesians . . . . .Eph

Philippians . . . . .Phlp

Colossians . . . . .Col

1 Thessalonians . . . . .1 Thes

2 Thessalonians . . . . .2 Thes

1 Timothy . . . . .1 Tim

2 Timothy . . . . .2 Tim

Titus . . . . .Titus

Philemon . . . . .Philem

Hebrews . . . . .Heb

James . . . . .Jas

1 Peter . . . . .1 Pet

2 Peter . . . . .2 Pet

1 John . . . . .1 John

2 John . . . . .2 John

3 John . . . . .3 John

Jude . . . . .Jude

Revelation . . . . .Rev

Apochryphal/Deuterocanonical Books

Tobit . . . . .Tob

Judith . . . . .Jdt

Additions to Esther . . . . .Add Esth

Wisdom . . . . .Wis

Sirach (Ecclesiasticus) .Sir

Baruch . . . . .Bar

1 Esdras . . . . .1 Esd

2 Esdras . . . . .2 Esd

Letter of Jeremiah . . . . .Let Jer

Prayer of Azariah and the Song
of the Three Jews . . . . .Song of Thr

Susanna . . . . .Sus

Bel and the Dragon . . . . .Bel

1 Maccabees . . . . .1 Macc

2 Maccabees . . . . .2 Macc

3 Maccabees . . . . .3 Macc

4 Maccabees . . . . .4 Macc

Prayer of Manasseh .Pr Man

Psalm 151 . . . . .Ps

Israel's Kings and Rulers

The United Kingdom

King	Ruled
1. Saul	1050–1010 BC
2. David	1003–970 BC
3. Solomon	970–930 BC

The Northern Kingdom (Israel)

King	Ruled
1. Jeroboam I	930–909 BC
2. Nadab	909–908 BC
3. Baasha	908–886 BC
4. Elah	886–885 BC
5. Zimri	885 BC
6. Omri	885–874 BC
7. Ahab	874–853 BC
8. Ahaziah	853–852 BC
9. Joram	852–841 BC
10. Jehu	841–814 BC
11. Jehoahaz	814–798 BC
12. Jehoash	798–782 BC
13. Jeroboam II	782–753 BC
14. Zechariah	753 BC

The Northern Kingdom (Israel) *Continued*

King . . . . *Ruled*

15. Shallum . . . . .752 BC
16. Menahem .752–742 BC
17. Pekahiah . . . . .742–740 BC
18. Pekah . . . . .740–732 BC
19. Hoshea . . . . .732–722 BC

The Southern Kingdom (Judah)

King   *Ruled*

1. Rehoboam .930–913 BC
2. Abijam . . . . .913–910 BC
3. Asa . . . . .910–870 BC
4. Jehoshaphat . . . . .870–848 BC
5. Jehoram . . . . .848–841 BC
6. Ahaziah . . . . .841 BC
7. Athaliah . . . . .841–835 BC
8. Joash . . . . .835–796 BC
9. Amaziah . . . . .796–792 BC
10. Uzziah (Azariah) . . . . .792–740 BC
11. Jotham . . . . .740–732 BC
12. Ahaz . . . . .732–715 BC
13. Hezekiah .715–686 BC
14. Manasseh .686–642 BC
15. Amon . . . . .642–640 BC
16. Josiah . . . . .640–609 BC
17. Jehoahaz . . . . .609 BC
18. Jehoiakim .609–598 BC
19. Jehoiachin .598–597 BC
20. Zedekiah . . . . .597–586 BC